About Language

CAMBRIDGE TEACHER TRAINING AND DEVELOPMENT

Series Editors: Ruth Gairns and Marion Williams

This series is designed for all those involved in language teacher training and development: teachers in training, trainers, directors of studies, advisers, teachers of in-service courses and seminars. Its aim is to provide a comprehensive, organised and authoritative resource for language teacher training and development.

Teach English – A training course for teachers
by Adrian Doff

Trainer's Handbook
Teacher's Workbook

Models and Metaphors in Language Teacher Training –
Loop input and other strategies*
by Tessa Woodward
This title was prepared with Roger Bowers as series editor.

Training Foreign Language Teachers – A reflective approach
by Michael J. Wallace

Literature and Language Teaching – A guide for teachers and trainers
by Gillian Lazar

Classroom Observation Tasks – A resource book for language
teachers and trainers*
by Ruth Wajnryb

Tasks for Language Teachers – A resource book for training and development*
by Martin Parrott

English for the Teacher – A language development course*
by Mary Spratt

Teaching Children English – A training course for teachers of
English to children*
by David Vale with Anne Feunteun

A Course in Language Teaching – Practice and theory
by Penny Ur

Looking at Language Classrooms
A teacher development video package

About Language – Tasks for teachers of English
by Scott Thornbury

Action Research for Language Teachers
by Michael J. Wallace

Mentor Courses – A resource book for trainer-trainers
by Angi Malderez and Caroline Bodóczky

* Original Series Editors: Ruth Gairns and Marion Williams

About Language

Tasks for teachers of English

Scott Thornbury

CAMBRIDGE
UNIVERSITY PRESS

PUBLISHED BY THE PRESS SYNDICATE OF THE UNIVERSITY OF CAMBRIDGE
The Pitt Building, Trumpington Street, Cambridge, United Kingdom

CAMBRIDGE UNIVERSITY PRESS
The Edinburgh Building, Cambridge CB2 2RU, UK
40 West 20th Street, New York, NY 10011–4211, USA
477 Williamstown Road, Port Melbourne, VIC 3207, Australia
Ruiz de Alarcón 13, 28014 Madrid, Spain
Dock House, The Waterfront, Cape Town 8001, South Africa

http://www.cambridge.org

First published 1997
Seventh printing 2003

Printed in the United Kingdom at the University Press, Cambridge

Typeset in Adobe Sabon 11/12pt.

A catalogue record for this book is available from the British Library

Library of Congress Cataloguing in Publication data
Thornbury, Scott, 1950–
   About language: tasks for teachers of English/Scott Thornbury.
   p.   cm. – (Cambridge teacher training and development).
   Includes bibliographical references (p.   ) and index.
   ISBN 0-521-56198-1 (hardback). – ISBN 0-521-42720-7 (pbk.)
1. English language – Study and teaching – Foreign speakers – Problems, exercises,
etc. 2. English language – Teacher training. I. Title.   II. Series
PE1128.A2T465   1997
428′.0071–dc21   96-37000
                                                                                            CIP

ISBN 0 521 56198 1 hardback
ISBN 0 521 42720 7 paperback

Contents

For my mother

Thanks

Teacher training is a collaborative enterprise and this book has grown out of many such collaborations: it would be impossible to list all the trainers and trainees who, over the years, have contributed, wittingly or unwittingly, to the development of this project. To them all, my sincere thanks. Thanks, too, to those who had a hand in the piloting process, and those whose enthusiasm kept my own enthusiasm from flagging.

I owe a special debt of gratitude to my colleagues at International House in Barcelona – Neil Forrest, Cathy Ellis, and David Clarke, in particular – who played an active part in helping develop these materials. And to my long-suffering Diploma trainees: I hope it was worth it!

The production of the book has involved a whole cohort of editors in Cambridge: I wish to record my gratitude to them all, and to thank Peter Donovan, in particular, whose support for the project at key stages was critical. Thanks also to Marion Williams and Tony Wright for their useful comments on parts of the text, and to Tallulah Forrest for her valuable help in compiling the index.

Finally, to my series editor, Ruth Gairns, I am especially grateful: without her encouragement, good-humour, perspicacity and sheer hard work this project would never have got off the ground.

Acknowledgements

The author and publishers are grateful to the authors, publishers and others who have given permission for the use of copyright material identified in the text. It has not been possible to identify the sources of all material used and in such cases the publishers would welcome information from copyright owners.

Mirror Syndication International for the extract on p.4 from the *Daily Mirror* 11.6.90; the extract on p.7 (Task 1) from *Hindoo Holiday* by J R Ackerley published by Penguin Books; Addison Wesley Longman for the following extracts: 5(a) on p.8 from *Use of English* by Quirk, Gimson and Warburg, 5(f) on p.9 from *The Teaching of Oral English* by H. E. Palmer, p.10 from *Opening Strategies* by B. Abbs and I. Freebairn, pp.13 and 70 from *Kernel Lessons Intermediate* by R. O'Neill, the entries for *angry* on p.15 from the *Longman Language Activator*, 3(a) on p.17 from *Word by Word* by S. Chalker, pp.45, 64, 106 and 124 from *Think First Certificate* by J. Naunton, pp.46 and 174 from *Sounds English* by J. O'Connor and C. Fletcher, pp.56, 96, 109 and 119 from *Intermediate Matters* by J. Bell and R. Gower, p.95 from *Living English Structure* by W. Stannard Allen, p.100 from *Beginners' Choice Workbook* by S. Thornbury, p.101 from *Longman English Grammar Exercises* by L. G. Alexander, p.102 from *Second Language Grammar: Learning and Teaching* by W. E. Rutherford, pp.108 and 123 from *The Sourcebook* by J. Shepherd and F. Cox, pp.115 and 241 from *A University Grammar of English* by R. Quirk and S. Greenbaum, p.116 from *Blueprint 2 Teacher's Book* by B. Abbs and I. Freebairn, p.125 from *Advanced Conversational English* by D. Crystal and D. Davy, p.130 from *New Proficiency English Book 1* by W. S. Fowler and J. Pidcock, p.134 from *Developing Strategies* by B. Abbs and I. Freebairn, p.135 from *Workout Advanced* by P. Radley and K. Burke, the answers on pp.191, 234 and 249 from *Think First Certificate Self-Study Guide* by R. Acklam, p.228 from *Language Issues* by G. Porter-Ladousse, all reprinted by permission of Addison Wesley Longman Ltd; Microsoft Corporation for extract 5(b) on p.8 from *MS-DOS 3.30 Operating System Manual*. MS-DOS® is a registered trademark of Microsoft Corporation. Portions reprinted with permission of Microsoft Corporation; Solo Syndication Limited for extract 5(c) on p.8 which appeared in *The London Evening Standard Magazine* Nov. 1991 and the extract on p.89 from the *Daily Express*; the stanza on p.8 (5d) from 'love is more thicker than forget' is reprinted from COMPLETE POEMS 1904–1962, by E. E. Cummings, edited by George J. Firmage, by permission of W. W. Norton & Company Ltd. Copyright© 1939, 1967, 1991 by the Trustees for the E. E. Cummings Trust; Tandem Press for extract 5(e) on p.9 from *Once Were Warriors* by A. Duff; Oxford University Press for the following extracts:pp.10, 19 and 136 from *Fast Forward 1* by V. Black, M. McNorton, A. Malderez and S. Parker (1986), p.15 from *Streamline English Departures* by P. Viney and K. Viney (1978), pp.19 and 154 from *English in Perspective Teacher's Book* by S. Dalzell and I. Edgar (1988), pp.31–2 and 38 from *Headway Upper-Intermediate Pronunciation* by B. Bowler and S. Cunningham (1991), pp.38 and 41 from *Headway Intermediate Pronunciation* by B. Bowler and S. Cunningham (1990), p.44 from *Headway Upper-Intermediate* by J. Soars and L. Soars (1987), pp.48 and 107 from *Headway Pre -Intermediate* by J. Soars and L. Soars (1991), p.71 from *A Handbook of Classroom English* by G. Hughes (1981), p.84 from *Headway Intermediate* by J. Soars and L. Soars (1986), p.108 from *Realistic English Drills* by B. Abbs, V. Cook and M. Underwood (1978), p.114 from *A Dictionary of 20th Century World Biography* edited by A. Briggs (1993), the adapted extract on p.122 from 'The illogic of logical connectives' by W. J. Crewe, *ELT Journal* 44:4 (1990), p.135 from *Grapevine 1* by P. Viney and K. Viney (1989), all by permission of Oxford University Press; the illustration on p.11 'All right, have it your way – you heard a seal bark!' Copr.© 1932, 1960 James Thurber. From *The Seal in the Bedroom*, published by HarperCollins; Cambridge University Press for the following extracts: p.13 (extract 1) from *A Way with Words 1* by S. Redman and R. Ellis, p.13 (extract 2) from *Writing Skills* by N. Coe, R. Rycroft and P. Ernest, p.13 (extract 3) from *Functions of English* by L. Jones, the adapted tables on pp.24 and 159 and the chart on p.28 from *English Phonetics and Phonology* by P. Roach, p.24 from *Ship or Sheep* by A. Baker, pp.25 (Task 8, exercise 1), 34, 37 and 99 from *The Cambridge English Course 1* by M. Swan and C. Walter, pp.25 (Task 8, exercises 2 & 3), 37, 45 and 135 from *The Cambridge English Course 2* by M. Swan and C. Walter, p.25 from *Clusters* by C. Mortimer, the illustrations on p.28 from *Clear Speech* by J. Gilbert, the diagram on p.29 from *The Cambridge Encyclopedia of Language* by D. Crystal, pp.35, 41 and 42 from *Speaking Clearly* by P. Rogerson and J. Gilbert, p.42 from *Intonation in Context* by B. Bradford, p.50 from *A Way with Words 2* by S. Redman and R. Ellis, pp.69 and 84 from *The New Cambridge English Course 2* by M. Swan and C. Walter, pp.92 and 115 from *Meanings Into Words Intermediate* by A. Doff, C. Jones and K. Mitchell, p.93 from *Language In Use Pre-Intermediate* by A. Doff and C. Jones, p.133 from *The New Cambridge English Course 1* by M. Swan and C. Walter; Phoenix ELT for the extracts on pp.13 and 25 from *How Now Brown Cow* by M. Ponsonby; Faber and Faber Ltd for the extracts on pp.18, 36 and 107 from *Tea Party and Other Plays* by H. Pinter (1967). Grove Atlantic, Inc for the extracts from *Tea Party and Other Plays* by H. Pinter (1967); Pitman Publishing for the diagram on p.29 from *Practical English Phonetics* by J. Wells and G. Colson; Heinemann for the following extracts: the chart on p.30 from *Sound Foundations* by A. Underhill, p.48 from *First Choice for Proficiency* by P. May, pp.63 and 88 from *Flying Colours 2* by J. Garton-Sprenger and S. Greenall, p.93 from *Target First Certificate* by N. Kenny and R. Johnson, p.119 from *Excel at First Certificate* by M. Vince, all reprinted by permission of Heinemann Educational, a division of Reed Educational and

Professional Publishing Ltd; Faber and Faber Ltd for the extracts on pp.40, 57, 58, 62 and 123 from *A Small Family Business* by A. Ayckbourn; IPC Magazines Ltd for the extracts on pp.43 (Task 2) and 72 from the *New Scientist* and the horoscopes on p.117 from *Options* June 1993 and April 1994; Reed Consumer Books Ltd for the extracts on pp.44 and 82 from *The Good and Faithful Servant* and the extract on p.68 from *The Ruffian on the Stair* in *The Complete Plays* by J. Orton published by Methuen; *The Good and Faithful Servant* copyright © 1970 by the Estate of Joe Orton, deceased; *The Ruffian on the Stair* copyright © 1967 by the Estate of Joe Orton, deceased. Used by permission of Grove/Atlantic, Inc; HarperCollins *Publishers* Limited for the extracts on pp.49–50 from *The Gate of Angels* by P. Fitzgerald and p.105 from *The Stories of Raymond Carver* by R. Carver; Cobuild for the entries for *fair* on p.51 from the *Collins COBUILD English Language Dictionary*, p.108 from *Collins COBUILD English Course Practice Book 1* by J. Willis and D. Willis, p.111 from *Collins COBUILD English Grammar*; The Royal Bank of Scotland plc for the extract on p.52 from Premium Account Leaflet ref L12 7/95 © The Royal Bank of Scotland plc; Attic Futura (UK) Ltd for p.52 from *Inside Soap*; the extracts on pp.54 and 55 from *I Left My Grandfather's House* by D. Welch published by Allison and Busby; New Zealand News UK for the text on p.61; Mirror Group for the extract on p.63 from *The People* 17.1.93; Reed Consumer Books Ltd for the extracts on pp.66 and 67 from *The Secret Diary of Adrian Mole* by S. Townsend published by Methuen. Copyright © 1982 Sue Townsend; *Which?* for the extracts on pp.71, 76 and 103. *Which?* is a monthly independent consumer magazine published by the Consumer's Association, 2 Marylebone Rd, London NW1 4DF. For further information including how to receive *Which?* on free trial for three months, please right to Department A3, Freepost, Hertford SG14 1YB or telephone free 0800 252100; *BBC On Air* for extracts 6(b) on p.72 and 5(b) on p.76. *BBC On Air* is the only monthly listings magazine for BBC World Service radio and BBC Prime and World television. Phone London 44 171 257 2211; Time Out Magazine Ltd for extract 6(c) on p.72; The Independent on Sunday for extract 6(d) on p.72; Chris Heath for p.74 from *The Face*; Private Eye for the extracts on pp.75 and 87–8 from *Private Eye's Colemanballs*; extract 5(a) on p.75 from *The Vanishing Hitchhiker: American Urban Legends and Their Meaning* by Jan Harold Brunvand. Copyright © 1981 by Jan Harold Brunvand. Reprinted by permission of W. W. Norton & Company, Inc; Penguin Books UK for the following extracts: 5(c) on p.76 from *The Mezzanine* by Nicholson Baker (Granta/Penguin Books, 1989) copyright © 1986, 1988 Nicholson Baker, p.106 from 'The Unicorn in the Garden' in *Fables For Our Time* from VINTAGE THURBER VOLUME 1 (p.185) by James Thurber (Hamish Hamilton, 1963) copyright © James Thurber, 1951, 1963, p.202 from *Penguin English Grammar A–Z for Advanced Students* (p.294) by Geoffrey Broughton (Penguin Books, 1990) copyright © Geoffrey Broughton, 1990, all reproduced by permission of Penguin Books Ltd; Grove/Atlantic, Inc for the extract on p.76 from *The Mezzanine* by Nicholson Baker copyright © 1986, 1988 Nicholson Baker; Macmillan General Books for the extract on p.76 from *An Unsuitable Attachment* by B. Pym; MORE Magazine New Zealand for the extract on p.77; International Herald Tribune for the extract on p.79 by Amy Hollowell, 20.9.93; the extract on p.83 from the *Adelaide Advertiser* 28.8.92 © The Advertiser, Adelaide; The European Limited for the extract on p.89; The Observer for examples 4(a–f) on p.90 from 'How will I vote' by Janet Watts, 4.4.92 Observer ©; the extract on p.94 from *The Kraken Wakes* by J. Wyndham published by Michael Joseph; the extract on p.98 © The World in 1991 – The Economist Publications; Employment Service for the JobCentre extracts on pp.101 and 230; the poem on p.104 from *The Fat Black Woman's Poems* by Grace Nichols and the extract on p.105 from *The Virago Book of Fairy Tales* edited by Angela Carter, both published by Virago Press; pp.105, 106, 120 (Task 1), 125 and 246 from *Pocket Encyclopedia* by Adrienne Jack published by Kingfisher. Copyright © Kingfisher Books Ltd 1983, 1987; the extract on p.106 from 'The Unicorn in the Garden' Copr. © 1940 James Thurber. Copr. © 1968 Rosemary A. Thurber. From *Fables For Our Time*, published by HarperCollins; Language Teaching Publications for the extract on p.107 from *Out and About* by M. Lewis; *London Property News Rentals* for the 'Hampstead' advert on p.111; the advert on p.111 from 'Resident Abroad, the FT Magazine for expatriates' © Pearson Professional Limited; the extracts on pp.111–12 from *Payment in Blood* by E. George © Susan George Toibin 1989. Published by Bantam Paperbacks, an imprint of Transworld Publishers Ltd. All rights reserved. *Payment in Blood* by E. George published by Bantam Books a division of Bantam, Doubleday, Dell Publishing Group, Inc; Hughes Massie Limited for the extracts on pp.117 and 118 from *Death on the Nile* by A. Christie. Copyright Agatha Christie Mallowan 1937; the extract on p.121 © The Times of India; Mitsubishi Electric Europe B. V. and CPS Golley Slater for the text on p.121. © CPS Golley Slater 1996; the extract on p.122 from 'Odd genius out' is reprinted by permission of Fourth Estate Ltd from THE BEDSIDE GUARDIAN 1991 edited by John Course, copyright © 1991 by Guardian Newspapers Ltd; split texts (1)/(e) on pp.126–7 appeared in *The Times* 16.9.93 © Times Newspapers Limited, 1993; Innovations plc for the extracts on pp.127, 128 and 253; the article on p.129 appeared in *Today* 7.6.94 © Today.

Introduction

The assumption underlying this book is that teachers of English not only need to be able to speak and understand the language they are teaching, but that they need to know a good deal about the way the language works: its components, its regularities, and the way it is used. It is further assumed that this kind of knowledge can usefully be gained through the investigation – or *analysis* – of samples of the language itself. Accordingly, the core of the book consists of sequences of tasks, the purpose of which is to raise the user's consciousness about language, that is, to promote language *awareness*.

What is language awareness?

In Molière's play *Le Bourgeois Gentilhomme*, Monsieur Jourdain was famously unaware that he was speaking 'prose' – until it was pointed out to him. He may have been equally surprised to know that he was speaking 'grammar', for example, or that he was pronouncing 'phonemes', or that he was producing 'discourse'. Most speakers of a language are similarly vague when it comes to identifying what it is they implicitly 'know' about their language that enables them to speak it – the underlying rule system that Chomsky termed their 'competence'. It usually requires someone to point it out to them – to make it explicit. This is what language awareness is: explicit *knowledge* about language.

But, so simply defined, the term allows multiple interpretations. In first language education the focus of language awareness is broad, encompassing not only the linguistic domain, for example, the grammar of the language, but the sociolinguistic and cultural domains as well. In the words of The National Council for Language in Education Working Party on Language Awareness: 'Language Awareness is a person's sensitivity to and conscious awareness of the nature of language *and its role in human life*.' (Donmal 1985, emphasis added). Typical activities for children might involve the exploration of the differences between written and spoken language, for example, or the researching of dialect diversity and its effects. In second language education the term has a narrower compass, referring – traditionally, at least – to linguistic knowledge only, and to the teacher's knowledge rather than the learner's. Put simply, language awareness is the knowledge that teachers have of the underlying systems of the language that enables them to teach effectively.

This is not to suggest that the broader picture – the role of language in human life – has no relevance to second language education. On the contrary, the learning of another language is significantly influenced by cultural and attitudinal factors and this is increasingly reflected in the content and approach of current EFL materials. Nevertheless, it is not within the scope of this book to explore these factors. So, if this book is 'about' language, it is about language in the narrower sense, that is *the analysis of the linguistic systems that constitute language*.

What is language analysis?

If language awareness is the goal, then language analysis is the route to it – or one route, at least. A more direct route might simply be to get hold of an up-to-date grammar and read it from cover to cover. It is a basic tenet of this book, however, that working out something for oneself pays greater dividends in terms of memory and understanding than simply having it explained. In other words, an inductive – rather than a deductive – approach to learning underpins the design of the tasks that follow. This is also consistent with the view that a discovery approach to grammar is an effective pedagogical option in second language classrooms. Language analysis, then, is a form of guided research into language. The aim of this research is to discover the language's underlying systems, in order to be in a better position to deal with them from a pedagogical perspective. Hence, the tasks do not stop at the point where the rules are laid bare – they are designed to invite the teacher to consider the pedagogical implications and classroom applications of these rules and systems.

It is perhaps important at this point to emphasise what language analysis is *not*. It is not the formal study of language known as 'linguistics'. The object of study is not language as an end in itself. The point of view is strictly a pedagogical one, i.e. what is it that a teacher needs to know about English in order to teach it effectively? While it is the case that most pedagogical descriptions of English might ultimately derive from linguistic models, or at least be accountable in terms of linguistic theory, they do not depend on these models and theories for their validity. Their validity is determined by their relevance to classroom practice – and, ultimately, learner outcomes. After all, languages were being taught successfully and pedagogical rules were being formulated long before the advent of linguistics as a science.

Why language awareness and language analysis?

It would seem to be axiomatic that knowledge of subject-matter is a prerequisite for effective teaching, whether the subject be mathematics, history, geography, or, as in this case, a second or foreign language. This is certainly the perception of learners: in a survey of several thousand former foreign language students who were asked to identify the qualities of 'outstanding' language teachers they had been taught by, the quality that was most frequently cited was that the teacher had had 'thorough knowledge of subject matter' (Moscowitz 1976). This was a characteristic quoted more often than, for example, the fact that the teacher was 'fluent in the use of the foreign language' or was 'enthusiastic, animated'.

This view is echoed throughout the literature on language awareness. For example, Wright and Bolitho (1993) are emphatic: 'The more aware a teacher is of language and how it works, the better'. It is an assumption that is manifested in the design of teacher training programmes, both at pre-service and in-service level: there are few courses that do not have a prominent language awareness component. And it is weakness in the area of language awareness that is a major cause of trainee failure on such courses. To quote from the Examinations Report for the RSA/UCLES Diploma in TEFLA examination for the year 1991/1992: 'It is a matter of concern that so many teachers of English seem to have such a limited knowledge of the language they are teaching'.

Among the consequences of such a limited knowledge of language are: a failure on the part of the teacher to anticipate learners' learning problems and a consequent inability to plan lessons that are pitched at the right level; an inability to interpret coursebook syllabuses and materials and to adapt these to the specific needs of the learners; an inability to deal satisfactorily with errors, or to field learners' queries; and a general failure to earn the confidence of the learners due to a lack of basic terminology and ability to present new language clearly and efficiently.

And yet there is a school of thought that argues that language awareness – or, at least, familiarity with the grammar – is incidental to effective teaching, and may even be prejudicial to it, especially when it becomes, not simply the means, but the object of learning a language. This view, which dates back at least to the late nineteenth-century Reform Movement and its reaction to grammar-translation methods, has been fuelled more recently by the work of Krashen (1982) and Prabhu (1987), among others. Each, independently and for different reasons, has argued that language proficiency is naturally acquired, rather than formally learned. For his part, Krashen claims that language acquisition takes place only through exposure to comprehensible input. The teacher's role is simply to facilitate comprehension and to provide the necessary input, by means, for example, of actions and simultaneous commentary. Krashen's claims for 'acquisition', as opposed to 'learning', are supported by a growing body of evidence that suggests that many grammatical items are learned in a predictable order (the 'natural order') irrespective of the order in which they are taught. Prabhu, meanwhile, argues for a strong form of the communicative approach: language learning takes place only when learners are communicating (and not before). The language learning programme is organised around a series of communicative tasks, first modelled by the teacher and then performed by the learners. Despite the differences in their methodology, both Krashen and Prabhu question the need for formal instruction, including explicit attention to grammar and error correction.

Krashen's, and, to a lesser extent, Prabhu's, views have had a wide following, despite critiques of their theoretical probity, on the one hand, and their research methods, on the other. There is a strong intuitive appeal in the idea that language acquisition simply 'grows', like a plant, given the right conditions of nurture. And it is this strong non-interventionist, 'anti-grammar' view that has led some language teachers to argue that they, unlike their colleagues in the mathematics or the history department, are exempt from the need to be authorities in their subject matter. They don't need to know their grammar.

The best that can be said about such a position is that it is somewhat ingenuous. (It is also a view that both Krashen and Prabhu would probably wish to disassociate themselves from.) Essentially, this argument confuses the needs of teachers on the one hand, and of learners on the other. If doctors choose not to baffle their patients with complex anatomical terminology, this does not exempt them from the requirement to know as much as they humanly can about anatomy. Likewise, language teachers, regardless of the methodology they adopt, are still *language* teachers. Whether or not they choose to make explicit to the learners the systems underlying the language they are teaching, they are still bound to be authorities in the language itself.

This is because, irrespective of the methodology chosen, one of the goals of language instruction is that the learners move in the direction of achieving the kind of proficiency in the language that native speakers have, what is now generally termed 'communicative competence'. This is the knowledge of what constitutes effective language behaviour in relation to one's communicative objectives. This knowledge includes not only the knowledge of what language is appropriate in a given situation for a given purpose ('sociolinguistic' competence) but of what is 'correct' – that is, 'linguistic' competence. Judgements about accuracy, therefore, inform teachers' decisions about learners at every stage of the learning process, right from the point where students are initially placed in classes of particular levels. Even the most basic pedagogical choices – between one task and another, or one text and another, or one test and another, or one textbook and another – will at some point require informed decisions to be made on the basis of the language content.

Of course, there have always been teachers who have been over-zealous in their desire to display their language awareness, and teachers who have been over-concerned with linguistic accuracy at the expense of fluency – teachers, in short, who have given grammar teaching a bad name. As Wright (1991) has pointed out: 'One great danger of acquiring specialist knowledge is the possible desire to show learners that you have this knowledge'. But this is not a problem of too much knowledge; it is a problem of not enough methodology. The remedy for 'chalk-and-talk' type teaching lies in (re-)training such teachers in the use of techniques that are more consistent with what we now know about the way people learn and what language proficiency consists of. That such teachers exist – and have always existed – is not sufficient grounds to reject the value of language awareness out of hand.

Moreover, to counter the non-interventionist theories of Krashen and Prabhu, there is a growing body of evidence to suggest that failure to balance communicative practice with 'a focus on form' (Long 1991) – whether it be in the form of grammar presentations, explicit correction or pattern practice drills – can result in premature 'fossilisation'. The pressure to communicate meanings that require the use of language beyond the learner's level of linguistic proficiency may result in the learner coming to depend on a simplified and lexicalised form of communication – a kind of personal 'pidgin'.

It seems that grammar instruction, while not necessarily changing the natural order of acquisition, may well accelerate the learner's progress along it. Accordingly, there has been a movement to promote the need for grammatical 'consciousness raising' techniques (Rutherford 1987): techniques that focus the learner's attention on salient features and recurring patterns in language data. It has also been claimed (e.g. Ellis 1993) that explicit attention to grammatical forms helps learners both to notice these forms when they occur in natural contexts – thereby improving the chances of input becoming 'intake' – and to 'notice the gap' between their own output and the target language input. Both kinds of 'noticing', it is claimed, accelerate the process by which the learner's developing 'interlanguage' system is restructured: noticing is necessary for acquisition.

This suggests that one of the teacher's key roles is to facilitate the process of noticing. This, in turn, presupposes that the teacher has sufficient language awareness to be able to alert the learner to the features of the language to be 'noticed' and to guide the process of consciousness-raising, whether through explicit rule-giving or guided discovery approaches. The teacher also needs to be sensitive to the learner's developing interlanguage so that consciousness-raising activities can be timed to coincide with the learner's optimal state of readiness.

In the context of a task-based approach, for example, at each stage of the teaching cycle – task-selection, task-setting, task-monitoring and task-checking – decisions will need to be made that demand a fairly sophisticated level of language awareness. And the language awareness will need to be of the kind that not only encompasses a wide range of systems (grammar, vocabulary, phonology and discourse), but is available at a moment's notice, according to the needs of individual learners each at different stages of readiness.

Who is this book for?

Once the need for language awareness is accepted, the question remains: how do you get it? The particular problem for many language teachers is that, unlike, say, teachers of mathematics or history, they may never have formally studied the subject that they are teaching. This is, of course, typically the case of teachers who are teaching their first language (their L1). It is a common experience of novice native-speaker teachers of English that their knowledge of English grammar is fragmentary at best, and, at worst, may well be below the level of their students.

Teachers for whom English is a second language (L2) are often at an advantage here, since they have experienced English learning first-hand. But, even for these teachers 'some reconversion and updating of awareness (e.g. from structural to functional, from prescriptive to descriptive) may be called for' (Britten 1985).

Who, then, is this book for? Essentially, for any teachers, or teachers-to-be, whether native speakers of English or not, either teaching in the public or the private sector, who need to fine-tune their language analysis skills. For example: trainee teachers on courses in preparation for an initial qualification such as the RSA/UCLES Certificate; or for teachers taking in-service training courses such as those in preparation for the RSA/UCLES Diploma, or for TESOL Diplomas awarded by universities. It is also intended for use by teachers whose first language is not English, such as participants on RSA/UCLES COTE, DOTE or CEELT schemes. Directors of studies responsible for providing in-service programmes to their teaching staff may find the tasks useful; so, too, may informal teacher development groups. Finally, it is hoped that the book will be of use to teachers studying on their own.

How is it organised?

There is an Introductory unit, whose main purpose is diagnostic, followed by 28 units, with about ten tasks per unit. The unit topics have been chosen to reflect the syllabus specifications of pre- and in-service training courses such as those mentioned above. These specifications, in turn, tend to match the content areas of current published EFL materials, both textbooks and pedagogical grammars. Despite the criticisms that have been levelled at the discrete-item, verb-phrase weighted nature of these kinds of syllabuses, it is nevertheless the case that most teachers will be working within this paradigm, and will need to familiarise themselves with the categories and terms they are likely to meet.

The sequence of topics adopts a 'bottom-up' approach to language: that is, the smallest unit of description, the phoneme, is the starting point, and the levels of analysis proceed through words (and morphemes), phrases and sentences, and finally, whole texts. It would be just as logical – or much more logical, genre analysts would argue – to start at the topmost level of analysis – the text – and work 'down'. This, in fact, is quite possible, and a progression through Units 1, 2 and 3, and then 26, 27, and 28 would be consistent with a discourse-centred view of language analysis.

Each unit typically consists of a variety of activity types, including (and often in this order):

- Identification/recognition tasks: 'Find all the examples of X'.
- Categorisation tasks: 'Classify all the examples of X'.
- Matching tasks: 'Match examples X with definitions Y'.
- Explanation/interpretation tasks: 'Explain all the examples of X'.
- Evaluation tasks: 'Assess the usefulness of this exercise to practise item X'.
- Application tasks: 'Design an exercise to practise item X'.

A key principle that has guided the preparation of these materials is that, as much as possible, the examples chosen to illustrate features of the language systems have been collected from authentic sources. This is consistent with a growing commitment on the part of grammarians and lexicographers to describe real usage, and to avoid at all costs a dependence on the kind of contrived examples often found in traditional grammars. (The costs, of course, include brevity and comprehensibility: authentic examples are by definition unsimplified.) Likewise, it is felt that language divorced from its co-text (not to mention its context of use) has little value for the purposes of analysis. Many teacher trainers will be familiar with the kind of fruitless arguments that often result from the attempted analysis of sentences in isolation. Does, for example, *I have been painting the car* represent a finished or an unfinished action? Is *It's going to rain* certain or just probable? Does *Can you drive?* refer to ability or is it a request? And so on.

Nevertheless, it is simply not practicable to provide the complete co-text for a citation, and many of the examples will have to be taken on trust. Moreover, most teachers have to work with materials that not only use decontextualised, manufactured examples of language for presentation and practice purposes, but often 'present' language rules that are contradicted by the evidence. Since this is essentially a practical introduction to language analysis, exposure to such materials is of key importance in terms of preparing teachers for some of the conundrums they will encounter in the classroom. That some of these conundrums are created by the materials themselves is a point worth making, even at the risk of occasionally presenting the trainee with conflicting views on certain issues.

At the same time, it is in the nature of language – essentially a unitary and fluid entity – to resist attempts at dissection and compartmentalisation. There are few easy answers in language analysis: even such fundamental categories as noun, verb, adjective and adverb are notoriously fuzzy. The trainer and the trainee should not be surprised, therefore, if there are often more questions raised than can be neatly and conveniently answered.

Nor is the material exhaustive. There is a great deal that has had to be left out, in the interests of clarity, of space, and of perceived usefulness. Readers should not expect that here they will find the last, or even the latest, word on every issue dealt with. But, if any frustration or disagreement that results from using these materials encourages teachers to research the areas in question more exhaustively, so much the better.

Key and commentaries

The answers to individual exercises and the commentaries that accompany them make up the latter part of the book, and should be used in conjunction with the tasks in the units. The commentaries are more than simply answers: they attempt to provide explanations for the answers, and are designed to be used by both the individual reader and by tutors using these on courses. An attempt has been made to anticipate sources of confusion, but, again, the commentaries are not exhaustive, and those readers interested in pursuing particular areas should consult the Bibliography.

How do you use this book?

It is not expected that all the material will be of equal relevance to different groups of users: teacher trainers are advised to use the material selectively, choosing those units, and those tasks within the units, whose content is both relevant to the courses they run and practicable within the constraints in which they are operating.

The material is designed for – and has been trialled extensively with – classes of trainee teachers working in pairs or groups, but it can also be used by trainees working individually.

A recommended basic approach to the material is the following:

- *Establish the topic*, for example, by reference to the the trainees' own classes – if the programme includes a practicum; or to a sample of typical learner errors relating to the language area in question; or to the teaching materials the trainees have used, and particular problems that they have met with regard to the topic. Alternatively, as a 'warmer', get the trainees to do a short activity designed for EFL students and targeted at the language area under study. *Grammar Practice Activities* by Penny Ur and *Five-Minute Activities* by Penny Ur and Andrew Wright are good sources for such activities.

- *Trainees work on the tasks*, either individually, in pairs or in groups. The tasks are designed to be used in sequence, but it is recommended that each task be checked before moving on to the next. Some tasks can be set for homework, to be done in advance of the next session. Alternatively, the trainees can be asked to read through the complete unit in advance of the session, in order to familiarise themselves with the content. If the training group is not too big, the tasks can then be discussed in open class.

- *To check the tasks*, the trainees can either be referred to the Key and commentaries at the back of the book, or the trainer can solicit feedback on the tasks from pairs/groups and lead a general discussion of the issues raised. Even if the task rubric does not specify it, it is important, where possible, to try to relate each task to the specific teaching context of the trainees.

- Possible *follow-up activities* might include:
  - collecting and analysing examples of student errors relating to the area under study;
  - collecting and analysing authentic (naturally occurring) examples of the area under study;
  - evaluating available EFL materials with regard to their treatment of the language area;
  - planning a lesson or a sequence of lessons to deal with the language area in question, targeted at a specific class of learners; and, if possible teaching the lesson(s), evaluating the effectiveness of the lesson in dealing with anticipated problems with regard to the language point;
  - if the trainees are to sit an examination, writing an essay related to the theme, to be done either in their own time or under examination conditions.

Further reading

Finally, for readers interested in following up any of the areas and issues raised in the book, here is a short list of those books that were particularly useful in the preparation of these materials. (Their inclusion in the list does not absolve the author from responsibility for any errors in the text that follows: any such errors are entirely his own.)

Broughton, G. (1990) *The Penguin English Grammar A–Z for Advanced Students*. Penguin.
Chalker, S. (1990) *English Grammar Word by Word*. Addison Wesley Longman.
Collins COBUILD English Grammar. (1990) Collins.
Comrie, B. (1976) *Aspect*. Cambridge University Press.
Comrie, B. (1985) *Tense*. Cambridge University Press.
Crystal, D. (1987) *The Cambridge Encyclopedia of Language*. Cambridge University Press.
Crystal, D. (1988) *Rediscovering Grammar*. Addison Wesley Longman.

Downing, A. and Locke, P. (1992) *A University Course in English Grammar*. Phoenix ELT.

Gairns, R. and Redman, S. (1986) *Working with Words*. Cambridge University Press.

Hatch, E. (1992) *Discourse and Language Education*. Cambridge University Press.

Huddleston, R. (1988) *English Grammar: An Outline*. Cambridge University Press.

Jackson, H. (1980, 1982) *Analyzing English*. Pergamon.

Leech, G. (second edition 1987) *Meaning and The English Verb*. Addison Wesley Longman.

Leech, G. (1988) *An A–Z of English Grammar and Usage*. Edward Arnold.

Leech, G. and Svartvik, J. (1975) *A Communicative Grammar of English*. Addison Wesley Longman.

Lewis, M. (1986) *The English Verb*. LTP.

McCarthy, M. (1990) *Vocabulary*. Oxford University Press.

McCarthy, M. (1991) *Discourse Analysis for Language Teachers*. Cambridge University Press.

Palmer, F. R. (1988) *Modality and the English Modals*. Addison Wesley Longman.

Quirk, R. and Greenbaum, S. (1973) *A University Grammar of English*. Addison Wesley Longman.

Roach, P. (second edition 1991) *English Phonetics and Phonology*. Cambridge University Press.

Swan, M. (1980) *Practical English Usage*. Oxford University Press.

Wells, J.C. and Colson, G. (1971) *Practical Phonetics*. Addison Wesley Longman.

References

Britten, D. (1985) Teacher training in ELT. *Language Teaching Abstracts* **18**, 2/3.

Donmal, B.G. (ed.) (1985) *Language Awareness: NCLE Reports and papers, 6*. CILT.

Ellis, R. (1993) *Second language acquisition and the structural syllabus*. TESOL Quarterly, *27*, 91–113.

James, C. and Garrett, P. (eds) (1991) *Language Awareness in the Classroom*. Addison Wesley Longman.

Krashen, S. (1982) *Principles and Practice in Second Language Acquisition*. Pergamon.

Long, M. (1991) Focus on form: a design feature in language teaching methodology. In de Bot, K., Coste, D., Ginsberg, R. and Kramsch, C. (eds) *Foreign Language Research in Cross-cultural Perspectives*. John Benjamins.

Moscowitz, G. (1976) The classroom interaction of outstanding foreign language teachers. *Foreign Language Annals 2*, 135–157.

Prabhu, N.S. (1987) *Second Language Pedagogy*. Oxford University Press.

Rutherford, W. (1987) *Second Language Grammar: Learning and Teaching*. Addison Wesley Longman.

Wright, T. (1991) Language awareness in teacher education programmes for non-native speakers. In James, C. and Garret, P. (eds), *Language Awareness in the Classroom*. Addison Wesley Longman.

Wright, T. and Bolitho, R. (1993) Language awareness: a missing link in language teacher education? *English Language Teaching Journal, 47*, 4, 292–304.

Tasks

Introductory unit

Introduction

This unit is designed to get you started, and invites you to consider some key issues related to the teaching of language – language being the operative word here – since the focus of this book is less on methodology than on the nature of language itself. Nevertheless, since it is written for language teachers, questions of methodology will inevitably enter into the discussion.

Tasks

1 **Opinions about language learning and teaching**   Consider these statements. To what extent and in what respects do you agree/disagree?

a) Learning a language is first and foremost a question of learning its grammar.

b) It is the language teacher's responsibility to know as much as possible about the language itself.

c) Grammar is best learned deductively – that is, by studying rules and then applying the rules to examples.

d) Grammatical terminology is best avoided in the classroom.

e) Giving learners complete rules, even if these are more complicated, is better than giving them half-rules.

f) Language should always be studied in its typical contexts of use, rather than in isolation.

g) English doesn't have very much grammar, compared to some languages.

h) The most important part of grammar is the verb system.

2 Read this text and answer the questions:

Webber blocks 'Evita' Madonna

By KEVIN SMITH

A PLAN to star pop queen Madonna in a film version of Evita has been vetoed by composer Andrew Lloyd Webber.

Angry Andrew, who co-wrote the stage blockbuster with Tim Rice, vowed that anyone BUT Madonna should play the part after she demanded to rewrite some of his songs.

Now Walt Disney, makers of the £30 million picture, are insisting that she must star.

And they have called for a meeting between her and Lloyd Webber in New York this week to sort out their differences.

Madonna was offered the part last year but was dumped when she clashed with Webber over the award-winning score.

She said then: "The music needs updating.

I told Oliver Stone, the director, that I was interested in working with Andrew and writing some new songs.

In the end Oliver thought I was going to be a huge pain in the butt."

(Reproduced by kind permission of the *Daily Mirror*)

Text type

a) In what sort of publication did this text appear? What features of the layout tell you this?

b) What is the overall purpose (or function) of the text – is it, for example, to advertise, to inform, to complain, to criticise?

c) Identify any stylistic features that are typical of this kind of text, for example, the use of the present tense in the headline.

Text organisation

Put these facts in chronological order:

a) Webber vetoed the choice of Madonna.
b) Webber co-wrote *Evita*.
c) Madonna demanded to rewrite some songs.
d) Disney called a meeting.
e) Madonna was offered the part.
f) Oliver Stone thought Madonna was a pain.

Why has the above order been chosen for the text, rather than the chronological one?

Cohesion

a) What do the following words refer to: *his* (line 8); *they* (line 12); *their* (line 14). How do you know?
b) *Composer Andrew Lloyd Webber*; *Angry Andrew*; *Lloyd Webber*; *Webber*; *Andrew* – is this the same person? If so, why is he referred to in five different ways?
c) How many words can you find that have something to do with (1) cinema; (2) music; (3) argument?
d) Identify these references: *Now* (line 9); *this* (line 14); *last* (line 16); *then* (line 20).
e) Why do the features in (a–d) help make the text cohesive?

Now that you have looked at the text as a whole, work through the following questions, which focus on specific parts of it.

Vocabulary

a) How are the following words formed: *rewrite*; *composer*; *award-winning*; *pop*; *to star*.
b) What is the connotation of the words *dumped* (line 17) and *clashed* (line 18)?
c) What is the style of the expression *a pain in the butt* (line 26)?

Grammar

a) Can you identify the part of speech of each of the following words in the text:

a plan vetoed by angry who after now

b) Can you match the phrase with the example

a noun phrase	then
a verb phrase	in the end
an adverb phrase	has been vetoed
an adjective phrase	a film version of Evita
a prepositional phrase	interested in working with Andrew

c) Can you analyse the headline in terms of subject, verb and object?

d) Do the same for the sentence beginning *Now Walt Disney* . . . (line 9).

e) Find an example of:

an infinitive
a present participle
a past participle
an auxiliary verb
a modal auxiliary

f) Find an example of:

present tense
past tense
perfect aspect
progressive aspect

g) Find an example of:

a transitive verb
an intransitive verb
a phrasal verb

Discussion

How useful do you think it is to be familiar with the kind of terminology dealt with above? Do you think it is possible to teach successfully (a) without knowing the terminology; (b) knowing it, but without using it?

1 Language standards and rules

Introduction

What English should we teach? What is 'correct' English? Who decides? This unit addresses these questions.

Tasks

1 **What is the rule?** A traveller in India was asked a question of usage that will be familiar to many teachers of English:

'If I am introduced to an Englishman, and he says "How d'you do?" to me, what do I reply? Shall I say "I am very well, thank you, how are you?" What is the rule, please?'

How would you answer this question?

2 Imagine a student of English asks you the following. How would you respond?

a) How do you answer the phone in English?
b) What is the correct spelling: *specialise* or *specialize*?
c) What is the past of *must*?
d) Why can you say *I'm absolutely furious* but not *I'm absolutely angry*?
e) Is it *different from* or *different than*?
f) How do you introduce your unmarried partner to a stranger?
g) Do you say *I didn't use to*…or *I usedn't to*…?

Consult with colleagues. Where do the answers come from – something you read in a book, something a teacher taught you, or simply a hunch?

3 **Prescriptive, descriptive and pedagogical rules** All of the following are presented as 'rules'. Can you categorise them according to whether they 'prescribe', 'describe', or are 'pedagogical' rules?

a) Use *a* before consonants and *an* before vowels.
b) '*Ain't* is merely colloquial, and as used for *isn't* is an uneducated blunder and serves no useful purpose.' (Fowler) ⎯⎯⎯
c) 'In the past, *whom* was normally used as the object of a relative clause. Nowadays, *who* is more often used.' (COBUILD)
d) When addressing an archbishop say 'Your Grace'. Begin an official speech 'My Lord Archbishop…'.
e) *i* before *e* except after *c*.
f) 'In British English, action verbs with *already* prefer perfect, not past, tenses: "I have already decided what to do." But in American English we can say: "I already decided".' (Chalker)

g) 'The simple past tense in regular verbs is formed by adding *-ed* to the infinitive.' (Thomson and Martinet)
h) 'Never use the passive when you can use the active.' (Orwell)
i) Use *some* in statements, *any* in questions and negatives.

How useful do you find the pedagogical rules in the above list?

4 Breaking rules   The fact that language seems to be rule-governed is apparent when the rules are broken. In which of the following are rules being broken? Which rules?

a) My dear Jane, make haste and hurry down. He is come – Mr Bingley is come.
b) If I'd have thought that this little film would have got so much exposure!
c) Well what's the what's the failure with the football I mean this this I don't really see I mean it 'cause the money how much does it cost to get in down the road now?
d) I love clothes just how I love money. I'm a star and I can't be in the same dotty boot every day, like things ain't happening for me.
e) I live in Sant Pol, is a village beautiful near the beach, the peoples is very happy.
f) The holiday I'm used to remembering with a wide smile is the one we went on when I was ten years old.

Who do you think the speaker (or writer) is, in each case? Are they, for example, native or non-native speakers of English?

5 Different Englishes   Can you identify the possible source of the following extracts? In what ways do they differ from 'standard English'? Why?

a) For the purposes of this Part of this Schedule a person over pensionable age, not being an insured person, shall be treated as an employed person if he would be an insured person were he under pensionable age and would be an employed person were he an insured person.

b) DISKCOPY does not recognize assigned drives. If you have used the ASSIGN command to change the drive assignment, you must reset the drives back to their original assignment before executing DISKCOPY. Do not use DISKCOPY on any drives that are being used in a JOIN or SUBST command. Do not use this command on a network drive.

c) Plaque. The biggest single cause of gum disease and tooth decay. Invisible. Doing its worst in those hard to get at places, in the gaps, out of reach of all but the most zealous brushers and flossers.

But now there's a simple way to dramatically reduce it.

d) love is less always than to win
less never than alive
less bigger than the least begin
less littler than forgive

e) The gathering gaining more and more as people strolled from up the street, down the street, from all over Pine Block as telephones passed the word around. And this flashly dressed Maori fulla addressing the growing crowd, and the venue the Heke place of all places. And boy was he laying it n the line toem: tellin em to jack their ideas up. Ta stop being lazy. …Ta stop feeling sorry for emselves. Ta stop blamin the Pakeha for their woes even if it *was* the Pakeha much to blame.

f) This is my head. That is your head.

Is this my head? Is this your head?

Is this my head or your head?

Is this my head or my foot?

g) The best day of my life was i borned. This day, my mother was very fat and her weight was seventy kilos. When the twelve o'clock, i can't to sleep very mutch and I said 'I want to go out!!' I screamed and danced in the bowels of my mother. Then the doctor loocked my mother, he said 'Good, good, your son is going out'!

6 **Researching usage**   In an attempt to find out what speakers actually *do* say – rather than what they *should* say – sociolinguists have devised ways of eliciting language behaviour such as the following 'discourse completion test'. Try it on yourself, and then compare your answers with a partner:

a) *A colleague at work drops into your office*:

Colleague: We're having a few friends round for dinner next Saturday night and I was wondering if you and your friend would like to join us?

You: …

Colleague: Oh, well, maybe another time then.

b) *You are sitting in a crowded open-air café and a person you don't know approaches you*:

Stranger: Do you mind if I share your table?

You: …

Stranger: I guess I'll just have to wait until someone leaves, then.

c) *In your school your colleague and flat-mate Bob is off work due to an illness. His student, Etsuko, approaches you*:

Etsuko: Excuse me, do you think I could have Bob's address so I could send him some flowers?

You: …

Etsuko: Thank you all the same.

Devise a discourse completion test to research the way people *disagree* in English. Try it on your colleagues.

7 **EFL materials**   Teachers (and writers of coursebooks) have to make choices with regard to the language they teach. Inevitably, a compromise has to be made between what is thought to be in current usage, what the teacher herself says, and what is in the best interests of the learner.

For example, look at the way the 'how do you do?' question is dealt with in different ELT texts. Do you think these reflect current usage?

Informal	*Formal*
This is Rita. She's from Bonn.	Rita, I'd like you to meet Mr ....
Hello, Rita. Nice to meet you.	How do you do?
Hello.	How do you do?

(from *Fast Forward 1* by V. Black, M. McNorton, A. Malderez and S. Parker)

DIANA:	Hello. Are you here for the video conference?
VINCE:	Yes, we are. Are you?
DIANA:	Yes, I am.
VINCE:	That's nice. I'm Vince and this is Joanne.
JOANNE:	Hi. Pleased to meet you.
DIANA:	Paul! Come and meet these people. Paul, this is Vince and Joanne. They're here for the conference, too.
PAUL:	How do you do.
VINCE:	That's neat! 'How do you do!' You British are very polite!

(from *Opening Strategies* by B. Abbs and I. Freebairn)

Finally, you might be interested to know how the traveller responded to the query about the correct response to How d'you do?:

'I said I did not think there was any rule, but that the best thing was to say "How d'you do?" too, and to try to get it in first and to say it with as little fuss as possible.'

2 Language systems and syllabuses

Introduction

The aim of these tasks is to help you think about what kind of linguistic knowledge speakers of a language draw on in order to express themselves. Attempts to identify and describe this 'knowledge' are often motivated by the need to devise programmes for language teaching. Programme designers are faced with the problem: What is it that language learners need to know?

Tasks

1 Spoken language   Let's start with a piece of spoken language:

'*All right, have it your way – you heard a seal bark!*'

(from *The Seal in the Bedroom* by J. Thurber)

Why don't these alternatives work as well as the original – 'You heard a seal bark'?

a) You heard a sill berk.
b) You heard a seal moo.
c) You heard bark a seal.
d) You've heard a seal barking.
e) Would you like to hear a seal bark?
f) Dear Albert, You heard a seal bark. Yours truly, Beryl.
g) A marine pinniped mammal going bow-wow was audible unto thee.

2 Language systems   Each of the alternatives above (a – g) represents 'incompetence' in one of the following systems. Can you match them? The first has been done for you:

- Vocabulary: knowledge of what words mean and how they are used. (b)
- Syntax: knowledge of how words are ordered and sentences constructed.
- Appropriacy and style: knowledge of what language is appropriate according to who one is speaking to, about what and by what means.
- Phonology: knowledge of how to pronounce individual sounds, words and chunks of speech.
- Grammar and morphology: knowledge of how words and phrases are marked for tense, person, case, etc.
- Knowledge of different types of texts and their conventions (sometimes called 'discourse competence').
- Knowledge of what forms are appropriate in order to realise one's communicative purpose (or function). This has been called 'pragmatic competence'.

3 Error analysis   Which of these systems is this student of English having trouble with?

Webber blocks Evita Madonna
The musical show Evita has been chosen as a candidate for a Walt Disney's millionary picture. On the beggining they thought on Miss Madonna to be the main star. She accepted, but the music compositor, Webber, refused her to take place in the film. The producter, decided to meet both involved to solve the problem. Madonna had some argues with the director Oliver Stone, who, I don't know why, had to think she was like a pain in the neck.

4 **Syllabuses**   These are ways of organising the language systems for teaching purposes. Look at these extracts from the contents pages of some language courses. Which of the language systems is each one dealing with?

1

Contents

Thanks   vi

1   Learning   1
2   Around the house   6
3   Clothes and shopping   12
4   Food and drink   18
5   People and relationships   23
6   Revision and expansion   28
7   Time   33
8   Holidays and travel   37

(from *A Way with Words 1* by S. Redman and R. Ellis)

2

Contents

To the student   4

1   Informal letters   5
2   Formal letters I   16
3   Formal letters II   26
4   Reports   41

(from *Writing Skills* by N. Coe, R. Rycroft and P. Ernest)

3

Contents

Acknowledgements   v

Introduction   1

1   Talking about yourself, starting a conversation, making a date   13

2   Asking for information: question techniques, answering techniques, getting more information   22

3   Getting people to do things: requesting, attracting attention, agreeing and refusing   28

4   Talking about past events: remembering, describing experiences, imagining 'What if . . .'   34

5   Conversation techniques: hesitating, preventing interruptions and interrupting politely, bringing in other people   38

6   Talking about the future: stating intentions, discussing probability, considering 'What if . . .'   42

(from *Functions of English* by L. Jones)

4

Contents

Introduction

1.	[p] pin	*A present for Penelope*
2.	[b] bin	*Brandy in the baby's bottle!*
3.	[t] tie	*Waiting for Templetons*
4.	[d] die	*All dressed up for a date with David*
5.	[k] cut	*Cash in the ice-cream carton*
6.	[g] gut	*Eggs from the Greek grocer*
7.	Syllable stress	*Photography or politics?*
8.	[f] fun	*A fine, flashy fox fur*
9.	[v] victory	*A visit to Vladivostok*
10.	[w] will	*Rowena, are you awake?*

(from *How Now Brown Cow?* by M. Ponsonby)

5

Contents

Foreword
Students' Introduction

Unit 1   Present simple and position of time adverbs
2   Present continuous
3   Simple past tense Regular and irregular verbs
4   Mass and unit
5   Some, any, a few, a little
6   Past tense with 'Ago' and questions with 'How long ago?'
7   Adjectives and adverbs
8   Comparison of adverbs

(from *Kernel Lessons Intermediate* by R. O'Neill)

5 Now, can you add these items to their respective syllabuses in Task 4? The first one has been done for you.

   a) Describing places and describing people. 3
   b) Entertainment.
   c) Going to do.
   d) Sentence rhythm.
   e) Moods and feelings: being sarcastic, being angry, being sad.
   f) Writing a story.
   g) Consonant clusters.
   h) Crime.
   i) Passive voice in present perfect and past.
   j) Business letters and memos.
   k) Complaining, apologetic responses, apologising.
   l) Reported speech.

6 Syllabus design   This involves making choices with regard to which items to include (selection) and in what order to include them (grading). Which of the items in Task 5 would you expect to find included in a beginners' general English syllabus? What factors determined your choice?

7 Grading   Items in syllabuses are often ordered in terms of their grammatical complexity. Can you order these structures from the most simple to the most complex?

   a) she has been working
      she worked
      she is working
      she works
      she will have been working
      she has worked

   b) where does she work?
      does she work?
      she works
      she doesn't work
      doesn't she work?

8 Natural syllabuses   Research into second language acquisition suggests that – irrespective of the teaching programmes designed for them – learners tend to acquire English grammatical items in a set order: what is sometimes called 'the natural order'.

Column 1 is an attempt to describe the natural order (after Krashen and Terrell). (The authors make no claims about the order of items within each group, only about the order of the groups themselves.) Column 2 represents the order in which the same items appear in a 'traditional' beginners' syllabus (*Streamline English* by Hartley and Viney). What differences and similarities do you note?

'The natural order'   *Streamline English*

-ing (progressive) plural copula (*to be*)

article (*a*)

verb *to be*

plural

auxiliary (progressive) article (*a, the*)

possessive (*'s*)

present progressive (auxiliary and *-ing*)

irregular past

present simple (+ third person singular)

regular past third person singular (*-s*) possessive (*'s*)

regular past

irregular past

What is the significance for teachers of there being a natural order of language acquisition?

9 **Lexical grading**   Just as with grammatical structures, choices often have to be made with regard to the teaching of vocabulary for active use. For example, these words and expressions are included in the *Longman Language Activator* under *angry*. Which of them would more likely feature in a beginners' course, which in an intermediate course, and which in an advanced course? What factors determined your decisions?

angry   mad   annoyed   cross

be in a temper   pissed off   pissed

be worked up   furious   irate   incensed

livid   seething   be on the warpath

3   Forms, functions, notions, texts

Introduction

In this unit we look at the relation between language forms and the functions these forms serve in their contexts of use. This is the area of language study sometimes called 'pragmatics'.

Tasks

1 **Meaning**   In talking about language we need to distinguish two kinds of meaning: 'semantic' meaning (the literal meaning of a text or utterance), and 'pragmatic' meaning (or the meaning the text/utterance takes on in its context of use).

a) Which picture most closely represents the 'literal' meaning of the following text?

This coach has powerful overhead ventilation. You will be more comfortable with windows closed.

b) What was the writer's probable intention?

– to inform
– to boast
– to warn against
– to promise

How do you know?

2 Context   Think of different contexts for the following utterances. What communicative function does the utterance perform, in each case?

a) I'm in the bath.
b) There's a policeman crossing the road.
c) It's ten to five.
d) How many fingers have I got?
e) That seat's taken.
f) Let him have it!

3 Text functions   Language does not exist in isolation. A starting point in the analysis of language is the text, and the function of the text in its context.

Look at the following short texts. In each case can you identify:
– the kind of text it is (its text type)?
– its probable context – that is, the situation in which it is used?
– its communicative function?

a) My grateful thanks to David Newby, for making valuable comments on the manuscript – and to Professor Sidney Greenbaum for allowing me to quote from the spoken and written texts that form the Survey of English Usage at University College London.

b) Dear Piet and Scott,

Thanks a million for those beautiful photos. Take care. I'll keep you posted *re* the exhibition. Best wishes.

Wali

c) JO, sleepy Dormouse huggle me, love Hamster Cheeks.

d) Hello, this is 374 8985. We don't value obscene phone calls from fundraisers, pollsters, or sales representatives. If you know us personally or otherwise have an appropriate and courteous reason for using a private phone line, please leave a message.

e) Your attention please. Passengers alighting at the next station are advised to be aware of the gap between the train and the platform.

f) Thank you for not smoking.

4 Functions, notions, grammatical forms and texts   Classify the following according to whether they are communicative functions, notions, grammatical forms, or text types (also called 'discourse' types):

a) duration   *notion*
b) complaining   *function*
c) comparatives   *grammatical form*
d) choosing
e) jokes
f) narrating
g) probability
h) guessing
i) past simple

j) futurity
k) biography
l) *can*
m) frequency
n) mass and unit
o) making arrangements
p) telephone conversations
q) passive

5 Form and function   There is no one-to-one match between form and function.

a) The following extracts (from *Tea Party and Other Plays* by Harold Pinter) are all requests of one kind or another. What grammatical structures do they use?

1 Could I have Newcastle 77254, please? *modal verb could*
2 Can I have a private word with you, old chap?
3 I was just wondering if you'd mind if I put my high-heeled shoes on your chair.
4 May I ask the reason?
5 Find that girl for me. As a favour.
6 Why don't you lend Wally a few pound, Mr Solto?

b) Identify the (probable) function of each of these utterances:

1 Have a custard tart, Mr Solto. *offer*
2 Ring Disley. Tell him to come here.
3 Come on. Annie, help me clear the table.
4 Buzz off before I call a copper.
5 Mind how you go.
6 Take my tip, Wally, wipe the whole business from your head, wipe it clean out of your mind.

What verb form do all the examples in (**b**) share?

c) Parts (**a**) and (**b**) of this task suggest that one function can be realised by any number of different linguistic forms, and that any one linguistic form can be used to express a number of different functions. Think of five functional uses of the 'first conditional' (*If you do X, I'll do Y*).

6 Functional syllabuses   For teaching purposes, certain functions are commonly associated with certain structures, and vice versa.

For example, this is part of the Contents page from *English in Perspective* by Dalzell and Edgar. Some of the main language points in the first nine units are on the left. Their corresponding notional and functional categories have been re-arranged on the right. Can you match up the two halves of the syllabus?

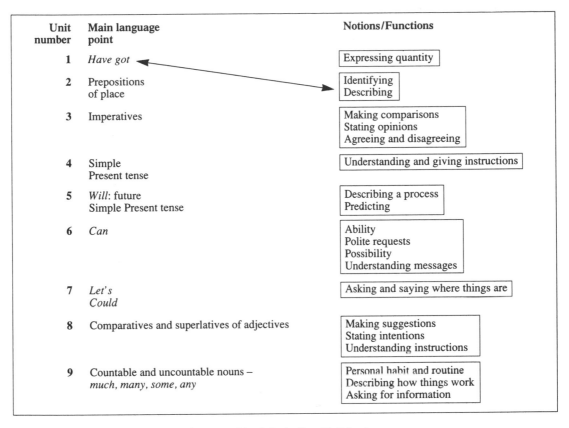

Unit number	Main language point	Notions/Functions
1	*Have got*	Expressing quantity
2	Prepositions of place	Identifying / Describing
3	Imperatives	Making comparisons / Stating opinions / Agreeing and disagreeing
4	Simple Present tense	Understanding and giving instructions
5	*Will*: future Simple Present tense	Describing a process / Predicting
6	*Can*	Ability / Polite requests / Possibility / Understanding messages
7	*Let's* / *Could*	Asking and saying where things are
8	Comparatives and superlatives of adjectives	Making suggestions / Stating intentions / Understanding instructions
9	Countable and uncountable nouns – *much, many, some, any*	Personal habit and routine / Describing how things work / Asking for information

(from *English in Perspective Teacher's Book* by S. Dalzell and I. Edgar)

7 Functional materials Look at this dialogue from a coursebook. It is designed to present exponents of particular functions. Can you identify the functions? How 'authentic' does the language sound? How would you use this (or a similar) dialogue to present the functional language?

Sue 32963.
Dave Hello, Sue. It's Dave.
Sue Oh! Dave! Hello!
Dave What are you doing tonight?
Sue Tonight? Well, er,...Oh, I'm having dinner with John.
Dave Oh well, are you free on Thursday then?
Sue Thursday? Er, no, I'm busy. I'm playing tennis with June.
Dave What a pity! On Saturday, then?
Sue Sorry, I'm washing my hair.
Dave Never mind. Another time perhaps.
Sue Yes, maybe. Bye-bye, Dave. Thanks for phoning.
Dave Yes, goodbye.

Val 29823.
Dave Hello, Val. It's Dave here. Are you free tonight?
Val Dave! Yes, I am. Why?
Dave Oh, good. Would you like to come to the cinema with me?
Val Oh, yes, I'd love to. What's on?
Dave Oh, it's an old James Bond film.
Val Great!
Dave I'll come round about seven then.
Val OK. See you then. Bye.
Dave Bye.

(from *Fast Forward 1* by V. Black *et al.*)

19

4 An introduction to phonology

Introduction

The smallest units of a language are the sounds of which it is composed. The teaching of pronunciation was once thought to involve little more than the identification and practice of these sounds. However there are other systems operating, over larger stretches of speech, which may be more important in terms of overall intelligibility. This unit introduces the general area of phonology by raising some of the pedagogical issues and establishing some basic terminology.

Tasks

1 **Attitudes to pronunciation teaching** Before looking at the phonological systems in more detail, you might like to consider some of the issues that English teachers have had to address over the years. On the basis of your experience as either a learner or a teacher, what is your opinion on these issues?

0 = strongly disagree
5 = strongly agree

a) Adult learners of English are unlikely to achieve native-like proficiency with regard to pronunciation.

   0   1   2   3   4   5

b) The best model for teaching pronunciation is RP (Received Pronunciation: the prestige accent of English).

   0   1   2   3   4   5

c) Intelligibility should be the criterion by which students' pronunciation should be judged.

   0   1   2   3   4   5

d) Stress, rhythm and intonation are more important than getting individual sounds right.

   0   1   2   3   4   5

e) Pronunciation should be integrated into other activities rather than taught as a separate system.

   0   1   2   3   4   5

f) Pronunciation teaching should start with listening.

   0   1   2   3   4   5

g) Students should be taught to read phonemic symbols – /æ/, /ɵ/, etc.

   0   1   2   3   4   5

h) Teaching pronunciation also involves teaching spelling.

   0   1   2   3   4   5

2 Terminology   Match the term with its definition:

phonology   the rise and fall of the voice when speaking

phonetics   the smallest element of sound in a language which is recognised by a native speaker as making a difference in meaning

phoneme   a vocal sound made without the audible stopping of breath

stress   the study of speech sounds and sound production in general

vowel   the greater emphasis of some syllables or words over others during speech

rhythm   the different phonemes that make up a language's phonology

sound system the regular repetition of stress in time

intonation   the study of how speech sounds are produced and used and distinguished in a specific language

3 The organs of speech   The starting point in a description of the phonological system is the identification of the organs of speech. Identify the following organs of speech in the diagram:

tongue   soft palate   alveolar ridge
lips   teeth   nasal cavity
hard palate   vocal cords and glottis   larynx

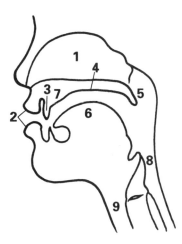

5   The consonants

Introduction

Now that the terminology has been defined, the next two units deal with phonemes.

Remember that a phoneme is not just *any* sound: it is the smallest element of sound that makes a difference in *meaning*. The sounds represented by the letter *l* in *like* and in *milk* are actually quite different (try saying them), but *milk* pronounced with the clear *l* of *like* is not a different word altogether. Pronounce the *v* in *van* as a *b*, however, and you change the meaning of the word. (In Spanish, though, this difference does not exist.)

Task

1 Articulation of consonants   Look at the following illustrations and written descriptions, can you identify which sounds are involved?

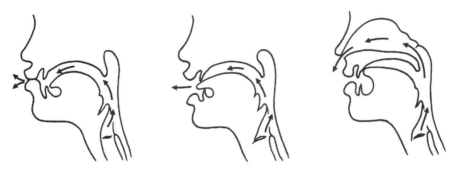

a) Close the lips tightly. Push air forward in the mouth. Open the lips quickly to let the air out.

b) Put the tongue between the teeth. Blow air out between the tongue and the teeth.

c) Touch the roof of the mouth with the tongue. Touch the side teeth with the sides of the tongue. Vibrate the vocal cords. The sound comes through the nose.

The three sounds illustrated and described above are all consonant sounds – that is, sounds that are produced when the flow of air from the larynx to the lips is obstructed in some way. Can you identify the point of obstruction in each case?

It is customary to describe and classify the consonants in terms of:
– the place where they are formed, that is, the point of major obstruction, for example, the lips

- the manner by which they are formed, for example, by the explosive release of air
- whether or not they are voiced, that is, whether or not the vocal cords are made to vibrate

2 Place and manner of articulation   Match these terms and their meanings:

PLACE

bilabial	formed at the teeth
labiodental	formed at the hard palate
dental	formed at the two lips
alveolar	formed at the tooth ridge
palatal	formed at the soft palate
velar	formed at the lips and teeth
glottal	formed in the gap between the vocal cords

MANNER

plosive (or *stop*)	by friction
fricative	through the nose
affricate	by explosion
semi-vowel	with little or no interruption or friction
nasal	by explosion ending in friction

So, any consonant sound can now be described in terms of its place and manner, using the technical terminology. Thus, the sound /f/, which is formed by friction at the juncture of lips and teeth, is a 'labiodental fricative'.

Now, can you describe (**a**), (**b**) and (**c**) in Task 1 according to where and how they are each produced, using the technical terms?

3 Voiced or voiceless   Hold your hand to your throat, and say 'ah'. You should be able to feel the vibration made as the vocal cords (or vocal folds) are engaged. Now, make a prolonged /h/ sound, as if sighing. Notice that there is a clear passage of air passing through the vocal cords, which are wide apart and not vibrating. When the vocal cords vibrate, the effect is called 'voicing'. 'Voiceless' or 'unvoiced' sounds are those produced without vocal cord vibration. Use the same 'hand on throat' test for the following consonant sounds (but try not to add a following vowel, as this will produce voicing, regardless of the consonant sounds):

m   d   b   g   t   th (as in thy)   th (as in thigh)

Now, can you produce a voiced bilabial nasal sound? A voiceless alveolar stop?

4 You should now be able to complete this chart of the English consonants:

Place of articulation	Bilabial	Labiodental	Dental	Alveolar	Palato-alveolar (Post-alveolar)	Palatal	Velar	Glottal
Plosive	p b			☐☐			☐☐	
Fricative		☐☐	θ ð	s z	ʃ ʒ			h
Affricate					tʃ dʒ			
Nasal	☐			☐			ŋ	
Lateral				l				
Approximant	w				r	j		

Manner of articulation (vertical label on left)

(after *English Phonetics and Phonology* by P. Roach)

5 You should now be able to read this /tekst/…

/nekst lets tʃek dʒenz freʃ breθ ðen sez dʒef/

and write this one:

'This thing is tinned fish mixed with gin'. The sound represented by the letter *i* in these words is /ɪ/.

6 Compared to another language you know, does English have more or fewer consonant sounds? How many sounds are shared between the two languages?

7 Look at the following exercise. What is it designed to practise? How could it be exploited?

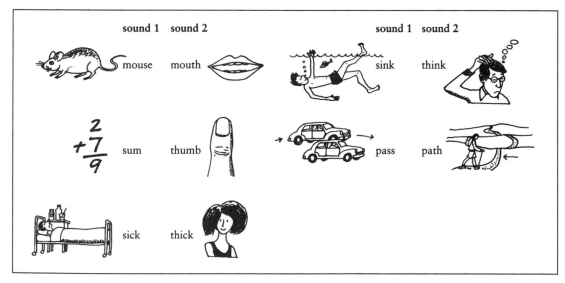

	sound 1	sound 2		sound 1	sound 2
	mouse	mouth		sink	think
	sum	thumb		pass	path
	sick	thick			

(from *Ship or Sheep?* by A. Baker)

8 Look at these exercises. What is the aim of each one? If they were done together, what would be the most logical order in which to do them?

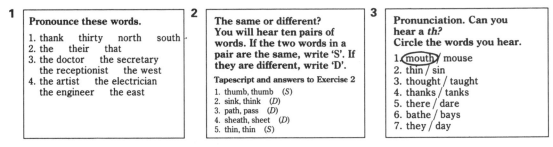

1
Pronounce these words.

1. thank   thirty   north   south
2. the   their   that
3. the doctor   the secretary
   the receptionist   the west
4. the artist   the electrician
   the engineer   the east

2
The same or different?
You will hear ten pairs of words. If the two words in a pair are the same, write 'S'. If they are different, write 'D'.

Tapescript and answers to Exercise 2

1. thumb, thumb   (S)
2. sink, think   (D)
3. path, pass   (D)
4. sheath, sheet   (D)
5. thin, thin   (S)

3
Pronunciation. Can you hear a *th*?
Circle the words you hear.

1. mouth / mouse
2. thin / sin
3. thought / taught
4. thanks / tanks
5. there / dare
6. bathe / bays
7. they / day

(from *The Cambridge English Course* by M. Swan and C. Walter)

9 What is the aim of this activity? In what way is it different from the last exercise in the preceding task?

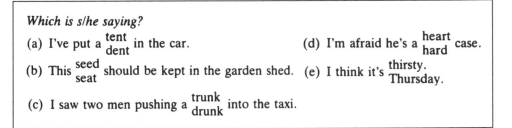

Which is s/he saying?

(a) I've put a tent/dent in the car.

(b) This seed/seat should be kept in the garden shed.

(c) I saw two men pushing a trunk/drunk into the taxi.

(d) I'm afraid he's a heart/hard case.

(e) I think it's thirsty./Thursday.

(from *How Now Brown Cow?* by M. Ponsonby)

10 What is the teaching objective of this exercise?

A	We were ro*bbed*!
B	Stri*pped* of everything!
A	They jum*ped* out into the road...
B	And when we sto*pped*...
A	They gra*bbed* me and thum*ped* me in the ri*bs*...
B	And said if we didn't 'shut our tra*ps**'...
A	We'd be sta*bbed*.
B	They tied us with ro*pes*.
A	And dum*ped* us in the back of a van.
B	Finally they dro*pped* us at the bottom of these ste*ps*...
A	And the **polite** one I descri*bed* to you...
B	Oh, yes – **he** said he was sorry we'd been 'distur*bed*'!
A	And ho*ped* the ro*pes* weren't too tight!
B	Actually **he** was rather charming!
	*traps: mouths (slang).

(from *Clusters* by C. Mortimer)

What 'consonant clusters' do your students have problems with? Why are final consonant clusters problematic in English? Think of words like *worked*, *lengths*, *sixth*, *child's*. What grammatical information can be carried at the end of a word?

Can you think of any techniques that might help learners overcome these problems? How, for example, could you help learners see how meaning is affected when final consonants are dropped?

6 The vowels

Introduction

The aim of this unit is to provide you with a working knowledge of the English vowel system, as well as suggesting a general approach to dealing with vowel problems. Don't worry if you have trouble trying to work out how the different vowels are formed – you may at least have a better appreciation of the problems learners face.

Tasks

1 **Accent** Vowels, more than consonants, distinguish accents. For example, the following couplets would rhyme in some parts of the English-speaking world, but not in others. Which, if any, of the following rhyme in *your* speech?

a) Who's that knocking? Could it be the Duke?
Give me the lantern – I'll go and take a look.

b) The day dawned clear, the sea was calm.
The sun rose up like an atom bomb.

c) Into the tomb stout Carter peered.
Let's go in! But no one dared.

d) Won't you come to the party, Kath?
Hang on a tick, I'm running a bath.

e) Open up, open up, in the name of the law!
If you don't open up we'll smash down the door.

2 **Vowels** There are 20 vowel sounds in RP English, and 24 consonant sounds. Which do you think are the most important in terms of intelligibility – vowels or consonants?

To help you, consider these two versions of a couplet – one with the written form of the consonants taken out, and one with the written form of the vowels taken out. Which is easier to reconstruct?

Version 1: _e __a___ __e __a_ _i_ _ __oo_e_ _a___

__o_e _o __e _u_ _i_ _o_e__ _a___

Version 2: H_ cl_sps th_ cr_g w_th cr__k_d h_nds

Cl_s_ t_ th_ s_n _n l_n_ly l_nds
(by Tennyson)

What does this – and the preceding exercise – suggest about the teaching of the English vowel system?

3 RP Vowels   Here is a list of RP vowels and their symbols. Compare it to your own vowel system. Do you distinguish between all of these vowels?

ɪ	as in 'pit' pɪt	iː	as in 'key' kiː
e	as in 'pet' pet	ɑː	as in 'car' kɑː
æ	as in 'pat' pæt	ɔː	as in 'core' kɔː
ʌ	as in 'putt' pʌt	uː	as in 'coo' kuː
ɒ	as in 'pot' pɒt	ɜː	as in 'cur' kɜː
ʊ	as in 'put' pʊt		

ə   as in 'about, 'upper'
əbaʊt, ʌpə

eɪ	as in 'bay' beɪ	əʊ	as in 'go' gəʊ
aɪ	as in 'buy' baɪ	aʊ	as in 'cow' kaʊ
ɔɪ	as in 'boy' bɔɪ		

ɪə   as in 'peer' pɪə
eə   as in 'pear' peə
ʊə   as in 'poor' pʊə

(from *English Phonetics and Phonology* by P. Roach)

4 Vowel position   Try saying these pairs of vowels, and note where the tongue re-positions itself in each case. Try and focus only on the tongue – this might mean reducing the movement of the lips as much as possible.

/iː/ → /uː/   (as in tea/two)

/uː/ → /ɑː/   (as in two/tar)

/ɑː/ → /iː/   (as in tar/tea)

Now, reverse the direction: /iː/ → /ɑː/ → /uː/ → /iː/.

Now, can you match these illustrations of the position of the tongue to the sounds: /ɑː/, /uː/, /iː/?

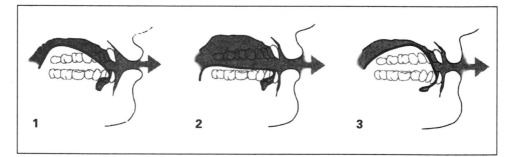

(from *Clear Speech* by J. Gilbert)

5 Tongue position   This chart represents the extent of the positions the tongue adopts in making the vowel sounds. The three vowels in the preceding task have been plotted onto the chart. They represent three extreme positions of the English vowel system.

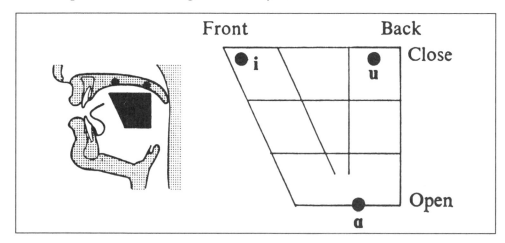

(from *Practical Phonetics* by J. Wells and G. Colson)

The rest of the vowel positions, except one, are shown in the following chart. The only vowel sound that needs to be added to the chart is the schwa (/ə/). Gimson (1970) describes it thus:

'/ə/ has a very high frequency of occurrence in unaccented syllables. Its quality is that of a central vowel with neutral lip position... In final positions, e.g. *mother, doctor, over, picture, China,* the vowel is articulated either in the half-open central position or in the most open region of the central area.'

Can you place it in the chart?

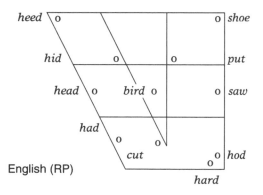

(from *The Cambridge Encyclopedia of Language* by D. Crystal)

Now, replace the words in the chart with the symbols that conventionally represent the vowel sounds of English. (These are listed in Task 3 above.)

6 Think about these questions:
  - Why do photographers make us say 'Cheese'?
  - Why do doctors make us say 'Aaahh'?
  - Why, when someone hits us in the stomach, do we make the sound 'Errgh'?

7 Diphthongs The following mnemonic includes the eight English diphthongs. Use the list in Task 3 to identify the diphthongs and complete the phonemic representation.

I	fear	no	boy	may	cure	their	cow
/ /	/f /	/n /	/b /	/m /	/kj /	/ð /	/k /

Do you notice that the diphthongs are of three different types?

8 The phonemic chart A useful classroom aid is a chart of the phonemic symbols. The layout of this one was devised by Adrian Underhill. Can you explain the rationale behind the way the symbols are distributed?

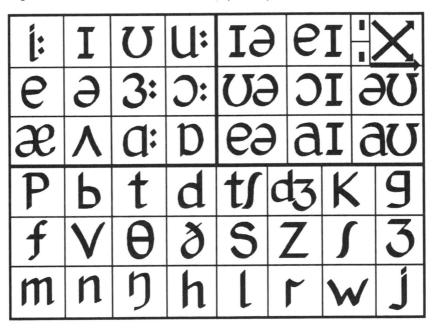

(from *Sound Foundations* by A. Underhill)

9 Transcribing from phonemic script You should now be able to read these sentences:

  a) /kʌm lɪv wɪð miː ænd biː maɪ lʌv/
  b) /swiːt biː nɒt praʊd ɒv ðəʊz tuː aɪz/
  c) /sləʊ sləʊ freʃ faʊnt kiːp taɪm wɪð maɪ sɔːlt tɪəz/
  d) /aɪ æm jet wɒt aɪ æm nʌn keəz ɔː nəʊz/

10   Try writing the following in phonemic script. (Check that you know what the words mean!)

phoneme   diphthong

vowel   schwa

consonant   phonology

pronunciation   syllable

11   Problems   Can you explain these invented, but plausible, problems of communication?

a) I asked where the boss was, but they sent me to the bus station.
b) I asked her if she was living here, and she said no, she was staying.
c) I told my landlady I needed a rag and she gave me a blanket.
d) I told him I had worked a lot in the weekend, and he asked me how many miles.

12   Activities   Look at these activities. They originally formed a sequence but here they are in the wrong order. Can you reconstruct the order?

What is the overall aim of the sequence? What is the aim of each exercise?

---

1   Listen to these sentences and underline all the / æ / sounds that you hear like this ____.

a. The young man was wearing fashionable sunglasses, black gloves, and a gangster's hat.
b. The wasp that's trapped in the jar of blackcurrant jam is buzzing angrily.
c. Thank you very much for coming to pay back that money you borrowed on Monday, Danny.
d. While cutting up lamb the drunken butcher hacked off his thumb with a hatchet.
e. My husband had a double brandy, my mother wanted apple juice, but I drank champagne.

Listen again and underline all the / ʌ / sounds that you hear like this 〰〰.

2   Listen to these pairs of words, and repeat them.

/ æ /	/ ʌ /
cap	cup
bag	bug
cat	cut
rag	rug
ankle	uncle
carry	curry
lamp	lump
paddle	puddle
hat	hut

Work with a partner. You say a word and your partner listens and points to the word he or she hears.

Continued overleaf

3 Practise saying the sentences five times each. Start by saying them slowly and then say them faster and faster. Make sure you pronounce the / æ / and / ʌ / sounds correctly.

4 Listen and circle the words you hear.

a. cap   cup
b. bag   bug
c. cat   cut
d. rag   rug
e. ankle   uncle

5 Practise making the sounds.

To make the sound / æ /, your mouth should be open like this, and your tongue should be down at the front of your mouth:

To make the sound / ʌ / your mouth should be less open, and your tongue should be a little higher in your mouth:

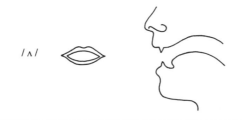

(from *Headway Upper-Intermediate Pronunciation* by B. Bowler and S. Cunningham)

13 Design a similar sequence for the pair /ɪ/ versus /iː/.

7 Stress, rhythm and connected speech

Introduction

So far we have looked at sounds in isolation, that is individual segments of the pronunciation system, both consonants and vowels. Obviously, there is more to pronunciation than simply the production of strings of phonemes. We now turn our attention to larger segments of the system, the 'suprasegmental' features of phonology.

Tasks

1 Sentence stress

a) Read these sentences, giving the main emphasis to the underlined words:
   – I <u>thought</u> you wanted to go out.
   – We always go to the <u>movies</u>.
   – I thought you hated <u>westerns</u>.
   – I didn't <u>go</u> to Hollywood because of the westerns.

b) Now, with a partner read this short conversation aloud – A reads naturally; B places the emphasis as in the preceding task:

   A: What's on the telly?

   B: I <u>thought</u> you wanted to go out.

   A: Well, let's go to the movies then.

   B: We always go to the <u>movies</u>.

   A: There's a new Clint Eastwood on.

   B: I thought you hated <u>westerns</u>.

   A: Speaking of which, have you ever been to Hollywood?

   B: Yes, but I didn't <u>go</u> to Hollywood because of the westerns.

What was the effect of placing stress this way? Read the dialogue again, assigning the stress correctly.

2 Information structure In each two-part exchange, mark the 'new' information, i.e. information that adds to, or contrasts with, what the previous speaker said. The first one is done for you:

   A: What's on the telly?
   B: I thought you wanted to go <u>out</u>.

   A: Well, let's go to the movies then.
   B: We always go to the movies.

   A: There's a new Clint Eastwood on.
   B: I thought you hated westerns.

A: Speaking of which, have you ever been to Hollywood?
B: Yes, but I didn't go to Hollywood because of the westerns.

How does the distinction between 'given' information and 'new' information relate to the placement of stress?

3 **Sentence stress in conversation**   We use stress to regulate the flow of conversations, by, for example, signalling what topic the speaker has chosen to introduce.

How does the speaker use stress to determine the kind of response required here?

You've got <u>two</u> sisters, haven't you?

This example comes from an exercise in *The Cambridge English Course*. Look at the rest of the exercise. How could you extend this kind of practice into a less controlled activity?

Stress. Listen carefully to these questions, and then write answers to them (beginning *No,* .....). When you have done that, practise saying the questions and answers.

1. You've got *two* sisters, haven't you?
   No, just one
2. You've got two *sisters*, haven't you?
   No, two brothers
3. You work in London, don't you?
4. Is that Mary's father?
5. Did you say you had a new red Lancia?
6. Do you need English for your work?

Now listen to this question. You will hear it three times, with three different stresses. Can you write suitable answers (a different answer each time)?

7. Would you like me to telephone Peter and Anne?

(from *The Cambridge English Course 1* by M. Swan and C. Walter)

In the recording which accompanies the above exercise the following words are stressed:

(3) work
(4) Mary's
(5) red
(6) English
(7) a) me   b) telephone   c) and

4   Rhythm   Read these sentences aloud, highlighting their rhythm:

a)   'Abercrombie argues that speech is inherently rhythmical.' (Brazil *et al.*)
b)   'The characteristic rhythm of one language may differ considerably from that of another.' (Brown)
c)   'The recurrence of stressed syllables at regular intervals gives speech its rhythmical qualities.' (Wells and Colson)
d)   'It is plain that this regularity is the case only under certain conditions.' (Crystal 1980)

What words carried the 'beat'? What happened to the words between the beats?

5   Rhythm   What is the purpose of this text and how could you use it in class?

A	B
Are you ready?	
Are you ready?	
	Not quite. Just a minute.
Hurry up!	
Hurry up!	
	Don't rush me.
	Don't rush me.
Come on, Allan,	
Hurry up!	
	I'm coming.
Hurry up.	
	I'm coming.
	I'm coming.
Hurry up!	
	All right!
We'll be late.	
We'll be late.	
	No, we won't. Don't panic.
We'll be late.	
	No, we won't.
	No, we won't.
	Here I am.
At last.	
At last!	
	What's the rush?

(from *Speaking Clearly* by P. Rogerson and J. Gilbert)

6 Weak forms   Many words in English have what is called a 'strong' form and a 'weak' form. Here are some examples – can you add another five to the list? What *sort* of words are these?

	strong form	*weak form*
an	/æn/	/ən/
some	/sʌm/	/səm/
of	/ɒv/	/əv/
them	/ðem/	/ðəm/
than	/ðæn/	/ðən/
was	/wɒz/	/wəz/
can	/kæn/	/kən/

Look at this extract. Identify any likely weak forms in the dialogue.

DISSON   How do you do, Miss Dodd? Nice of you to come. Please sit down.

That's right. Well now, I've had a look at your references. They seem to be excellent. You've had quite a bit of experience.

WENDY   Yes, sir.

DISSON   Not in my line, of course. We manufacture sanitary ware…but I suppose you know that?

WENDY   Yes, of course I do, Mr Disson.

DISSON   You've heard of us, have you?

WENDY   Oh yes.

(from 'Tea Party' in *Tea Party and Other Plays* by H. Pinter)

Using evidence from the extract, can you formulate a rule as to when auxiliary verbs take their strong form, as opposed to their weak form or a contraction?

7 Sounds in connected speech   Weak forms are just one of the ways in which sounds change 'in the stream of speech'. Try transcribing this dialogue into its written form:
(Note: the symbol /ʔ/ represents a glottal stop – the sound that replaces the /t/ sounds in *hot water bottle* if you speak with a London accent.)

A: /wɒdʒʊ θɪŋk wɪ ʃəd duː ðəs iːvnɪŋ/

B: /əi kn traɪm bʊk səm siːts fərə muːvɪ/

A: /wɒtsɒn/

B: /ðəz reɪm mæn ɔː ðə naɪp pɔːtə ɔː bæʔmæn tuːwət ðɪɟəʊdəɟɪn/

A: /lets gəuwənsɪ bæʔmæn weəz mɪ hæmbæg/

What words in the phonemic transcription of the dialogue differ from the 'dictionary' versions of those words? For example:

	dictionary	*dialogue*
what do you:	/wɒt duː juː/	/wɒdʒʊ/

8 Sound change Here is a list of the main changes sounds can undergo in natural RP speech. Can you find an example of each in the dialogue in Task 7?

a) Assimilation: this is when a sound is influenced by a neighbouring sound so that it becomes more like its neighbour – as the first /n/ in *ten pence* becomes an /m/ under the influence of the neighbouring /p/.

b) Elision: this is when a sound is left out altogether – this typically happens to /t/ and /d/ as in *hand stand, past perfect*.

c) Liaison: this is where a sound is introduced at word boundaries, typically the /r/ as in *raw (r) egg*. It is also sometimes called 'linking', especially when used to describe the way final consonants link up with initial vowels, or vice versa: *I scream for ice cream!*

9 Coursebook exercises Look at these different exercises. What feature(s) of connected speech does each one focus on? In each case, is it a production or recognition activity?

---

1 Listening to fast speech. How many words are there? What are they? Contractions like *what's* count as two words.

a. Who were you waiting for?
b. He's sold the flat.
c. They found some money in the street.
d. We like the hotel.
e. They'd been waiting for ages.
f. I've failed my driving test.
g. She's enjoying her new job.
h. We washed the car on Sunday.
i. She cycled home.
j. How are you hoping to get there?

(from *The Cambridge English Course 1* by M. Swan and C. Walter)

---

2 Say these sentences in two ways: first with an ordinary pronunciation of *must* (/ms/) and then with an emphatic pronunciation (/mʌst/).

1. You must tell me.
2. You must tidy up afterwards.
3. You must get everybody out.
4. They must go today.
5. We must have them by the end of the month.

(from *The Cambridge English Course 2* by M. Swan and C. Walter)

3

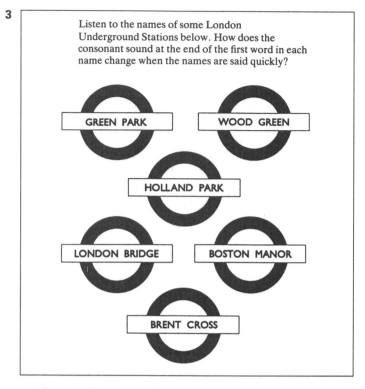

Listen to the names of some London Underground Stations below. How does the consonant sound at the end of the first word in each name change when the names are said quickly?

GREEN PARK

WOOD GREEN

HOLLAND PARK

LONDON BRIDGE

BOSTON MANOR

BRENT CROSS

(from *Headway Intermediate Pronunciation* by B. Bowler and S. Cunningham)

4 Sometimes when people are speaking very quickly, it is difficult to hear the difference between past and present tenses. Listen to these sentences and write *past* if a Past Simple, Past Continuous or Past Perfect tense is used. Write *present* if a Present or Present Perfect tense is used.

a. _____   f. _____

b. _____   g. _____

c. _____   h. _____

d. _____   i. _____

e. _____   j. _____

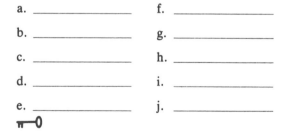

a. Who were you waiting for?
b. He's sold the flat.
c. They found some money in the street.
d. We like the hotel.
e. They'd been waiting for ages.
f. I've failed my driving test.
g. She's enjoying her new job.
h. We washed the car on Sunday.
i. She cycled home.
j. How are you hoping to get there?

(from *Headway Upper-Intermediate Pronunciation* by B. Bowler and S. Cunningham)

8   Intonation

Introduction

This unit introduces an area of phonology that is not easily described nor understood. At the risk of over-simplifying the subject, the following tasks will sidestep some of the more abstruse areas of intonation theory.

Tasks

1 **Tone units**   The tone unit functions as a means of 'packaging' information in spoken discourse. Say these pairs of utterances aloud, pausing slightly where marked (|), and see if you can distinguish the differences of meaning in each:

a) – I like Elizabethan drama and poetry.
    – I like Elizabethan drama | and poetry.
b) – The passengers who didn't have tickets | were fined.
    – The passengers | who didn't have tickets | were fined.
c) – She went to answer the phone hopefully.
    – She went to answer the phone | hopefully.
d) – We prefer dancing to music.
    – We prefer dancing | to music.
e) – I didn't marry him because of his looks.
    – I didn't marry him | because of his looks.

Did you notice what happened to the pitch of your voice just before each of the marked pauses?

Now, mark the main stressed word in each tone unit in each pair of sentences.

2 **Pitch range**   Here are three situations. How do A and B say *Hi* in each case? Practise the 'dialogues' in pairs.

a) A and B are old friends who haven't seen each other in six months and they bump into each other at a party.

    A: Hi

    B: Hi

b) A and B are work colleagues and friends. They are greeting each other in the lift at the start of another day's work.

    A: Hi

    B: Hi

c) A and B are old friends and haven't seen each other in a long time. During this time B has heard that A has been saying unpleasant things about him/her.

A: Hi

B: Hi

What does this task suggest about the relation between pitch and attitude?

3 Pitch direction   In each (one-word) tone unit in this invented conversation what is the probable direction of pitch – does it go up or down, up and down; or even, down and up?

A: (*politely*)   Tea?

B: (*firmly*)   No.

A: (*surprised*)   No?

B: (*considering*)   Well...

A: (*handing tea*)   Here.

B: Ta. (*B drinks tea greedily*)

A: (*sarcastically*)   Well!

Try the dialogue with a partner.

4 Pitch direction   In the following extract from a play, divide the text into tone units. Then identify the main stressed syllable in each tone unit. Finally, decide the probable direction of pitch change at each of these main stresses (you may find that there is more than one possibility):

POPPY   What's that?

JACK   What's what?

POPPY   (*indicating*) That. What's that?

JACK   That? That's a – that's a briefcase.

POPPY   Is it yours?

JACK   No.

POPPY   Oh. What's in it, then?

JACK   Nothing. Just paper. Bits of – bits of paper.

(from *A Small Family Business* by A. Ayckbourn)

With a partner, read the extract aloud, with the appropriate intonation.

Does this exercise suggest any rules – or at least tendencies – with regard to the relation between changes in pitch and types of sentence?

5 Activities   Look at the following textbook activities. What feature of intonation does each one target: tone group division, pitch range or pitch direction? What general principle is it designed to practise? Finally, is it a recognition or a production activity?

a)   Write down five facts about your partner that you
think you are sure of, and five facts that you are not
really sure of and need to check. Then say things to
your partner like this.

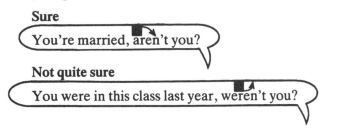

Sure

You're married, aren't you?

Not quite sure

You were in this class last year, weren't you?

(from *Headway Intermediate Pronunciation* by B. Bowler and S. Cunningham)

b)   Listen to the conversation between Peter and Sarah. Listen
particularly to how Sarah replies. Is she enthusiastic or not very
interested? After each 'bleep', draw the appropriate mouth.
Example:
   Peter: Sarah, I'm going to a party tomorrow night, would you
            like to come?

1 Sarah: Oh.
   Peter: It's just an office party really.

2 Sarah: Oh.

Now continue:

3

4

5

6

7

8

9

(from *Speaking Clearly* by P. Rogerson and J. Gilbert)

c) Listen and then practise saying this dialogue. Make sure you
group the right couples together!

A: Who's coming tonight?
B: John.
A: Just John?
B: No, John and Susie.
A: No one else?
B: Well, there's Bob.
A: Alone?
B: No, with Anne.
A: So, that's John and Susie and Bob and Anne. Is that it?
B: Oh, and Gordon. On his own.
A: So that's John and Susie and Bob and Anne and Gordon.
B: Yes, that's right.

(from *Speaking Clearly* by P. Rogerson and J. Gilbert)

d) Work with a partner if possible. In the first part of the reply B reminds A of
things they both know, and then in the second part introduces a new idea.
Listen to the example first, and then listen and repeat B's part.

A: I'm really enjoying my stay here. Where shall we go tonight?
B: We've seen all the good films, and we've been to the theatre and to a
concert. Let's go to a nightclub.

Now go on in the same way. The intonation is not transcribed for you this
time. Try first and then listen to the recording.

i)   A: Did you get everything for the office?
     B: Here are the envelopes and the stamps. But there wasn't any paper.

ii) A: Who's coming to the dinner party?
     B: As you know, we've invited the Whites and the Robsons. But I also
        invited the Jenkins.

iii) A: Have we prepared everything for the party now?
     B: Well, we've organised the music and the drinks. But we haven't got
        the food yet.

iv) A: What have you got for the fruit salad?
     B: We've got apples and pears and peaches. We ought to get some
        oranges.

v)   A: Where shall we go for our holiday this year?
     B: It's difficult. We've been to Italy and Greece and Austria. How do
        you feel about Turkey?

(from *Intonation in Context* by B. Bradford)

9   Word formation, spelling and word stress

Introduction

This unit introduces the area of vocabulary, or lexis, in English. The two terms 'vocabulary' and 'lexis' are frequently used interchangeably and that convention is followed here. In this unit we look at the *form* of words. In the next unit we look at how words relate to other words in terms of their *meaning*.

Tasks

1 **Word formation**   There are a number of common ways of constructing words. For example:

   – through the use of affixes (prefixes and suffixes), for example *replay*; *playful*
   – by combining two or more existing words, for example *windscreen*; *screenplay*
   – by converting words from one part of speech to another, for example *to screen* (from *a screen*); *input* (from *to put in*)
   – by some form of shortening. This may entail abbreviating, or clipping, words, for example, *pram* (from *perambulator*); *advert* (from *advertisement*). Or it may entail using acronyms – initial letters – as, for example, in *scuba* (*self-contained underwater breathing apparatus*) *diving*; *AIDS* (*acquired immune deficiency syndrome*)

   Do these same word-formation processes operate in another language you know?

2 In this extract, can you identify which of the above principles of word formation is exemplified in each of the underlined words?

   Example: <u>versatility</u> — affixation (*–ity* added to <u>versatile</u>).

   Such is the <u>versatility</u> of the SV-3900, it can be used equally <u>successfully</u> to record music or as a scientific <u>research</u> tool. You can, for example, <u>interface</u> it with a wide variety of digital devices – <u>CD</u> players, <u>workstations</u>, <u>recorders</u>. Or, alternatively, it can be <u>networked</u> with up to 31 other SV-3900 <u>DAT</u> machines.

3 **Multi-word units**   There are many types of multi-word units, or 'lexical phrases', that have become fixed and behave as if they were a single word. They include phrasal verbs (see Unit 25); idioms and proverbs (*if looks could kill*); social formulae (*how are you?*, *long time no see*); binomials (*to and fro*, *back to front*); discourse markers (*mind you*, *by the way*); and sentence

builders (*the problem is (that)…, if you ask me…*). There are also many semi-fixed phrases such as *a month/year/hour ago; see you soon/later*, etc.

Identify the multi-word units in this extract from Orton's *The Good and Faithful Servant*:

MRS VEALFOY How can I help you?

DEBBIE   I was more or less bludgeoned into coming to you by a friend of mine. You may recall helping her out in a sticky spot when she was up before the council about the rateable value of her flat?

MRS VEALFOY Yes. I remember the girl well.

DEBBIE   She left the firm under a cloud, but she certainly profited by your advice. (*pause, she bites her lip*) I don't know where to begin. I'm nearly at my wit's end.

MRS VEALFOY Take your time. Speak slowly and distinctly. I'll be listening to every word.

          (*Debbie twists her fingers together. Her lip trembles.*)

DEBBIE   Well, you see, Mrs Vealfoy, I've become intimately attached to a boy who means all the world to me. Against my better judgement, I allowed him to persuade me to do something which I knew to be wrong. Oh, you'll never know what I've been through these last few weeks…

4 What principles of word formation are the following exercises designed to practise?

---

1 Complete the following sentences using a verb (in an appropriate tense) which denotes a part of the body.

Example
You have no money. *Face* the facts. You can't go on spending money as though you were a millionaire.

a. Could you _____ me that book on the table next to you? Thank you.

b. In the final minutes of the football match, Robson _____ the ball into the back of the net.

c. She _____ the car carefully out of the garage, and drove off.

d. After his father's death, Tom had to _____ the responsibility for his family's debts.

e. She _____ the material gently. It felt as smooth as silk. From this she could make the most beautiful gown.

f. The bank robber was _____ with a knife and a gun.

g. I ran out of petrol on the motorway, so I had to _____ a lift to the nearest petrol station.

(from *Headway Upper-Intermediate* by J. Soars and L. Soars)

2 VOCABULARY
Word building

1 *Now you can strengthen the thin green line.*
Strengthen is a verb which is made from the adjective
strong.
Work in pairs and complete this table.

ADJECTIVE	NOUN	VERB
wide		
strong		
deep		
weak		
short		
high		

2 Complete these sentences using one of the words
from the table. Make any changes that are necessary.

1 They wanted to .... the harbour to allow
 oil tankers in.
2 These country roads are dangerously narrow. They
 need ....
3 Greenpeace has .... our understanding
 of the environment.
4 Industry is laughing at the .... of the
 new regulations.
5 Only people over a certain .... can join
 the army.

(from *Think First Certificate* by J. Naunton)

3 **A person with dark hair is *dark-haired*.
Somebody who writes with his or her left hand
is *left-handed*. What are the adjectives for
these people?**

1. a person with brown hair
2. somebody with blue eyes
3. a person who has broad shoulders
4. people who write with their right hands
5. a person with a thin face
6. somebody with long legs

Now say these in another way.

1. a blue-eyed girl
 'a girl with blue eyes'
2. a brown-haired man
 'a man . . .'
3. a left-handed child
 'a child who . . .'
4. a fat-faced person
 'somebody who has . . .'
5. a dark-eyed woman
 '. . .'
6. a long-sleeved pullover
 '. . . with . . .'

(from *The Cambridge English Course 2* by M. Swan and C. Walter)

5 Spelling   In *Sounds English*, common sound–spelling correspondences are signalled like this:

Spelling

Units 1–6 and 23–32 contain a Spelling box. English spelling is not always a good guide to pronunciation. There are often different ways to write a sound. The Spelling box shows you the common and less common ways of spelling each sound in that unit and looks like this:

Common ways of spelling the sound /eə/.

ALL means that all words with this spelling are pronounced with this sound.

MANY means that many words with this spelling are pronounced with this sound, but some are not. (Other headings are MOST and SOME.) The headings help you work out the likely pronunciation of a new word.

Exceptions – useful words with unusual spellings.

(from *Sounds English* by J. O'Connor and C. Fletcher)

Can you devise similar 'spelling boxes' for the sounds /dʒ/ as in *judge*, and /ɑː/, as in *car*?

6 Spelling rules   Some basic spelling rules can be demonstrated using nonsense words. For example:

a) How is *stin* pronounced? And *stine*?
b) What is the present participle of the verb *stin*?
c) A person who teaches is a teacher. What do you call a person who *stines*?
d) What is the plural of the noun *gimmy*?
e) How do you think the word pronounced /greɪk/ is spelt?
f) I *splo*, you *splo*, he or she…?

What spelling rule are you applying in each case?

7 Word stress

a) Put the words below into the appropriate column, and see if you can work out some general tendencies in the stressing of two-syllable words.

teacher   student   repeat   English   listen   begin   written
explain   study   discuss   reading   describe   phone me
grammar   complete

Stress on first syllable	Stress on second syllable
teacher	repeat
_____	_____
_____	_____
_____	_____
_____	_____
_____	_____
_____	_____
_____	_____
_____	_____

b) The following words can be used as both verbs and nouns:

present   record   discourse   converse

What is the rule of stress here?

c) Now group these polysyllabic words. What is the effect of certain suffixes?

Stress on fourth to last syllable	Stress on third to last syllable	Stress on second to last syllable
	syllable	

syllable   syllabic   comprehension   phonemic   presentation
lexical   grammatical   authentic   dictation   dictionary
linguistic   vocabulary   lexicography

d) **Compound words**   Where is the stress on these compound words?

homework   blackboard   classroom   workbook   roleplay

notepaper   flashcard

8 Word stress   What teaching points are the following exercises designed to make? How effective do you think they are?

---

1   Word families and word stress

1 The words below have all appeared in the previous four units of *Headway Pre-Intermediate*.
Put them in the correct row according to their stress pattern.

discovery	invention	disappearance
discussion	computer	advertisement
celebration	argument	development
authority	government	accommodation
	existence	behaviour

1 ●●●	
2 ●●●	
3 ●●●●	
4 ●●●●	*discovery*
5 ●●●●●	

2 The words in exercise **1** are all nouns.
What are the verbs? Be careful with word stress!

3 Put the following words into the correct row according to their stress pattern.

generous	determined	valuable
reliable	comfortable	scientific
	technological	

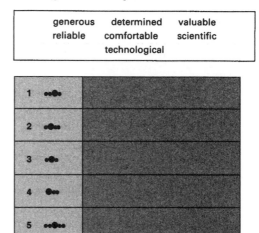

4 The words in exercise **3** are all adjectives. What are the nouns? Be careful with word stress.

(from *Headway Pre-Intermediate* by J. Soars and L. Soars).

---

2   Parts of speech

Some words are stressed according to whether they are acting as verbs, nouns or adjectives.

a Look at the following and work out the rule.

1 Customs have seized some <u>sus</u>pect packages.
2 I am writing to pro<u>test</u> about the treatment of conscientious objectors.
3 There is a <u>con</u>trast between their attitude to defence spending and overseas aid.

b Write sentences using the following words:
<u>con</u>flict   <u>reb</u>el   <u>add</u>ict   con<u>vict</u>
es<u>cort</u>   con<u>script</u>   de<u>sert</u>   <u>per</u>fect

---

(from *First Choice for Proficiency* by P. May)

10 Lexical meaning

Introduction

When you learn a new word it is not enough simply to know how it is spelt and pronounced. You need to know what it means, what it means in one context but not in another, and how this meaning relates to other words and other meanings. This unit looks at ways of classifying words in terms of their meaning.

Tasks

1 Lexical errors   Identify the lexical errors in these examples from students' writing. What *kinds* of errors are they – errors of form (the right word but the wrong form) or errors of meaning (the wrong word or words?) How would you explain the correction to the students?

a) He liked to climb some tryes and to play witch his dog.
b) I turned on the radio and heard a very bad new: Freddie Mercury is dead.
c) There was a lot of people who wearing masks and they song a sing for me.
d) Her husband is an artist too. They both are working hardly.
e) Marilyn Monroe was very famous. She did films as *The Men Like Fairs*.
f) I have chosen to describe Stephen Hawking, a notorious cientific of our century.
g) In London I took a two floor bus and of course crossed the city in the highest floor.
h) I tried to shout up but the voice didn't go out from my neck.

2 Semantic meaning   Words are often defined by reference to their similarities or differences with other words. For example:
  – different words but same or similar meaning (synonyms)
  – different words and opposite meaning (antonyms)
  – different words but same word family or lexical field (hyponyms)
  – same word but different meaning (homonyms)
  – same word and similar meaning (polysemes)

Using the above categories, identify the sense relation between the underlined words in the following extracts (from *The Gate of Angels* by Penelope Fitzgerald). The first is done for you.

a) He took a <u>taxi</u> to St Angelicus to fetch his gown.
    Fred asked the <u>cab</u> to wait. *synonyms*
b) 'I hope you young gentlemen slept <u>sound</u>,' she asked us the first morning.
    There was a <u>sound</u> like a vast heap of glass splintering…

c) She crossed the river and turned <u>left</u> down Jesus Lane. That was a mistake, she would have to go <u>right</u> again somewhere…

d) Daisy suggested taking the <u>lift</u> up to the Tea Gardens.
She crossed the road and stood by the ditch, waiting for a <u>lift</u>.

e) There was a cupboard inside from which he took a <u>broom</u>, a <u>dustpan</u> and a <u>brush</u>, and began to sweep up the nave.

f) 'By the way, who was that man, your <u>friend</u>, or <u>enemy</u>, with a beard?'

g) There will be no <u>possibility</u>, or let us call it <u>likelihood</u>, of her being buried alive.

h) 'What are those <u>birds</u>? Daisy asked. 'Were they <u>quails</u>, Fred?'
'No, I'm afraid not, I'm afraid they were <u>fieldfares</u>.'

i) 'Run out and buy me a morning <u>paper</u>.'
The house, like all houses which have stood vacant for any length of time, seemed full of bits of <u>paper</u>.

3 Synonyms Do this activity.

We often repeat information in a text but choose different words to do so. Can you find synonyms in the following article for the words which are underlined in the text?

<u>Holiday travellers</u> <u>faced long delays</u> today after a <u>French air traffic control dispute</u> and a double <u>computer failure</u> threw Europe's airways into <u>chaos</u>.

A number of flights were held up for more than six hours and one group of holidaymakers was <u>unable to leave</u> Portugal today, as scheduled. So far, they have been stranded at Faro Airport for more than 20 hours.

A row over working conditions is responsible for the problems with the French air traffic control, but the confusion has been made worse by the simultaneous breakdown of important computers at Brest and Prestwick.

(from *A Way with Words* 2 by S. Redman and R. Ellis)

Can you think of other ways of using texts like the one above to sensitise learners to the different way words are related?

4 Connotation   Dictionaries often provide coded information concerning the connotation of words. The *Cambridge International Dictionary of English*, for example, uses the following labels:

fml Formal: words and phrases used in a serious way…Formal language is often used when people want to appear polite.

infml Informal: used with friends or family or people you know in relaxed situations. Informal words are more common in speech than in writing.

slang Informal language which might include words which are not polite.

taboo Words which are likely to offend someone and are not used in formal situations.

literary Words and phrases which are mainly used in literature.

dated Words or phrases which sound old-fashioned.

How would you categorise the following dictionary entries using the above terms?

knackered   whacked   fatigued   buggered   ennervated
dog-tired

What value might there be in doing this kind of task with language students?

5 Polysemes and homonyms   Is there a single word *lift*, which has got two related meanings – that is, is it polysemous? Or are there two different words: *lift* and *lift*?

For example, how many meanings of the word *fair* can you identify in these citations (from *Collins COBUILD English Language Dictionary*)? And/or how many *different* words (homonyms) having the form *fair* can you identify?

a) This isn't fair on anyone, but it does happen.
b) Does he do his fair share of household chores?
c) That is a very fair point I think.
d) The trials accorded to them were fair.
e) He must have made a fair amount of money.
f) We have a fair size garden and we may as well make use of it.
g) She was only a fair cook.
h) She had long fair hair.
i) This fair city of ours…
j) It will be fair and warm.
k) My pig won first prize at Skipton Fair.
l) The Leipzig Trade Fair.

6 Hyponyms Draw a 'tree-diagram' to show the relationship between these words.

verse   book   novel   chapter   encyclopedia   anthology
paragraph   poem

Devise a similar tree-diagram for transport to include *taxi* and other related items.

What application could this type of organisation have to language teaching?

7 Collocation Read this text and underline any strong verb–noun collocational pairs. The first is done for you.

With a Premium Account you don't need to <u>give</u> any <u>notice</u> before withdrawing money from your account and there's no loss of interest.

You can issue Premium Account cheques for any amount, large or small – many High Interest Cheque Accounts insist that cheques be for at least £200. You can draw cash by cheque at any branch of the major UK banks. Many banks make a small charge for this service.

8 Idioms *Idiom*: A lexical item (usually a phrase or clause) whose meaning cannot be derived from the sum of its parts. (McCarthy 1990)

Identify the idioms in these texts:

12.55 Home and Away	**7.30 East Enders**	**4.40 Island**
ITV Angel is none too happy when Jo returns to Summer Bay and immediately starts to wind up poor Mrs Parrish. Just what is Jo up to? Angel doesn't want to hang around to find out and starts to wonder if it's time she and her family upped sticks and moved away from Summer Bay.	**BBC1** Nervous Phil shies away from telling Peggy his and Kathy's choice of godparents for Ben. Sarah bunks off school, only to run into trouble while out window shopping.	**ITV** Dominic must face the music in the wake of his rave, and Theresa discovers what terrible fate his father has in store for him. Romance looks rocky for Philip.

(from *Inside Soap*)

9 Error analysis Identify the vocabulary problems in these texts. Which do you think are problems of *collocation* and which of *connotation*?

a) As you will realise at the view of the CV I enclose to this letter, I own a certain experience in teaching tasks.
b) I taught at State Lycée…This work gave birth to these techniques – French of all levels, commercial…
c) I would be pleased to meet you to envisage my contribution towards excellency of your establishment…

d) Enclosed I'm sending my curriculum vitae, expressing my desire to collaborate with your school as a professional Spanish teacher, with 15 years of experience as particular professor.

e) By chance, from October, first, I'll get rid of my present job, and I shall be able to dedicate completely to 'teaching', my real and favourite task.

11 Word classes and phrases

Introduction

One of the standard processes of any kind of language analysis is the identification and labelling of the individual words that make up a sentence or a text. Although this kind of analysis does not provide much helpful information about how texts or even sentences are constructed, a basic knowledge of 'parts of speech' provides the teacher with a useful tool.

Tasks

1 **Word classes**   Can you match the term in this list with its definition below? The first is done for you.

   noun   pronoun   verb   adjective   adverb   preposition
   determiner   conjunction

   a) A word that functions either to specify the time, place or manner of the verb, or as an intensifier, or a connector. *adverb*
   b) A word that can substitute for a noun.
   c) A word used in front of a noun to express, for example, number and quantity.
   d) A word which names things: people, places, objects, activities, feelings, ideas, etc.
   e) A word that relates nouns to other elements, the relation being one of time or place, for example.
   f) A word that joins one clause to another, or one word to another.
   g) A word that typically expresses an event, process or state.
   h) A word that typically identifies an attribute of a noun.

2 **Word classes**   Now can you find an example of each word class in this extract?

   In the early summer of 1933 I started out for my first walking tour. I left my grand-father's house at Henfield in Sussex one evening and walked towards the river. My aunt seemed pleased to be rid of me. She speeded me on my way rather too gaily and quickly.

   (from *I Left My Grandfather's House* by D. Welch)

3 **Groups**   In the text in Task 2 above, it should be clear that many of the words in the sentences cluster into groups. For example, which 'analysis' of the first sentence best reflects the way the words are grouped?

   a) In the early | summer of 1933 I | started out for | my first walking | tour |
   b) In the early summer | of 1933 | I started | out for | my first walking tour |
   c) In the early summer of 1933 | I | started out | for my first walking tour |
   d) In the early summer of 1933 | I | started | out for my first walking tour |

4 Phrases   These 'groupings' of words – traditionally called 'phrases' – have functions like individual parts of speech. There are five types of phrase in English:

noun phrase (NP)
verb phrase (VP)
adjective phrase (AdjP)
adverb phrase (AdvP)
prepositional phrase (PP)

Look at the following examples from the extract. Identify the phrase type for each one.

a)   pleased to be rid of me
b)   rather too gaily
c)   my grandfather's house at Henfield in Sussex
d)   started out
e)   towards the river

5 Phrase heads   Notice that in the first four phrase types, the phrase can be reduced to just one word: *pleased, gaily, house,* and *started.* This is the 'head' of the phrase. The word class of the head indicates the type of phrase: *gaily* is an adverb; *rather too gaily* is an adverb phrase.

What phrase type is each of the underlined phrases, and what is the head of each?

I felt excited, but also <u>a little unhappy</u> and alarmed. I wished that I <u>had not started out</u> in the evening.

When I got to <u>the river banks</u> the sun <u>still</u> seemed <u>high</u> but it <u>was turning</u> orange. I spoke to <u>an old man who was smoking his pipe near the water</u> and asked him if it was Steyning that I <u>could see</u> on <u>the other bank</u>.

(from *I Left My Grandfather's House* by D. Welch)

6 Modification   The words which precede the head are called its 'premodification' and those which come after are called its 'postmodification':

PREMODIFICATION	HEAD	POSTMODIFICATION
my grandfather's	house	at Henfield in Sussex

Subdivide the following underlined phrases in the same way:

I made my way from Exmoor to <u>the edge of Dartmoor</u>. I had <u>yet another great-aunt in view</u> to provide <u>my next night's bed</u>. She was <u>the sister-in-law of the uncle I had stayed with at Petersfield</u>, and she had a house <u>not very far from Okehampton.</u>

(from *I Left My Grandfather's House* by D. Welch)

7 Prepositional phrases   Prepositional phrases have two parts – a preposition followed by a noun phrase:
– at Henfield
– on my way

Identify the prepositional phrases in the extract in Task 5.

8 Phrases   What kinds of phrases do the following activities practise?

1

> Write down five dates or time expressions that
> have some significance to you. Examples:
> *5th May 1972*   *last Monday*
>
> Then tell other people in the class why your dates
> are important to you and what happened. Example:
> *'On the 5th of May 1972 my son was born.'*

(from *Intermediate Matters* by J. Bell and R. Gower)

2

**Discuss the disadvantages of having the following animals as pets.
Use *too* and/ or *enough*:**

An elephant is too big to put in the car.

A lobster is not aggressive enough to scare off intruders.

A SNAKE   A WALRUS   A BAT

A KANGAROO   AN OYSTER

A PORCUPINE

3

I went to the *Antique shop*....:
a memory game.

Student 1 starts by saying: 'I went to the antique shop and I
bought a table', for example. Student 2 continues by adding a
modifier: 'I went to the antique shop and I bought a big table'.
And so it continues, each student adding a modifier, and
inserting it in the correct place: '...and bought a lovely big old-
fashioned handmade Moroccan coffee table'.

12 Sentence structure: the simple sentence

Introduction

The basic unit of language analysis is the sentence. A grammar is essentially (or, at least, traditionally) a description of how the sentences in a language are formed. Although sentences are neither the smallest nor the largest units in a language, they are more tightly constructed than the other larger elements. This unit and the next look at ways of analysing sentences and describing their construction.

Tasks

1 **Sentences and 'non-sentences'**   Identify those groups of words that form grammatically complete sentences in these two extracts (from Alan Ayckbourn's *A Small Family Business*). What are the other groups of words?

a) We appear to be looking at a cross-section of a modern or recently modernized house, perhaps on an executive-type estate. Ours is a rear view. Four rooms, two up and two down. Downstairs, to one side, is the sitting room. Modern furnishings, fitments with hi-fi, etc., a settee, armchairs, low tables. Neutral carpeting. It is a fairly large area, being two rooms knocked into one.

b) POPPY   How did it go, then?

   JACK   All right. You know. Fond farewells. Usual thing. We shall miss you for ever thank God he's gone at last...I'm not that late, am I?

   POPPY   Only a little.

2 **Sentence elements**   Look at this sentence from the Madonna text (Unit 1). Which of the following groupings best represent its internal structure?

a) A plan to star | pop queen Madonna | in a film version of Evita has been | vetoed by composer | Andrew Lloyd Webber.
b) A plan to star pop queen Madonna in a film version of Evita | has been vetoed | by composer Andrew Lloyd Webber.
c) A plan | to star | pop queen Madonna in a film version | of Evita | has been vetoed | by | composer Andrew Lloyd Webber.

Can you divide the following sentences up into their basic elements? (The number of elements is shown in brackets.)

d) Australia's most senior female politician has resigned. (2)
e) The All Black side to play the British Lions in the first test in Christchurch on Saturday was predictable. (3)
f) Hundreds of angry Afghans sacked the Pakistan embassy. (3)
g) The counting of votes from thousands of expatriates gave the Prime Minister a majority of one seat. (4)
h) A Pakistani court cleared Asif Ali Zardari, husband of the Prime Minister, Benazir Bhutto, of bank fraud charges. (4)

3 Sentence elements Traditional sentence analysis identifies five different types of sentence elements: subject, verb, object, complement and adverbial (S, V, O, C, A).

Can you match these terms with their definition?

subject	gives further information (or completes what is said) about some other element
verb	identifies what or who is topic of the clause and/or the agent of the verb
object	adds extra information about the time, manner, or place, etc. of the situation
complement	identifies who or what is affected by an action
adverbial	the clause element that typically expresses an event, action or state

4 Subjects Identify the subject in each of these sentences. (*Note*: the examples in Tasks 4–8 all come from *A Small Family Business* by A. Ayckbourn)

a) We all steal things. *We all*
b) Your mum steals things, does she?
c) Of course I don't.
d) Neither does Tina.
e) From now on this family's going to be subject to a few hard and fast rules.
f) Well, perhaps a small gin with just a dab of tonic would be very pleasant.
g) Someone's trying to break in the back door.
h) Who did that?
i) Look, what's the matter with you lot?
j) What are you saying?
k) Am I the only one with any moral values at all?
l) There speaks the expert.
m) What I'm saying is we're trying to keep this in the family.

5 Complements and objects Can you identify which of the underlined phrases are objects, which are complements, and which are neither?

a) This is <u>a very well-appointed kitchen</u>. *complement*
b) Dad threw <u>him</u> out. *object*
c) Everybody steals <u>things</u>.
d) I thought that was <u>her</u>.
e) I feel <u>so ashamed</u> even saying it.
f) Ice is <u>in the freezer</u>.
g) We're doing <u>nothing illegal</u>.
h) The Italians are proving <u>a bit difficult</u>.
i) She gave me <u>a false name</u> as well.
j) She gave <u>me</u> a false name as well.
k) That makes him out <u>a complete idiot</u>, doesn't it?

6 Adverbials   Identify the adverbials in the following sentences. (Note that in several cases there is more than one.) How is each one realised – by a prepositional phrase, an adverb phrase, or noun phrase?

a) I'm expecting a phone call *any minute*. *noun phrase*
b) She always listens to Tina.
c) I'll be there all day.
d) I was educated privately in Dorset.
e) We manage perfectly well.
f) Would you step in here for a moment first?
g) I have to sleep in our spare room these days.
h) Perhaps we can hide him somewhere.

7 Sentence elements   Now, you should be able to identify the elements of the underlined sentences in the following extracts. The first group have been done for you:

JACK: Cliff!

ANITA: How many more times, he's not here. He's <u>down the pub</u>. *S V A*

I promise you, he is. He's got some darts match. *S V   O   S V S V   O*

JACK: Then call him and get him back here.

ANITA: I can't do that. It's a match.

CLIFF: It's Jack. He knows everything. He knows about you.

DESMOND: Jack does?

CLIFF: It's probably him at the door. …

JACK: …I pay him the money. Clear the family name. Then that's it. …

POPPY: It's my fault. I got you into this.

    (from *A Small Family Business* by A. Ayckbourn)

8 Sentence analysis   Now you should be able to analyse a simple sentence according to:

1   the elements that make it up (S, V, O, C, A)

and the way these elements are realised, both in terms of

2   phrases and
3   word classes

For example:

	It	's	probably	him	at	the	door
1	S	V	A	C	A		
2	NP	VP	AdvP	NP	PP		
3	pn	verb	adverb	pn	prep	det	noun

Do the same for these sentences:

a) It's a free country.
b) My friend lent them to me.
c) She gave me a false name.
d) I was educated privately in Dorset.
e) We'll use the front door this time.
f) Poppy doesn't get on too well with Harriet.

Now can you label the elements (S, V, O, C, A) in sentences (**d** – **h**) in Task 2?

9 Sentence structure of other languages   Look at these word-for-word translations from different languages. In what way does the basic syntax of each of these languages appear to differ from English syntax? What is the significance of this for the teacher of English?

a) *Arabic*: Kataba al-mu'allimu al-darsa 'ala el-sabburati. Wrote the teacher the lesson on the board. (The teacher wrote the lesson on the board.)
b) *Hindi*: kalam méz par nahiñ hai. Pen table on not is. (The pen is not on the table.)
c) *Spanish*: Tú no nos lo prestas nunca. You do not us it lend never. (You never lend it to us.)
d) *Turkish*: Ahmet bugün şehirde bana hikaye anlattı. Ahmet today town-in me-to a story told. (Ahmet told me a story in town today.)
e) *German*: Wir haben es nicht gekauft, weil es zu teuer war. We have it not bought because it too expensive was. (We didn't buy it because it was too expensive.)
f) *French*: J'aime les films de science-fiction bien faits. I like the films of science-fiction well made. (I like well made science-fiction films.)

13 Sentence structure: the complex sentence

Introduction

In the preceding unit we looked at the simple, one-clause, one-verb, sentence. Complex sentences are those that consist of two or more clauses, hence two or more verbs. This unit introduces you to the ways clauses can be combined in sentences.

Tasks

1 **Finite and non-finite verbs**   Finite verbs are those that are marked for tense and/or number and/or person, as in *she works* and *she has worked*. Non-finite verbs do not express these contrasts. They are the participles and infinitives: *working, worked* and *(to) work*. Read this text and identify the verb phrases. Which verb phrases are finite and which are non-finite?

Desperate action

A YOUNG Dunedin man suffered a severe electrical shock in the Income Support Service office after walking out of an interview.

The incident left staff as well as the man badly shaken.

The young man walked out of the interview room before the interview had finished.

He pulled a wire from his clothing and plugged it into a wall socket, receiving a severe shock.

A staff member swiftly disconnected the plug and the man was taken to hospital.

(from *New Zealand News UK*)

2 **Clauses**   In the text in the preceding task there are more verb phrases than sentences. Each verb phrase marks the presence of a clause. Use these definitions to find examples of the following (some of these categories overlap):

– a simple sentence: A sentence that contains only one clause.
– a multiple sentence: A sentence that contains more than one clause. It can be either complex or compound (see the definitions of these below).
– an independent clause: A clause that can stand on its own to form a

sentence. It is sometimes called a main clause.

– a compound sentence:	A sentence consisting of two independent clauses linked by co-ordination, for example, *and*, *or* or *but*.
– a dependent clause:	A clause that cannot stand on its own to make a sentence. It is sometimes called a subordinate clause.
– a complex sentence:	A sentence that contains a main clause and one or more dependent clauses. The dependent clause is subordinate to the main clause.
– a finite clause:	A clause whose verb is finite.
– a non-finite clause:	A clause whose verb is non-finite.

3 Noun clauses   Dependent clauses are often classified into three broad groups:

– relative clauses:	There was an old woman *who lived in a shoe*.
– noun clauses:	She had so many children she didn't know *what to do*.
– adverbial clauses:	*As I was going to St Ives* I met a man with seven wives.

(Relative clauses are dealt with in Unit 23.)

Noun clauses (or nominal clauses) function the same way as noun phrases. That is, they function either as the subject, object or complement of a clause.

Identify the noun clauses in these sentences (from Ayckbourn's *A Small Family Business*). What is their function – subject, object or complement?

a) I don't know *what he's supposed to have done*. noun clause as object
b) So. That is *what's going to happen*. noun clause as complement
c) Are you saying I steal things?
d) Anybody here object to killing people?
e) She does what she likes, I do what I like.
f) All I did was stand up to blackmail.
g) What I'm saying is we're trying to keep this in the family.
h) I'll see what he wants.
i) Listen, I don't know what you think you're doing.

4 Reported speech   Two kinds of noun clause, the *that*-clause, and the *wh*-clauses, are often used to report what someone is saying or has said:

– Uberto said *(that) he liked your speech*.
– Won't you tell me *where you're going*?

Identify the reporting clauses in the following extract. What, do you think, were the actual words spoken? How are the reporting clauses affected by the choice of reporting verb? What would happen if the reporting verbs were in the past ('Charles said…')?

EXTRACTS of Charles and Di's ding-dong involves a potentially embarrassing squabble over the custody of their children.

On the transcript Charles says he's doing nothing but think of Di and the children ever since their troubles started.

Di replies that she doesn't believe that and tells him to stop being so self-centred...

Their conversation reveals that Charles was determined to have the children with him at Sandringham over Christmas.

Charles says three days is hardly a lifetime.

Diana asks him exactly what he means by three days.

Di asks him if he has considered the implications of a custody battle over the children.

Charles tells her not to be silly and that he hasn't.

Di warns him that this is what would happen and that the boys would suffer...

(from *The People*)

5 Activity Here is an activity designed to practise reported speech. How language-productive do you think it might be? To what extent does it reflect real-life language use?

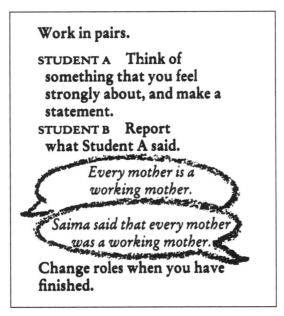

Work in pairs.

STUDENT A   Think of something that you feel strongly about, and make a statement.

STUDENT B   Report what Student A said.

Every mother is a working mother.

Saima said that every mother was a working mother.

Change roles when you have finished.

(from *Flying Colours 2* by J. Garton-Sprenger and S. Greenall)

6 Adverbial clauses These supply circumstantial information about time, place, manner, purpose, etc. They can be finite or non-finite.

Adverbial clauses are traditionally classified according to their meaning – time, place, condition, purpose, etc.

– I listen in the mornings *when I'm jogging*. (This is a time clause.)
– I'll shout *if I need you*. (This is a conditional clause.)
– Jack's coming home *to run the business*. (This is a purpose clause.)

Look at these examples of student writing. Each example contains a problem with adverbial clauses. Can you identify the type of adverbial clause, correct the error, and provide an explanation of the rule that has been broken?

a) When I'll come back, I'll phone you to go out.
b) He's from New Jersey but he went to Chicago for look for a job.
c) In spite of you're less free I'm more interested in a cars than in a motorbikes.
d) All the sky over Tibidabo was really lighted, like if they will be stars.
e) If you would have worked more hard you would have passed the exam.

7 Verb chains   There are a number of verbs in English that tend to be followed by other verbs, forming 'chains' of two or more verbs. Thus, in:

– She keeps saying that word lately
– I'm inclined to agree with her

keeps saying is a verb chain, and *inclined to agree* is another.

Identify the verb chains in the following sentences. What form of the verb follows the primary verb? The first one is done for you.

a) He was *attempting to blackmail* me. *attempt + to-infinitive*
b) Also I resented paying for them.
c) He doesn't seem to be breathing.
d) We stop doing business with them, to start with.
e) Let me make this quite clear.
f) Help me stop him.
g) I want to get home and have my dinner.
h) I don't want him working for me.
i) I'd like you and Anna to consider coming on to the board.

8 Look at the following exercise on verb chains. Is it designed to teach, practise, or test? Can *you* do it?

Look at these pairs of sentences. Decide where there is:
- little or no change in meaning.
- an important change in meaning.

1 It started to rain. It started raining.
2 He remembered to close the window. He remembered closing the window.
3 I like to play tennis. I like playing tennis.
4 My car needs working on. I need to work on my car.

5 They stopped to look at the map. They stopped looking at the map.
6 She tried to learn Japanese. She tried learning ten new words a day.

(from *Think First Certificate* by J. Naunton)

9 Can you write some classroom instructions using chain verbs (*Remember…; Try…; Stop…*)?

10 Sentence analysis You should now be able to analyse these sentences into their clauses, and the clauses into their respective clause elements. The first one has been done for you.

a) I didn't know before I came.

I	didn't know	before	I	came.
S	V	A		
		conjunction	S	V
(main clause)		(adverbial clause of time)		

b) I listen in the mornings when I'm jogging.
c) I'll shout if I need you.
d) I'm at Des's so I won't talk for long.
e) They say this is what happens.

If you are in the mood for more sentence analysis, try analysing the sentences of the news article in Task 1 'Desperate action'. Identify their main and dependent clauses, and analyse each clause into its elements: S, V, O, C, A.

14 Negatives and questions

Introduction

The way negative statements and questions are formed varies from language to language. English employs a number of syntactic and lexical features to mark negation and to form questions. Some of these features are common to both negatives and questions.

Tasks

1 Negation Can you identify all the examples of negation in this extract? (There are seven.)

> **Sunday January 4th**
> SECOND AFTER CHRISTMAS
>
> My father has got the flu. I'm not surprised with the diet we get. My mother went out in the rain to get him a vitamin C drink, but as I told her, 'It's too late now'. It's a miracle we don't get scurvy. My mother says she can't see anything on my chin, but this is guilt because of the diet.
>
> The dog has run off because my mother didn't close the gate. I have broken the arm on the stereo. Nobody knows yet, and with a bit of luck my father will be ill for a long time. He is the only one who uses it apart from me. No sign of the apron.
>
> **Monday January 5th**
> The dog hasn't come back yet.

(from *The Secret Diary of Adrian Mole aged 13¾* by S. Townsend)

2 Types of negation In the examples of negation in the preceding text, can you find any instances of the following:

a) *not*-negation (using *not* to negate the verb)

b) dummy operator (*do/does/did* + *not*)

c) a negative pronoun, that is, a word that stands for a noun

d) a negative determiner, that is, a word that precedes a noun

e) a non-assertive form (see Task 4)

3 *Not*-negation   Read this explanation of negation using *not*.

To make a negative statement in English, all you do is add *not* to the auxiliary verb. So, for example: *I can swim – I can't swim; she is swimming – she isn't swimming.*

In what way is this explanation insufficient? Can you improve on it? Consider, for example, how you would negate these statements:

– I am a swimmer.
– She swims.
– She has been swimming.

4 Non-assertive forms   Look at these examples from the extract in Task 1:

– My mother says she can't see anything on my chin.
– The dog hasn't come back yet.

Any and its compounds (*anything, anybody, anywhere*, etc.) and *yet* are examples of non-assertion: these, rather than their assertive forms (*some, already*), tend to be used in negative statements and in questions.

Can you identify the non-assertive forms in the following? What is the equivalent assertive form?

a) My father was first in the queue at the bank this morning. When he got inside, the cashier said he couldn't have any more money because he hadn't got any left.
b) Mr Lucas came in this morning to see if my mother needed any help in the house.
c) My mother cut the dog's hair. It looks worse than ever.
d) Mrs Kane, the proprietor, has refused to keep Sabre any longer.
e) Nothing happened at all today, apart from a hail storm around six o'clock.
f) My father seemed to be the only one doing any work.

(from *The Secret Diary of Adrian Mole aged 13¾* by S. Townsend)

5 Questions   How many different types of question can you identify in this extract? Can you categorise them according to the following types? *Note:* some questions will fit more than one category.

a) *yes-no* questions
b) *wh*-questions
c) indirect questions
d) subject questions – where the questioner seeks information about the subject of the verb
e) object questions – where the questioner seeks information about the verb, its object or its adverbials
f) intonation questions – where the question is signalled by means of intonation alone
g) tag questions

WILSON	Well, I'm sorry I can't stay. I must be going then. Before I say goodbye would you mind telling me, as briefly as possible, why you killed my brother.
MIKE	I didn't!
WILSON	You did. You were paid two hundred and fifty quid. Exclusive of repairs to the van.
MIKE	No!
WILSON	It was on October the twenty-first he was killed. What were you doing that day?
MIKE	I was fishing.
WILSON	Where?
MIKE	In the canal.
WILSON	Did you catch much? …Did you have the good fortune to find a salmon on the end of your line?
MIKE	No. Whoever heard of catching salmon in a canal?
WILSON	You killed my brother. Your denials fall on deaf ears. (*pause*) You're a liar. That's what it amounts to.
MIKE	(*frightened*) What are you going to do?
WILSON	Nothing I can do, is there? (*He picks up his suitcase and goes to the door*) I'll be off. (*He smiles, deliberately*) Give my love to Maddy.

(*Mike grabs Wilson's arm*)

MIKE	Why did you call her Maddy?
WILSON	She asked me to. In private. It's her trade name.
MIKE	She never saw you till two days ago.
WILSON	She told you that? Do you believe her?
MIKE	Yes.

(from *The Ruffian on the Stair* by J. Orton)

6 Questions   How do you form questions in English? Formulate a rule for question formation that takes account of these questions:

– Do you believe her?
– What were you doing that day?
– Why did you call her Maddy?

7 Practising questions   One obvious but, nevertheless, effective way of practising questions is to play 'Twenty questions'. Students ask each other a maximum of twenty *yes-no* questions in order to guess the name of, for example, an object, a famous person, an animal, etc. Can you think of other guessing games involving questions? What sort of questions are practised in each case?

8 Common errors   Here are some examples of questions that a group of learners produced by playing 'Twenty questions'. What rules of question formation have they not yet acquired?

a)   You are man? Or woman?
b)   Are famous?
c)   Speak you English?
d)   Do you can play tennis?
e)   Do you was born in America?
f)   You are André Agassi, isn't it?

9 Activity   Look at this exercise. What grammar point is it practising? How could you prepare students to do this exercise?

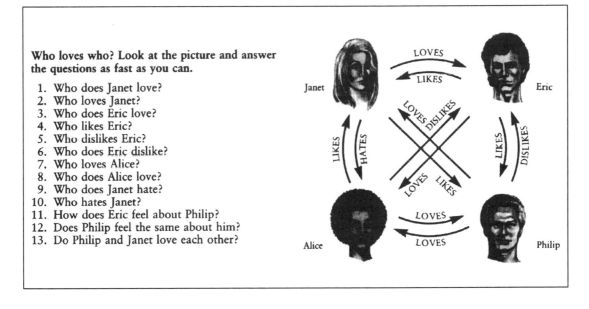

Who loves who? Look at the picture and answer the questions as fast as you can.

1. Who does Janet love?
2. Who loves Janet?
3. Who does Eric love?
4. Who likes Eric?
5. Who dislikes Eric?
6. Who does Eric dislike?
7. Who loves Alice?
8. Who does Alice love?
9. Who does Janet hate?
10. Who hates Janet?
11. How does Eric feel about Philip?
12. Does Philip feel the same about him?
13. Do Philip and Janet love each other?

(from *The New Cambridge English Course 2* by M. Swan and C. Walter)

10 Classroom questions   Learners often want to ask questions about the language they are learning, but may lack the means. Make a list of questions that students could usefully be taught (for example, 'What preposition does it take?') and indicate the level at which you would introduce them.

15 The verb phrase

Introduction

This unit introduces the area of grammar which, more than any other, is the main focus of most pedagogical grammars, and therefore of most language teaching materials (and, of course, of much classroom teaching). You might like to consider why this is the case.

Tasks

1 Verbs The following note appears towards the end of the teacher's book of an intermediate course. So far the syllabus has covered present, past, and future verb forms, as well as continuous and perfect aspect.

How is the learning of the verb-forms going? If students are still making mistakes, begin regular testing of all the verbs. If necessary, start the students learning the forms again from the beginning. THESE MUST BE KNOWN CORRECTLY.

(from *Kernel Lessons Intermediate* by R. O'Neill)

Do you consider the verb forms to be this important? Why is so much emphasis placed on the verb phrase in many language courses?

2 Types of verbs Look at the note to teachers in Task 1 and see if you can find examples of the following:

a) irregular verbs: How do they differ from regular verbs?
b) auxiliary verbs: What *are* auxiliaries – as opposed to lexical verbs?
c) participles or infinitives: Why are these types of verbs called 'non-finite'?
d) imperatives
e) chain verbs – lexical verbs that are followed by other lexical verbs.
f) intransitive verbs: What *is* an intransitive verb?
g) passive constructions
h) stative verbs and dynamic verbs: What is the difference?
i) verbs marked for aspect
j) verbs marked for modality

3 Irregular verbs Irregular verbs are 'regularly' irregular – that is, there are several basic patterns of irregularity. Can you add at least two examples of each pattern to these lists?

a) buy   bought   bought
   teach   taught   taught
b) write   wrote   written
   rise   rose   risen
c) begin   began   begun
   swim   swam   swum

d) cut   cut   cut
    hit   hit   hit

Do you think this kind of organisation would be helpful for learners? At what stage and for what purposes do learners need to be familiar with past participle forms?

4 Imperatives   Find examples of imperatives in these classroom instructions:

Look at me!
Pay attention now!
Could I have your attention please?
Try to concentrate now!
Don't look out of the window!
Eyes to the front, please!
I'm sorry to interrupt you, but could you look this way for a moment?
Be quiet!
Everyone listen!
Sit still!
Don't move!
Nobody move!
Settle down, all of you!
Everybody stay where they are!

(from *A Handbook of Classroom English* by G. Hughes)

Use the data in the above examples to answer the following questions:

a) How do you form the imperative in English?
b) How do you form the negative imperative?
c) Can imperatives have a subject?
d) How do you 'soften' an imperative?

5 Passive voice   Read this text and identify examples of the passive. What tenses are used? Why do you think the passive has been chosen, in each case?

Jessica Johnson was out walking with her husband when she was attacked by an unsupervised Alsatian dog. Jessica's leg was bitten, and she had to have stitches in two wounds. Two days later, because the wounds had become infected, Jessica was admitted to hospital. Even after she was discharged, she needed further treatment from her GP – and she was told to rest for two weeks.

Jessica is self-employed, and her business was affected while she was sick. Also, the trousers and shoes she'd been wearing at the time of the attack were ruined by bloodstains, and had to be thrown away.

Jessica told us, 'I'm now trying to get compensation from the owners of the dog'.

(from *Which?*)

How could you use this text with intermediate learners of English, in order to focus on the passive?

6 Stative verbs There are a number of verbs in English that are generally only used to express states rather than events or actions and, therefore, do not generally allow progressive forms.

How many can you find in these extracts? For example, *knows* in (**a**)

a)

> Imedeen is sold in 40 countries, including Britain. No one knows how the product works. The label on the package states that each tablet contains 190 milligrams of "deep-sea protein".

(from the *New Scientist*)

b)

> This radio measures 19.1 x 11.8 x 3.2cm and it weighs 615g with batteries. It is therefore quite portable and suitable for the international traveller.

(from *BBC On Air*)

c)

> ●**PRETTY, INDEPENDENT WOMAN,** loves travel, has good friends, many interests, doesn't meet the kind of man she wants – single, intelligent, good company, trustworthy, no hang-ups, 30's – where are you?

(from *Time Out*)

d)

> This baguette also got the thumbs down. "It looked and tasted dreary. For health freaks only," said Steve Job.

(from the *Independent on Sunday*)

7 Verb forms Can you complete these grids?

ACTIVE

	simple	progressive	perfect	perfect progressive
present	I watch			
past		I was watching		
future			I will have watched	

PASSIVE

	simple	progressive	perfect	perfect progressive
present				——
past	I was watched			——
future		I will be being watched		——

8 Can you identify the underlined verb forms in this text? The first one is done for you.

share: *present simple*

> **ALISON WALL AND** her partner Simon <u>share</u> a small, colourful inner city house with Eastwood the cat and one or two flatmates.
>
> 'I<u>'ve had</u> this house for two years. I <u>bought</u> it after I<u>'d done</u> some TV work after the sharemarket crash. …I used to be really cynical about people who did gardening and home renovating – but that's exactly what we<u>'ve been doing</u>. Simon's very handy with a hammer – he <u>likes</u> smashing things up. As soon as we<u>'ve finished</u> with the carpentry I<u>'ll ditch</u> him and take up with a plumber.'

(from *Metro Magazine*)

As a preview to the following units, you might like to consider *why* each verb form has been chosen.

16 Time and tense

Introduction

This unit attempts to unravel the relationship between real time and grammatical tense.

Tasks

1 How many tenses are there in English? Two, three, eight, sixteen or twenty-one?

   What are they?

2 **Time and tense**   Look at these sentences. What is the *tense* of the verb in each case. What is the *time* reference?

   a) ## The Chelsea Flower Show opens next week

   b) ## SIR CHARLES GROVES DIES

   Can you think of other examples of the present tense that do not refer to present time, and examples of the past tense that do not refer to past time?

   c) Present tense with future reference — *The Chelsea Flower Show opens next week.*
   d) Present tense with past reference.
   e) Past tense with present reference.
   f) Past tense with future reference.

3 **Present simple**

   a) Identify all the examples of the present simple in this text:

   > Rosie really likes Prince. She listens to his music and she knows he has love in his heart. ...She is still talking about how she'd rather have her voice than be skinny, when Levi saunters in. He tells me how he and Prince listen to other artists' records together...

   (from *The Face*)

b) Can you find examples in the above text of the following uses of the present simple?

- to talk about present states
- to talk about present events
- to talk about present habits (or repeated events)

c) Now, match these time lines to each of the above uses (the symbol ↓ indicates the present).

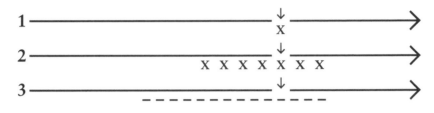

4 **Present simple**   Look at the examples in the left-hand column. They represent at least six of the ways the present simple is used in English. Can you match each example with its corresponding concept in the right-hand column?

1 The concert *finishes* at 8.00 p.m. so you'll have plenty of time to get home for the last bus.
2 Noah always *beats* Curren. He has a sort of Houdini against him.
3 I'll never play at Wembley again, unless I *play* there again.
4 She *puts* her head down and *bangs* it straight across the line.
5 She *comes* from a tennis-playing family. Her father's a dentist.
6 POLICE *DISCOVER* CRACK IN AUSTRALIA.

A present and timeless states
B repeated events in the present
C instantaneous events in the present
D past events
E future scheduled events
F adverbial clauses of time and conditional clauses

(Examples 1–5 from *Private Eye's Colemanballs*)

Can you think of typical contexts for uses A–E of the present simple? In what order, and at what levels, might you introduce these uses to a group of learners?

5 **Present and past**   Identify the kinds of texts the following extracts come from. Change the verbs in the present into the past simple. What is the effect?

a) …a family goes mushroom hunting, and, upon returning home, begins worrying about toadstools. So they feed a mushroom to their cat – that's nice – and since the beloved pet survives, they begin eating mushrooms at a great rate. Suddenly, somebody looks out the window, and there's the cat on the lawn, stone cold dead…

b) WEDNESDAY. I take Lily and the other three children to our local park. It is bitterly cold, almost freezing. My kids are wrapped up like Eskimos but there are other children wearing just thin cotton T-shirts and no socks.

c) Nicholson Baker lives in Mount Morris, New York, with his wife and child. His stories have appeared in *The Atlantic* and *The New Yorker*. *The Mezzanine* is his first novel. His second, *Room Temperature*, is also published by Granta Books.

6 Past simple Identify the past simple verbs in this extract. As in Task 3, distinguish between past states, past events and past habits.

Ianthe always hurried past the vet's house... The basement cattery seemed to her a sinister place... On the crowded train a man gave up his seat to Ianthe and she accepted it gracefully. She expected courtesy from men and often received it.

(from *An Unsuitable Attachment* by B. Pym)

7 Past simple In which of the following text types are you likely to find a high frequency of past simple verb structures? In these text types what other linguistic features are likely to co-occur with the past? The first one is done for you.

a) biographical sketch (written) *frequent past simple; time expressions (in 1982, etc.)*
b) joke (spoken)
c) weather report (written or spoken)
d) complaint about faulty merchandise (spoken)
e) holiday postcard
f) film review (written)
g) news broadcast
h) insurance claim (written)

What does this exercise suggest about possible approaches to teaching the past simple?

8 Past perfect Identify the examples of the past perfect in this passage:

Penny and Ian Muirhead installed their smoke alarm just in time. 'We'd bought the alarm and hadn't got round to fixing it up for weeks,' said Penny. 'I'd been nagging Ian to do it.' A fortnight after
Ian had put the alarm in place, their solid fuel stove overheated in the middle of the night and set fire to wooden panelling behind it...

(from *Which?*)

9 Past perfect Which of these statements most satisfactorily explains the examples of the past perfect in the preceding text?

a) 'If you want to talk about a past event or situation that occurred before a particular time in the past, you use the past perfect.' (*Collins COBUILD English Grammar*)

b) 'If the speaker looks back from a remote point to a point further in the past, we get the past perfect...' (Lewis 1982)

c) 'The past perfect is used to make it clear which event or state in a sequence preceded which.' (Close)

10 Tenses in context Read this text and identify the different verb phrases that refer to past time; then add the verbs to the timeline below.

> CLARE STRACK was working in Edinburgh, 'cooking and cleaning, and getting pretty fed up', when she discovered an interesting alternative.
>
> 'Way, way back, I had actually trained to be a teacher and I had a degree in English, but I had never used those qualifications. When I heard about teaching English as a foreign language, I realised it was something that fitted my qualifications and lifestyle.'
>
> She enrolled at the Basil Paterson college in Edinburgh, completed the RSA certificate, and was immediately hired by the school to teach for two hours a day – Spaniards, Italians and Arabs mostly.

(from *More Magazine*)

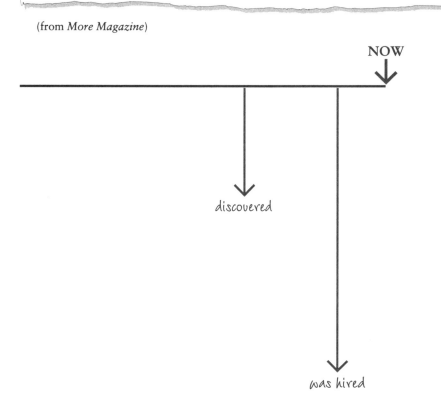

NOW

discovered

was hired

11 Time and tense   Correct the tense mistakes in these extracts from students'
writing. How would you explain your corrections to the students?

a) When we arrived in my house and I opened the door others friends were
inside yet. They had been prepared a party and I was surprising.

b) I didn't realise it was so late and the underground didn't work yet.

c) When we arrived, the train leaved the station and we stayed in three long
hours until the next train arrived.

d) My mother said me that my boyfriend, Andrew, was having a accident
and he stayed in the General Hospital.

e) It seems difficult think that I had been arrived here two weeks ago.

f) In this afternoon my cousin was killed the cat of his mother because the
cat was in the road and my cousin don't he looked.

17 Progressive aspect

Introduction

The different ways of marking the verb phrase to convey the speaker's perception of the event – its 'aspect' – are commonly called 'tenses'. It is important, however, not to confuse tense and aspect, since the latter has less to do with time than with 'shape'. It is another 'dimension', if you like.

Tasks

1 **Aspect**   English verbs are marked for two aspects: progressive (or continuous), and perfect. These are not mutually exclusive – they combine freely. Can you identify examples of either progressive or perfect aspect in this interview with the novelist William Kennedy?

> Q. "Very Old Bones" has just been published in Europe. Your work is so much about Albany, New York. What is the appeal for Europeans?
> A. They seem to take to it. I've had about seven or eight interviews this week. Some of the interviewers have read every book, and they want to know all about Albany. ...
> Q. Are you working on another novel?
> A. Yes, I'm on page 12. I've been working on it since 1977. But it wasn't cooked until about three weeks or a month ago, and I finally got it started. I've got the ...

(from the *International Herald Tribune*)

2 **Progressive aspect**   Look at these explanations of the progressive aspect:

'Forms containing (*be*)+-*ing* express the speaker's view of the event as having *limited duration*.' (Lewis 1986)

'Progressive *be* is so called because its basic meaning is that it presents the situation as being in progress.' (Huddleston 1988)

'The basic meaning of the progressive is...its depiction of an activity or event as incomplete, changing, temporary, etc.' (Richards 1985)

Which of these explanations best fits *all* the following examples?

a) Inflation and interest rates are going up, growth is going down.
b) The eighteen-year-old is living in squats or sleeping rough and is probably using a false name, detectives believe.
c) In December 1989, 208 English hotels were being built, extended or refurbished.

d) I was putting the milk bottles out when I heard the planes.
e) The Portuguese have been fighting bulls for as long as their Spanish neighbours.
f) A lot of weekends have to be given up to writing when I'm writing books.
g) 'This is my first interview and I'm being very frank,' she says.
h) 'I get a real kick out of showing people what to do. I'm always learning.'
i) Everyone around me was crying and screaming.
j) Up-and-coming Camden venue Pullit, in Jamestown Rd NW1, is putting on a Norman Jay special on June 6.

3 Progressive aspect   The use of the *-ing* form to focus on events in progress can be seen when it is combined with verbs of perception. What is the difference in meaning between these two sentences?

a) ...I see out of the corner of my eye a middle-aged woman crossing over towards the car...
b) ...I see out of the corner of my eye a middle-aged woman cross over towards the car...

How does this difference relate to the inherent meaning of the progressive?

4 Present progressive   Teachers' grammars list a number of different uses for the present progressive. For example:

1   To describe events/situations in progress at the moment of speaking.
2   To describe temporary situations in the present, though not necessarily at the moment of speaking.
3   To describe changing or developing situations in the present.
4   To describe repeated events or situations (with *always, constantly, forever*, etc.).
5   To describe the background to an event in the present.
6   To describe a present arrangement for a future event.

Can you find an example of each use in the extracts (**a–j**) in Task 2?

What do all these uses have in common? For example, to what extent do they fit this diagram?

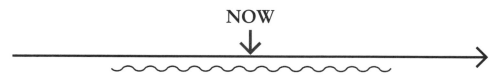

NOW

5 Present progressive   Can you think of natural contexts for introducing and practising uses (1–4) in Task 4 of the present progressive? For example:

1   Events/situations in progress at the moment of speaking: *Describing on-going events to someone not present, e.g. in a postcard or over the phone.*

6 Past progressive   Look at these examples from Task 2 again. Convert the past progressive verbs into past simple. How does this seem to affect the meaning?

a)   In December 1989, 208 English hotels were being built, extended or refurbished.
b)   I was putting the milk bottles out when I heard the planes.
c)   Everyone around me was crying and screaming.

7 Past progressive   How is the past progressive used in narrative? Consider this opening line from a story by Raymond Carver:

The telephone rang while he was running the vacuum cleaner.

What does this suggest about ways of introducing and practising the past progressive?

18 Perfect aspect

Introduction

Continuing our exploration of aspect, we now look at the perfect.

Tasks

1 Perfect aspect   As with the progressive, the auxiliary system allows different combinations of tense and aspect. Can you identify the perfect verb structures in the following sentences and decide what aspectual meaning, if any, they all have in common?

a) My attitude was, I've had my name for twenty years, why change it?
b) By 2000 every age group over 50 will have increased.
c) I have experienced winning the League once with the club and it's something you don't forget.
d) She has been rehearsing for months and looks fitter and in better shape than ever before.
e) Warnings that a major storm was approaching had been issued.

2 Present perfect   Identify examples of the present perfect in this extract:

BUCHANAN	Is this the Personnel section?
EDITH	Yes.
BUCHANAN	I've found it at last. I've had a long journey.
EDITH	Didn't they provide a map?
BUCHANAN	No. I was offered a guide, but I turned it down.
EDITH	Are you expected?
BUCHANAN	Yes. I'm retiring today. They're making a presentation. I'm the oldest living employee. My photograph will be in the firm's magazine. They've already arranged the particulars. I gave them every assistance, of course. ...How long have you worked here?
EDITH	Fifty years. I have breaks, of course. For pregnancy and the occasional death of a near relative.
BUCHANAN	I've been here for fifty years, too. How strange we've never met.
EDITH	Which gate do you use?
BUCHANAN	Number eight.
EDITH	Ah, well, you see, that explains it. I've always entered by number fifteen.
BUCHANAN	I've a feeling we have met. ...You've the look about you of the only woman I ever loved. ...(*Edith stops, looks up, gives a startled cry*) I'm sorry if I've offended you.

(from *The Good and Faithful Servant* by J. Orton)

3 Present perfect   Swan (1980) identifies two ways in which the present perfect is used:

A) for actions and situations continuing up to the present
B) for finished actions and events

Look at the examples of the present perfect you identified in Task 2. For each example, decide whether it belongs to category A or B. Are there any which could belong to both categories?

4 Present perfect   Some writers (such as Comrie 1976) elaborate on the two basic categories described above:

– Perfect of result: in which a present state is viewed as being the result of some past situation.
– Experiential perfect: where a situation has occurred at least once during some time in the past leading up to the present.
– Perfect of persistent situation: to describe a situation that started in the past and persists until the present.
– Perfect of recent past: the past situation is very recent.

Can you match the concept with the appropriate example?

a) I have just found out that my husband has a four-year-old daughter by another woman.
b) Have you ever had smoked mackerel pâté?
c) And he said: 'I've worked damn hard with England for eight years and I am not about to quit.'
d) Her housekeeper said: 'She's gone away, but I've no idea where.'

5 Present perfect   The present perfect is often used in conjunction with certain time expressions. Which of the following time expressions *cannot* be used with the present perfect sentence *She's been here*? Why not?

before   already   once   last year   since three o'clock   two weeks ago   recently   often   for half an hour   at three o'clock just   yesterday morning   this morning

6 Present perfect   The present perfect is often used to announce news. Identify the tenses of the verbs in the headline and in the first two sentences of this news article. What determines the choice of verb tense in each case?

Surfer survives white pointer shark attack

A South Australian teenager has been attacked by a white pointer shark – and lived to tell the tale.

Student Jason Bates, 17, suffered only minor cuts when he was attacked by a 4m white pointer while surfing at Lipson Cove, north of Tumby Bay, on Tuesday.

(from *The Advertiser*)

7 Present perfect   Can you think of situations that you could use to present each of the four uses of the present perfect in Task 4?

For example:
– Perfect of result: *The aftermath of a burglary — They've smashed the door in; they've taken the video . . .*

8 Present perfect progressive   Can you do this exercise? What does it suggest about the way the present progressive is used?

Results of past activity

PRESENTATION

A   You look tired. What have you been doing?
B   I'm exhausted. I've been getting ready to go on holiday.

A   Have you done everything?
B   Nearly. I've packed the cases, and I've been to the bank, but I haven't checked the flight yet.

● Grammar questions

Underline with a solid line _____ the examples of the *Present Perfect Simple*.
Underline with a broken line - - - - - the examples of the *Present Perfect Continuous*.

Why does A ask:
What have you been doing?
but
Have you done everything?

(from *Headway Intermediate* by J. Soars and L. Soars)

9 Present perfect   Now can you do this exercise?

Here are some rules for the use of the Present Perfect (Simple and Progressive). Some of them are good rules; some of them are wrong. Which are the good ones?

1. We can use the Present Perfect when we are talking about things which are still happening now.
2. We cannot use the Present Perfect when we are talking about a finished action.
3. We cannot use the Present Perfect when we give the time of a finished action.
4. We use the Present Perfect for actions which happened recently, and the Simple Past for actions which happened longer ago.
5. We often use the Present Perfect to give news.
6. We often use the Present Perfect to talk about experience.

(from *The New Cambridge English Course 2* by M. Swan and C. Walter)

19 Modality

Introduction

We have seen how verbs can be marked for tense and aspect. They can also be marked for 'modality'. Modal verbs are auxiliary verbs that function as an indicator of the speaker's (or writer's) judgement about the likelihood or desirability of the situation in question. This unit looks at the way modal verbs work and the range of meanings they convey.

Tasks

1 Modal verbs   Identify the modal verbs in this text:

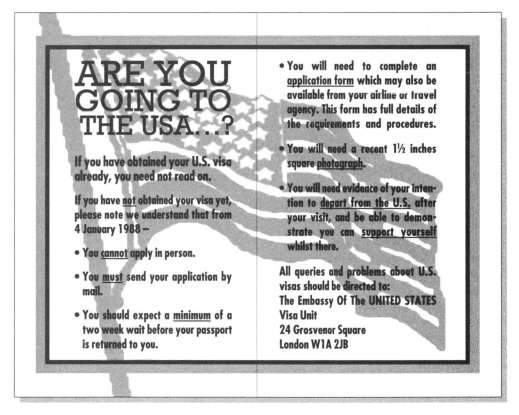

ARE YOU GOING TO THE USA...?

If you have obtained your U.S. visa already, you need not read on.

If you have **not** obtained your visa yet, please note we understand that from 4 January 1988 –

- You **cannot** apply in person.

- You **must** send your application by mail.

- You should expect a **minimum** of a two week wait before your passport is returned to you.

- You will need to complete an **application form** which may also be available from your airline or travel agency. This form has full details of the requirements and procedures.

- You will need a recent 1½ inches square **photograph**.

- You will need evidence of your intention to **depart from the U.S.** after your visit, and be able to demonstrate you can **support yourself** whilst there.

All queries and problems about U.S. visas should be directed to:
The Embassy Of The UNITED STATES
Visa Unit
24 Grosvenor Square
London W1A 2JB

2 Modal structures   Compared to 'lexical verbs' (*work, live, want,* etc.) modal verbs function in syntactically special ways. There are also a number of verbs that share some of the characteristics of modals and some of the characteristics of lexical verbs.

Look at the features listed in the left-hand column of the chart below. For each of the verbs in the chart, put a tick (✔) where the features apply and a cross (✘) where they do not apply.

	can	must	need	want
It takes the infinitive without '*to*'				
There is no special third person form				
The negative is formed simply by adding '*not*'				
The question is formed by inversion				
It cannot be preceded by other auxiliaries				
There is a past form				

3 In another language you are familiar with, are there equivalent forms to the English modals? Do they function in syntactically similar ways? For example, how would you translate the following dialogue:

A. I must go.

B. Can't you stay?

A. I would stay if I could. But I have to work tomorrow.

B. You shouldn't work so hard. Will you be able to find a taxi?

A. It might be difficult. May I use your phone?

If your first language is not English, to what extent does your language use verbs to express the meanings of these modals? What other means are available? How might these differences influence your teaching of modals to your language group?

4 **Error analysis**   Correct any problems of modality in these extracts. How would you explain your corrections to the students who wrote the sentences?

a) A motorbike is cheaper and is faster in a city. You can leave it anywhere because you shouldn't look for a park place.

b) The hotel was overbooked and they sended us to another hotel at London. There it was only one room and all of us must sleep together.

c) The best activity was a kind of competition: things have been hide and the teams should to find them.

d) At the end, a policeman could get the man and he gave the bag back to the woman.
e) If don't rains we will can swim in the beach.
f) If my money isn't refunded I'll be able to go to a lawyer to resolve the question.

5 Two types of meaning   Every modal verb expresses at least two meanings:

– *All* modals can be used to talk about probability/possibility: this is sometimes called their 'extrinsic' meaning.
– Each modal has another set of particular meanings which may be loosely classed as relating to human wishes, abilities, and obligations: these are sometimes called their 'intrinsic' meanings.

Can you now complete this chart, indicating which modals commonly express which concepts. Think of an example, in each case.

	can *can't*	*could* *couldn't*	*may* *may not*	*might* *mightn't*	*should* *shouldn't*	*must* *mustn't*
likelihood/ probability	✔					
ability						
permission						
prohibition						
obligation/ duty						

In the text in Task 1 above, find uses of modals that express:

– probability
– ability
– prohibition
– obligation/duty

6 Meaning   Classify the following examples of modals (1) according to whether they are being used in their extrinsic ('probability') sense, or in their intrinsic sense; and (2), if intrinsic, according to whether they express obligation, permission, prohibition, or ability. The first one is done for you.

a) There <u>must</u> be something on Gooch's mind, and he wants to get it off his chest. (Farokh Engineer) *extrinsic*
b) I'm going to make a prediction – it could go either way. (Ron Atkinson)
c) I must apologise to the deaf for the loss of subtitles. (Angela Rippon)
d) That should arrest the non-movement of the scoreboard. (Neville Oliver)
e) The Dutch boxer, Turr, can speak four languages, which is amazing for someone so short. (NBC Commentator)

f) In the rear, the small diminutive figure of Shoaif Mohammed, who can't be much taller or shorter than he is. (Henry Blofeld)

g) It looks as though that premature excitement may have been premature. (Brough Scott)

h) He should put his foot down with a firm hand. (Radio Broadland)

i) The two superpowers cannot divide the world into their oyster. (Michael Heseltine)

j) At times he gave us what Barnes and Waddle could have given us but couldn't because they didn't play. (Bobby Robson)

(from *Private Eye's Colemanballs, Colemanballs 2, 4, 5, and 6*)

7 Obligation   Do this exercise. What modal expressions does it include, apart from the modal auxiliary *must*?

Read the statements below. Decide if they mean:
must/have to   mustn't   don't have to

You aren't allowed to carry a gun.
You are required to carry an identity card all the time.
It isn't necessary to tell the police if you want to have a demonstration.
You are obliged to carry vehicle documents when you drive.
You don't need to wear a seatbelt in town.
It's forbidden to criticise the government.

Now complete the chart below with phrases from the statements.

must/have to	mustn't	don't have to
you are required to		

Work in pairs. Say if the statements in activity 2 are true or false for your country.

In Holland we don't have to carry ID cards.

(from *Flying Colours 2* by J. Garton-Sprenger and S. Greenall)

8 Functions   Because of the range of meanings expressed by modal verbs, particularly with regard to their intrinsic senses, modals are used to fulfil a variety of important communicative functions.

a) How many ways of making a request, using modal verbs, can you think of?
b) How many functions can be expressed using *can*?
c) Devise a short functional syllabus for beginners that uses *only* modal verbs.

9 Teaching order   Can you guess which is the most frequently occurring modal auxiliary in English? And which is the least? Try putting the nine modals (*can, could, will, would, shall, should, may, might, must*) in order of frequency of occurrence. Then have a look at the commentary. Does anything surprise you about the frequency order? What implications might this order have in the selection of modals for teaching?

20 Futurity

Introduction

This unit looks at the ways futurity is expressed in English, with special attention to the modal auxiliary *will*.

Tasks

1 **Future tense**   There is no future tense verb ending in English. Futurity is expressed in a number of different ways, some of which are exemplified in these extracts. Can you identify them?

a)

Senator Ted Kennedy is in for a busy year, marriage-wise at least. His niece Kerry, daughter of the late Robert F. Kennedy, is getting married to New York Governor Mario Cuomo's son Andrew in Virginia in June. Now comes word that Ted's daughter Kara, 30, will tie the knot with Washington architect Michael Allen this autumn.

(from the *Daily Express*)

b)

For the time being, at least, Kuravsky is going to stay. But this too may change. 'I have a son, aged 11,' he says. 'In a few years' time he will have to serve in the army and maybe I will have to start thinking about going too.'

(from *The European*)

c)

There are some good concerts in the offing, especially as Decker returns during June and July to work with the NZSO. On June 20 he will be conducting Bruckner's *Sixth* with Schoenberg's *Transfigured Night*; on July 15 the great violinist Ida Haendel plays Beethoven's *Violin Concerto*...

(from *Metro Magazine*)

2 Will   The modal auxiliary *will* is considered by many learners (and a number of grammarians) to be the nearest thing to a 'pure' future in English. But *will* does not always express futurity. In each of the following examples decide whether *will/won't* is used with future reference. Can you explain what *will/won't* means in those instances where it does not have future reference?

a) But there will come a time during even the happiest visit to Madrid when one will want to leave in a hurry.
b) After the 17th, although you will still be active, you will also feel more introspective. Keep your spending to a minimum.
c) It's difficult. Deb won't speak to me or see our children. Oliver's mother blames me and won't meet me.
d) On a good day I'll get home at around six in the evening but most days it's after seven and sometimes much later.
e) Dry and sunny in many areas. The best of the sunshine will be in the West, especially Scotland and Wales.
f) Readers of *The Daily Telegraph* will have recently noticed several lengthy articles about the BBC.
g) I was the only person who knew where the restaurant was, so he said 'I'll ride with you, Lee.'
h) He neither drinks nor smokes and will not touch tea or coffee.
i) If you *will* smoke in bed, what can you expect?
j) 100,000 people in Britain will have died from AIDS by the year 2000.

3 Will   What kind of texts do extracts (**b**) and (**e**) in the preceding task come from? In what other contexts would you expect to find *will* used for making predictions? If possible, look for authentic texts, and check if you were right.

4 Exponents of futurity   Faced with so much complexity, learners invent rules. Two common assumptions are that the choice of future form is determined (a) by the degree of certainty; or (b) by how soon the future event will occur.

In a survey conducted by a newspaper on the eve of a general election, the following statements were made about voting intentions. What ways of expressing futurity do they choose? Is there any relation between the exponent chosen and the degree of certainty each respondent expresses – or the proximity of the elections?

a) I will vote Conservative. Of course, I will.
b) I will probably vote Labour, if I can find out who my candidate is.
c) If it's a fine day, I will perhaps vote for Paddy Ashdown.
d) I'm voting Labour. The country needs an integrated housing policy.
e) So in Cambridge I'll be voting for Shirley Williams.
f) First let me say how I am not going to vote. I am not going to vote tactically…

5 *-ing* forms   We have seen (in Unit 17) how progressive aspect conveys the meaning of activities 'in progress'. How does this apply to progressive forms with future reference? What is 'in progress' about these examples?
a) His niece Kerry is getting married in June.
b) A new album of songs to help foreign students learn English is being released this Autumn. (*EFL Gazette*)
c) For the time being, at least, Kuravsky is going to stay.
d) 'I'm nearly 32,' he says without a hint of self-pity, 'and I am going to get old very quickly.'
e) It is going to be an intriguing few days between now and next Thursday. I do not have a single shred of doubt we are going to get a working majority. (*The Independent*)

6 Arrangements, schedules, etc.   In the following situations, which future verb forms would you expect to feature prominently? Why?

a) Two people trying to agree on a mutually convenient time to have a meeting.
b) An enquiry at a train station information office.
c) A person describing projected renovations to a house.

What sort of classroom activities are suggested by these situations?

7 Future forms   The choice of future form is determined less by factors such as nearness or certainty, than by the speaker's perception of how the future event is to come about. Match the exponent on the left with its concept on the right:

a) Kim's meeting Chris at 6.	1 There's *evidence* for X event occurring.
b) I tell you what: I'll phone the station.	2 X event is *predicted*.
c) The train leaves at 10.17.	3 I'm *deciding* to do X.
d) I think I'm going to be sick.	4 X event is *scheduled* to happen.
e) There will be showers on the coast.	5 X event has been *arranged* to happen.
f) I'm going to order a salad.	6 X event will happen *as a matter of course*.
g) The plane will be landing shortly.	7 I have *decided* to do X.

8 Will/going to   Despite the fact that *will* and *going to* can each be used to make predictions and to talk about plans and intentions, there are often factors that determine the choice of one over the other.

Look at this presentation idea, designed to highlight a difference between *will* and *going to*. What *is* the difference that is being highlighted? How clear is it?

WILL & GOING TO

Presentation

Four friends have just won £800,000 on the football pools. They celebrate in a restaurant:

Later, a reporter interviews them:

Why do the friends use **I'll** in the restaurant, and **I'm going to** in the interview?

(from *Meanings Into Words Intermediate* by A. Doff, C. Jones and K. Mitchell)

Can you devise an activity either to practise or to test the contrast that is being made?

9 Future progressive   Look at these two examples, from previous tasks, in which the future progressive form is used:

a) I'll be getting the plaster off next Tuesday.
b) I'll be voting for Shirley Williams.

What difference in meaning do you detect when the simple form is used?

c) I'll get the plaster off next Tuesday.
d) I'll vote for Shirley Williams.

Do the same for these examples – convert the progressive forms into simple ones and note any differences in meaning:

e) Christian Brando will be pleading 'not guilty' to the charge of murder.
f) The House of Love won't be releasing 'Shake and Crawl' as a single.

10 Activities   Look at these examples of coursebook activities. To what extent do you think they help learners express futurity in English?

1   **Answer these questions. If you're sure, use *I'm going to*.
    If you're not sure, use *I'll probably* or *I expect I'll*.**

What are you going to do ...
        ... tomorrow night?
        ... on your next birthday?
        ... when you retire?

(from *Language In Use Pre-Intermediate* by A. Doff and C. Jones)

2   Look at these sentences and decide if they
    are right or wrong.

Examples:
My plane leaves at 18.00   (right)

(It's the same time for everybody,
and I can't change it)

I meet my sister at 2 p.m. tomorrow   (wrong)

(I can change the time because it
only involves me and my sister)

1 Tomorrow is the first day of term.
2 I go to the theatre tomorrow.
3 Angelo starts English classes next week.
4 The party starts at 8 p.m.
5 My exam is next Monday.
6 The restaurant closes at 6 p.m.
7 I meet my friend tomorrow evening.
8 Next year is a leap year.

(from *Target First Certificate* by N. Kenny and R. Johnson)

21 Hypothetical meaning and conditionals

Introduction

To complete this sequence on modality (and on the verb phrase) this unit takes a look at ways hypothetical and conditional meaning is expressed in English.

Tasks

Use this text to answer Tasks 1–3 below.

1 'I don't think I can stand this much longer, Mike. Take me away, please.'
'Where is there to go? – if we could go,' I said.
'The cottage, Mike. It wouldn't be so bad there, in the country. ...'
'But even if we could get there, we'd have to live,' I pointed out, 'we'd need food and
5 fuel and things.'
'...We could find enough to keep us going for a time until we could grow things.
...It'd be hard – but, Mike, I can't stay in this cemetery any longer – I can't. ...Look at it,
Mike! Look at it! We never did anything to deserve all this. ...If it had only been
something we could fight – ! ...
10 'I can't stand it here any more, Mike. I shall go mad if I have to sit here doing
nothing any longer while a great city dies by inches all around me. It'd be different in
Cornwall, anywhere in the country. I'd rather have to work night and day to keep alive
than just go on like this. I think I'd rather die trying to get away than face another winter
like last.'
15 I had not realized it was as bad as that. It wasn't a thing to be argued about.
'All right, darling,' I said. 'We'll go.'

(from *The Kraken Wakes* by J. Wyndham)

1 **Hypothetical meaning** *It wouldn't be so bad there*. Does she know – or is she hypothesising? Can you identify any other examples of hypothetical meaning in the above passage?

2 **Conditional clauses** 'When you want to talk about a possible situation and its consequences, you use a *conditional clause*.' (*Collins COBUILD English Grammar*) How many conditional clauses can you find in the extract?

3 **Modals** 'When you are using a conditional clause, you often use a *modal* in the main clause.' (*ibid*.)

Find examples in the text to support this.

4 **Would** The modal *would* commonly expresses hypothetical meaning. But it can also express a variety of other meanings. Identify the examples in these extracts that have a conditional meaning, and then categorise the others.

a) When I was on tour with Hothouse Five we would do a gig, travel all night and play music all the time.

b) To carry on working and making it in the film business here would have meant coming to live in London, which was an appalling prospect.

c) I would, of course, vote Conservative if I were in Taunton, where my vote is: except I won't be there, and therefore can't vote.

d) Major Phillips said Mark would continue to run the Gatcombe estate.

e) Buckingham Palace would not be drawn on whether the Princess had any plans to remarry.

f) I would advise would-be patients to be accompanied for the moral support.

g) Sometimes I would give them food, because I was thinking that if my son was in the same position, I hope someone would do the same for him.

h) I suppose in my heart I already knew I wouldn't see her again.

5 Conditionals 'Foreign learners are often taught that there are three kinds of conditional sentence... This is largely correct, but does not fully describe the normal patterns of tense in conditional clauses'. (Collins *COBUILD op. cit.*)

Why not? Look at this grammar summary which lists the three types of conditional:

Conditions and Unreal Past

(1) He *will come* if you *call* him. – something will happen if a certain CONDITION is fulfilled.

(2) He *would come* if you *called* him. – the probable result of a certain condition that we suppose or imagine. The *if*-clause names action that is not taking place at this moment, but I can imagine the probable result. We include here all the unreal *ifs*, like: *if you were a fish, the cat would eat you.*

(3) He *would have come* if you *had called* him – but he didn't come! Why? Because you didn't call him.

All No. (3) types are impossible ideas, because we know the condition was not fulfilled, but we like to imagine the result if . . .

So we have:

TYPE (1) Main clause – FUTURE; *if*-clause – PRESENT. (Likely or probable.)

TYPE (2) Main clause – *would*; *if*-clause – PAST. (Unlikely or improbable; imaginary.)

TYPE (3) Main clause – *would have*: *if*-clause – PAST PERFECT. (Impossible.)

(from *Living English Structure* by W. Stannard Allen)

Which of the following examples conform to one of the three above types?

a) It'll be a miracle if I make it (to the White House) but God is still in the miracle business.

b) If I met Margaret Thatcher I couldn't feel any violence towards her. All I could do is laugh at her.

c) He said: 'If we are not going to win the World Cup then I do want England to win it.'

d) 'You get me out and I give you Terry Waite,' he told his counsel.

e) 'If they had panicked and run off, we would have been perfectly within our rights to shoot at them' said a spokesman.

f) If you grow vegetables in conventional long rows, digging helps to control weeds.

g) She is more surprised than anyone. 'If I'd have thought that this little film would have got so much exposure!' she says in genuine astonishment.

h) If I go in a room and I don't know anyone, I won't be the loud one, I'll sit back and take it all in.

i) If he never returns, I would not be greatly surprised.

j) I'd get up about 10 to 11. If I had no money I'd go shoplifting…

k) I am not a member of the Government now. If I were a member of the Government, I would say: 'For goodness' sake, don't do anymore about it'.

l) Maybe if somebody would dye greengage jam to look like strawberry I might get to like it.

6 Conditionals Look at this coursebook exercise. Which of the three conditionals is it focused on? Evaluate the usefulness of this kind of exercise.

Which two of the following sentences are *not* correct?

a) If someone will scream in the house next door, I'll call the police.

b) I wouldn't tell her if she asked me.

c) I wouldn't be surprised if somebody were listening to our conversation.

d) I might go and see him if he wanted me to.

e) If the money market would collapse I wouldn't lose all my savings.

(from *Intermediate Matters* by J. Bell and R. Gower)

7 Real versus unreal conditions MacAndrew (1991) says, of conditionals, that 'the division into two is more pedagogically useful than the division into three'.

What does he mean? For example, which of the extracts in Task 5 refer to 'real' and which to 'unreal' conditions? What do you notice about the tense of the verbs in the *if*-clauses in the unreal conditions?

8 Conditionals and language functions   Given the wide variety of conditional clause types, the importance of using realistic contexts for presentation and practice should be obvious.

Can you think of some typical language functions that might be expressed using different conditional clause types? Give an example for each function and classify them according to whether they are real or unreal conditions. For example:

Function	Example	Real/Unreal
making threats	If you don't go, I'll phone the police!	real

Now, can you order the items you have listed for teaching purposes, i.e. in what order and at what approximate levels would you introduce them?

9 Hypothetical past   'Apart from conditional clauses, hypothetical meaning may occur in a few other special constructions.' (Leech and Svartvik)

Can you think of any other ways of expressing unreal meaning using the hypothetical past? For example: *I wish I had a car*.

22 The noun phrase

Introduction

It may be the case that the preoccupation with the verb phrase in language teaching materials has been at the expense of due attention to the noun phrase: a simple count of errors in the writing produced by intermediate students often reveals a higher proportion of noun-phrase-related errors than errors in the verb system. This unit, and the following unit on determiners, attempts to redress the balance.

Tasks

1 **Noun categories**   In the following text, find an example of each of the following:

a) A proper noun: the name of a specific, and unique, person, place, etc. (Be careful: a capital letter does not necessarily make something unique!)
b) A common noun: any noun that is not a proper noun, often divided between concrete and abstract nouns.
c) A count noun: a noun that refers to an object that can be counted, and therefore allows a plural form, or takes a plural verb.
d) A non-count noun (also called 'mass' noun): a noun that is uncountable and always takes a singular verb.
e) A collective noun: one that refers to a group, and may take either a singular or a plural verb.
f) A noun modifier: when a noun functions like an adjective and modifies the meaning of the noun that follows.
g) A pronoun: a word that can substitute for a noun.
h) An adjective functioning as a noun.

A nanny became a Princess. A Boomtown Rat became an Honorary Knight. And, to cap it all, Wimbledon won the Cup.

We've just emerged, pinching ourselves, from a decade when we got rather used to the unexpected. But in the motor industry, the 'eighties saved their biggest surprise until the very end.

Last year, Vauxhall unveiled a car called Calibra. Those present – the press at previews and the public at the major European motor shows – couldn't have been less prepared for what they saw.

Because it's not every day, not even every decade, that a new car appears which bucks so many trends and owes so little to prevailing thinking.

(from *The Economist: The World in 1991*)

2 Countability   Which of the following combinations are permissible?

	1	2	3	4
	Kim	cup	furniture	stone
	the Kim	the cup	the furniture	the stone
I saw	a Kim	a cup	a furniture	a stone
	some Kim	some cup	some furniture	some stone
	Kims	cups	furnitures	stones

(after *A University Grammar of English* by R. Quirk and S. Greenbaum)

Can you identify each of the noun groups in columns (1–4) in the above exercise?

3 Count/Non-count nouns   What is the language point that is being practised in this exercise?

With or without *a*?
Match the words and the pictures.

potato
a potato
paper
a paper
glass
a glass
hair
a hair
lamb
a lamb

1. ....   2. ....   3. ....   4. ....   5. ....

6. ....   7. ....   8. ....   9. ....   10. ....

(from *The Cambridge English Course 1 Workbook* by M. Swan and C. Walter)

4 Number   English distinguishes between singular and plural. The formation of the plural is relatively easy for learners to grasp. But there are a few inconsistencies.

Which is the 'odd one out' in each group. Why?

a)	book	watch	coat	clock
b)	mouse	man	child	goose
c)	wife	thief	chief	wolf
d)	trousers	skirts	jeans	tights
e)	cow	fish	sheep	salmon
f)	sheep	cattle	police	people

Which of the above irregularities are learners likely to encounter at beginner level?

5 Nouns in groups When two nouns are put side by side a relationship is implied, and this is often one of possession. But there are constraints as to what nouns can go together and how. Look at these examples of student errors. Can you correct them?

a) I didn't know what to do with the refrigerator of my sister.
b) The hair of Yolanda is very long and very curly.
c) This hit the policeman's head that was standing at the house's corner.
d) He had filmed *T2*, the most expensive film in cinema's history.
e) Few months later his daughter died in a car's accident.
f) He is a mechanic of cars.
g) We have also a buses network.
h) My investigations led me to the prison where there was a Frank's old friend.

What rules about the use of possessive *'s* can you generalise from these examples?

In another language you are familiar with, can nouns be combined in similar ways to English?

6 Can you think of contexts and activities for presenting and practising the use of the possessive *'s*?

For example:

(from *Beginners' Choice Workbook* by S. Thornbury)

7 Modification   The main noun of a noun phrase can be described (or *modified*) by words that precede it – typically adjectives (see Unit 24) – or words that follow it, as in:

a   new   car   called Calibra
   premodification   *head*   *postmodification*

Identify examples of pre- and postmodification in the text that follows. What form does the modifier take? Is it, for example, an adjective, a noun, a prepositional phrase or something else? (Note that some examples of modification are embedded in others.)

Example:
- a gap *in an existing team*: postmodification of gap using a prepositional phrase
- *an* existing *team*: premodification of team using a participle

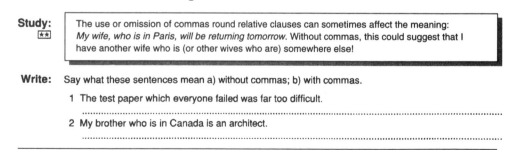

> # Before we sent them fitters we made sure they'd fit.
>
> Filling a gap in an existing team isn't just a case of finding someone with the correct skills and experience. So, before we send anyone for a job, we check they'll fit it.
>
> Carlyle Parts, who amongst other things replace damaged coach windscreens, discovered this recently. They hadn't been able to find anyone suitable for their vacancies. But we did. The people we found were offered to Carlyle Parts on a work trial. Within days they had taken them on permanently. We'll also find the people you need. Whatever the job. Give your local Jobcentre a call. They'll give you all the help you need.

8 Relative clauses   Relative clauses are a form of postmodification. Here is part of an exercise which exploits the ambiguity of relative clauses. Can you do the exercise and invent some examples of your own?

Sentences with two meanings

Study: The use or omission of commas round relative clauses can sometimes affect the meaning:
★★   *My wife, who is in Paris, will be returning tomorrow.* Without commas, this could suggest that I have another wife who is (or other wives who are) somewhere else!

Write: Say what these sentences mean a) without commas; b) with commas.

   1 The test paper which everyone failed was far too difficult.
   ....
   2 My brother who is in Canada is an architect.
   ....

(from *Longman English Grammar Exercises* by L. G. Alexander)

How would intonation resolve the ambiguity, if these sentences were spoken?

9 Pronouns   As noted in Task 1, there are a number of different types of pronoun. For example:

personal pronouns (both subject and object)
possessive pronouns
demonstrative pronouns
relative pronouns
indefinite pronouns

Identify the pronouns and their referents – the person or thing the pronoun stands for – in the Jobcentre advertisement (Task 7). Do you know what kinds of pronoun they are? *Note*: there is at least one pronoun in every sentence in the advert.

How could you use or adapt the Jobcentre text to focus on pronoun use in English?

10 Nominalisation   Look at these two texts. One is from an encyclopedia and the other was written by a learner. What is the approximate proportion of nouns to verbs in each case? (Combinations of auxiliary and participle – *have bought* – count as one verb.)

1 Newspapers have a distribution that is wider than that of television news. Since the invention of the telegraph, which enormously facilitated the rapid gathering of news, newspapers have bought their services from the great news agencies. Improvements in typesetting and in printing have made possible the publication of huge news editions at great speed. Modern newspapers are supported primarily by the sale of advertising space, as they are sold at only a fraction of the cost of production. In recent years newspapers have wielded vast influence through their controlling interests in other media, including radio and television.

(from *The New Columbia Encyclopedia* cited in *Second Language Grammar: Learning and Teaching* by W. E. Rutherford)

2 My country famous newspaper is 'Times of Mukar'. It establish around 1920. It publish in three other city. Circulation are 270,000 copy. There are many people buy copy and read all news about current topic, education and etc. It print much advertising and are distribute all over my country.

(from *Second Language Grammar: Learning and Teaching* by W. E. Rutherford)

What exercises or activities can you think of that might help learners increase the noun–verb ratio in their writing? Here is one possibility:

Re-write the following sentences by changing the underlined verb into its noun form, and make any other necessary changes:

She <u>knows</u> her grammar thoroughly.

She <u>succeeded</u> because she <u>worked</u> hard.

23 Determiners

Introduction

Nouns stand for people, things and so on, but often it is important to establish which particular person or thing is being referred to, or how many. Determiners are a class of words that are used with nouns and have the function of defining the reference of the noun in some way. They answer, for example, the question *Which?* or *Whose?* or *How many?* of the thing(s) named in the noun phrase.

Tasks

1 Determiners There are eight different determiners in this text (although some are repeated). Can you identify them? The first is underlined for you:

> Wayne and Shirley Dwyer snapped up a bargain Nikon camera in the duty free shop at Charles de Gaulle airport in Paris last summer. The couple were off to Berlin a few weeks later, and were still on the first roll of film when the camera broke, which meant missed photo opportunities in Berlin.
>
> They contacted Nikon UK to find out what their rights were under the guarantee. Nikon agreed to look at the camera, and to repair any fault free of charge, but when the camera was returned, it was still faulty. In the end Nikon did replace the camera, as a gesture of goodwill – but they were under no obligation to do so.

(from *Which?*)

2 The zero article In the previous text some noun phrases, such as *Paris* have no determiner at all. Since the presence of a determiner is the norm, determiner absence is called the 'zero article' (and marked Ø). Other examples from the text are: *Ø Charles de Gaulle airport; roll of Ø film; Ø missed photo opportunities; free of Ø charge.*

Identify six 'zero articles' in this text:

103

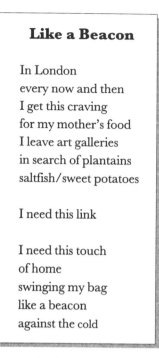

Like a Beacon

In London
every now and then
I get this craving
for my mother's food
I leave art galleries
in search of plantains
saltfish/sweet potatoes

I need this link

I need this touch
of home
swinging my bag
like a beacon
against the cold

(by G. Nichols)

Now, find an example in the text of each of these rules for zero article use:

a) Use zero article with non-count nouns, where the reference is indefinite.
b) Use zero article with plural count nouns, where the reference is indefinite.
c) Use zero article with proper nouns.
d) Use zero article with certain common expressions of time and place, means of transport, and so on.

Can you think of more examples of Rule (**d**)? For example: *by train, in bed.*

3 Articles: definite versus indefinite   In the text in Task 1, *a bargain Nikon camera* is subsequently referred to as *the camera*. The indefinite article is used here to signal new information, while the definite article is used for given information. Complete the spaces in these limericks with either *a* or *the*. What 'rules' determine your choice?

There was ____ young man of Verdun
Who lay several hours in ____ sun.
____ people who milled
Round ____ man said: 'He's grilled –
Not just medium-rare, but well done!

—— certain young woman of Thule
Fell in love with —— man with —— mule.
Said ____ girl to ____ man:
If we marry, we can
Go to Thule on ____ back of ____ mule.

How does the 'new versus given' distinction account for the use of *the*, in each case?

4 **Definite article**   What is definite, i.e. 'given', about each of the underlined examples of *the* in the following two texts, both openings of stories?

a) There was once a rich man who had a very beautiful wife and a beautiful daughter known as Nourie Hadig. Every month when <u>the</u> moon appeared in <u>the</u> sky, <u>the</u> wife asked: 'New moon, am I <u>the</u> most beautiful or are you?' And every month the moon replied, 'You are the most beautiful.'

   (from *The Virago Book of Fairy Tales* edited by A. Carter)

b) Carl got off work at three. He left <u>the</u> station and drove to a shoestore near his apartment. He put his foot on <u>the</u> stool and let <u>the</u> clerk unlace his workboot.

   (from *The Stories of Raymond Carver* by R. Carver)

5 **Generic reference**   Look at the following four-sentence text about dodos. Which sentences are generalisations, and which refer to specific events and entities? How are dodos referred to in each case?

> **DODO**
> <u>The dodo</u> was a flightless bird which lived on the island of Mauritius in the Indian Ocean. <u>The dodo</u> was clumsy and helpless, but it had no natural enemies. Then sailors brought dogs, pigs and rats to the island. <u>The dodos</u> were killed and their eggs were eaten. <u>The last dodo</u> died in 1681.

   (from *Pocket Encyclopedia* by A. Jack)

6 **Generic reference**   Look at two more texts from the *Pocket Encyclopedia*. Which of the following combinations of article + noun are <u>not</u> used in English to talk about things in general, i.e. as a class?

<u>Count nouns</u>

a) *a(n)* + singular: A tiger...
b) *the* + singular: The tiger...
c) *the* + plural: The tigers...
d) *zero article* + plural: Tigers...

<u>Non-count nouns</u>

e) *the*: The carbon...
f) *zero article*: Carbon...

> **TIGER**
> The tiger is the largest of the big cats. Its home is Asia.
> Tigers hunt alone and at night. They prey on deer, wild cattle and pigs. Only an old or sick tiger will attack people. The tiger's stripes camouflage it in long grass. Unlike other cats, tigers often bathe to keep cool.

(from *Pocket Encyclopedia* by A. Jack)

> **CARBON**
> Carbon is one of the chemical elements. All living things contain carbon. If you hold a plate above a candle flame, a black deposit of carbon forms on it. Both charcoal and coke are forms of carbon.

(from *Pocket Encyclopedia* by A. Jack)

7 Articles   You should now be able to account for all uses of zero article (Ø), *a/an* and *the* in this extract:

Once upon a sunny morning a man who sat in a breakfast nook looked up from his scrambled eggs to see a white unicorn with a gold horn quietly cropping the roses in the garden. The man went up to the bedroom where his wife was still asleep and woke her. 'There's a unicorn in the garden,' he said. 'Eating roses.' She opened one unfriendly eye and looked at him. 'The unicorn is a mythical beast,' she said, and turned her back on him. The man walked slowly downstairs and out into the garden. The unicorn was still there; he was now browsing among the tulips...

(from *Fables For Our Time* by J. Thurber)

8 Articles   Look at these matching exercises. Can you do them? How useful are these rules? Which of the different rules for the use of *the* have been dealt with in Tasks 2–6 in this unit?

The natural world is under assault from man.
The can be used for many different reasons. Match each reason with an example sentence or phrase.

1 There was a man outside. **The** man was tall.
2 **The** moon and **the** world both go around **the** sun.
3 I can't find **the** pen I bought yesterday.
4 Where's **the** cat? (*the cat that lives in this house*)
5 Paul is in **the** garden.
6 She plays **the** piano well.
7 It was **the** best film I have ever seen.
8 **the** rich, **the** poor, **the** unemployed
9 **the** United States of America, **the** Queen of Spain

A with superlatives
B when only one exists
C when the object or person is mentioned for a second time
D when we make something definite by adding extra information
E with musical instruments
F with adjectives to describe a class or group
G when location means only one thing is being referred to
H with titles and place names that have the idea of
I when the object is known by everybody

When we do **NOT** use the article
Match the examples with their descriptions.

1 love/hate/beauty
2 Cats are beautiful.
3 petrol/sugar/milk/wood
4 home/work/hospital
5 New York/Brazil

A most names of towns, cities and countries
B uncountable nouns
C countable objects in general
D abstract nouns
E some places/locations

(from *Think First Certificate* by J. Naunton)

9 Some/any   Look at these two descriptions of the use of *some* and *any*. In what way do they differ?

---

1 Countable nouns are used with **some** +
a plural noun in positive sentences, and
any + a plural noun in questions and
negatives.
I've got some books.
Are there any eggs?
We don't need any potatoes.

Uncountable nouns are used with **some**
in positive sentences and **any** in
questions and negatives, but only with a
singular noun.
There is some milk.
Is there any butter?
We haven't got any wine.

(from *Headway Pre-Intermediate* by J. Soars and L. Soars)

---

2 **Both *some* and *any* are used for indefinite
quantities.**

***Some* is used if the quantity is restricted or
limited in some way.**

***Any* is used if the quantity is unrestricted or
unlimited.**

**The restriction may be a real one (There's some
cheese in the fridge) or in the mind of the speaker
(Would you like something to eat?).**

**The choice of *some* or *any* is not determined by
grammatical form but by meaning.**

(from *Out and About* by M. Lewis)

The following examples are taken from *Tea Party and Other Plays* by
Harold Pinter. Can you account for them using the above descriptions?
Which of the descriptions do you consider to be more helpful for learners?

a) I brought some chocolates for her.
b) I bet you some woman could have made you a good wife.
c) I've never spoken to any other woman on the subject.
d) Can I get you some cocoa? Some hot chocolate?
e) If you have any complaints, just tell me.
f) Anyone could do that for you.
g) Get dressed, will you? It'll be any minute now.

10 Determiners   Look at these activities. What particular uses and kinds of determiners is each one dealing with?

1

The two speakers are going round a zoo. The first speaker points out a group of animals and the second exclaims that he dislikes those animals. Before doing the drill look at the picture of the zoo.

There are the snakes.
Oh, I hate snakes!

There are the lions.
Oh, I hate lions!

There are the crocodiles.
Oh, I hate crocodiles!

There are the parrots.

There are the camels.

There are the owls.

There are the apes.

There are the snakes.

There are the wolves.

There are the tigers.

(from *Realistic English Drills*
by B. Abbs, V. Cook and M. Underwood)

2

For each phrase with *the* ask yourself the question 'Which one?' Use the phrases underneath to help you answer.

Johann was on a walking holiday in Britain. He arrived at *the youth hostel* early one evening, only to realise that he had left his guide book in *the mountain restaurant* where he had had lunch. 'Oh dear' he thought, '*the book* doesn't even belong to me; I'll have to go back and find it.' So he left all his things in the Youth Hostel, explained to *the man* what he was doing, and set off up *the mountain* again. He hoped *the girl* in *the restaurant* would still be awake when he got there. It was getting dark when he finally arrived back at *the top*. There were no lights on in the *restaurant*; *the door* was locked.

Jenny Willis

1 *the youth hostel* = The Youth Hostel ....
2 *the restaurant*   = The restaurant ....
3 *the book*   = The book ....
4 *the man*   = The man ....
5 *the mountain*   = The mountain ....
6 *the girl*   = The girl ....
7 *the top*   = The top ....
8 *the door*   = The door ....

a he had left behind.
b where he had had lunch.
c who worked in the Youth Hostel.
d of the restaurant.
e who owned the restaurant.
f of the mountain.
g where he was going to stay.
h where the restaurant was.

(from *Collins COBUILD English Course Practice Book 1* by J. Willis and D. Willis)

3

Make a chart of your own normal diet – what you usually eat – and then discuss it and compare it with your partner's eating habits.
Example:
A: *I don't eat any chocolate.*
B: *Don't you? I eat a lot of chocolate, I love it!*
A: *Do you eat much fruit?*
B: *I eat a little fruit, and a lot of cakes and ice-cream!*

(from *The Sourcebook* by J. Shepherd and F. Cox)

24 Adjectives and adverbs

Introduction

The function of adjectives is, typically, to add extra information to a noun phrase, while adverbs, very generally, expand on the information conveyed in the verb phrase. These definitions are necessarily vague: this unit explores some of the problems related to these two important word classes.

Tasks

1 **Adjectives and adverbs**   It is sometimes difficult to tell them apart. Can you, for example, do this coursebook exercise?

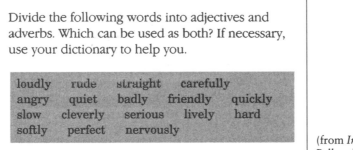

Divide the following words into adjectives and adverbs. Which can be used as both? If necessary, use your dictionary to help you.

loudly	rude	straight	carefully
angry	quiet	badly	friendly	quickly
slow	cleverly	serious	lively	hard
softly	perfect	nervously

(from *Intermediate Matters* by J. Bell and R. Gower)

2 **Adjectives**   Identify the adjectives in this text:

No more fumbling about at the bottom of your bag when you buy our

ORGANISER HANDBAG

Once you get your hands on one of these terrific soft leather bags, you'll know exactly where that elusive pen is or where those house keys are securely placed.

Made from soft leather, which is smooth to the touch and fully lined, our bag has a host of useful features that you'll be grateful for whenever you use it. On an everyday basis it is a must and for holidays you'll find it indispensable for keeping all those needed bits and pieces together.

It is available in black (B), navy (N) or cream (C), and costs just **£25.95** including postage and packaging.

Can you identify any common adjectival suffixes in the above adjectives?

3 Adjectives 'Some adjectives, it seems, are more adjective-like than others'. (Crystal 1987)

There are five main criteria used in identifying an adjective, but not all adjectives meet all the criteria. They are:

a) Adjectives occur after forms of *to be*: *it's soft*.
b) They occur after articles and before nouns: *an everyday basis*.
c) They occur after intensifiers, such as *very, rather, so, extremely*: *very elusive*.
d) They occur in the comparative and superlative form: *more useful*.
e) They occur before *-ly* to form adverbs: *secure – securely*.

The following grid lists some of the words from the advertising text in Task 2. Look at each word and put a tick against each of the criteria (a – e) it fulfils. To what extent can each word be called a 'pure' adjective?

| | Criteria | | | | |
	a	b	c	d	e
soft					
available					
needed					
everyday					
house					
your					

4 Participles and participial adjectives In the following advertisements, say which of the underlined words are:

a) participles, either present or past, and are functioning as components of a verb phrase (e.g. the woman was <u>drowning</u>; the book <u>left</u> on the train).
b) participles acting as qualitative adjectives, i.e. they describe the quality of something and they can be qualified with <u>very</u> (e.g. a <u>boring</u> book; a <u>frightened</u> rabbit).
c) participles acting as classifying adjectives, i.e. they classify things and they cannot normally be qualified with <u>very</u> (e.g. the <u>setting</u> sun; a <u>broken</u> leg).
d) adjectives formed by adding -<u>ing</u> or -<u>ed</u> to noun phrases (e.g. a <u>talented</u> musician).
e) compound adjectives formed by adding a verb participle to a noun, adjective or adverb (e.g. a <u>good-looking</u> actor).

HAMPSTEAD

An <u>interesting</u> modern <u>detached</u> home on 2 floors. Warm <u>inviting</u> reception area (as <u>illustrated</u>) <u>opening</u> onto patio/garden. Lavishly <u>equipped</u> kitchen area. <u>Galleried</u> master bedroom + second double bed, with separate shower room. Well <u>furnished</u> in comfortable modern style.

£420 per week

Killarney, Ireland

<u>Three-bedroomed</u> bungalow in over an acre of mature gardens, five minutes' walk from the sea in Ireland's southwest. <u>Approached</u> by a <u>curving</u>, <u>tree-lined</u> driveway, the property includes a <u>sitting</u> room, <u>oak-fitted</u> kitchen, two bathrooms, conservatory and double garage. Central heating, double glazing, carpets and blinds <u>included</u>. Price £97,000.

(from *London Residential Rentals*)

(from *Resident Abroad*)

5 Adjectival order   *One of these terrific soft leather bags.* What is the preferred order of adjectives before the noun?

'When you use more than one adjective in a noun group, the usual order of the adjectives is: qualitative adjectives (i.e. adjectives that identify a quality that something has, such as *pretty, healthy, old*), followed by colour adjectives, followed by classifying adjectives (i.e. adjectives used to identify the particular class something belongs to, such as *wooden, electric, foreign, Italian*).' (*Collins COBUILD English Grammar* – parentheses added)

Do these examples follow the above pattern?

a)   Saritta wears *tight black dress* £191 from Katherine Hamnett. (*The Face*)
b)   Relax in this *comfortable Victorian country house*…(*The Observer*)
c)   *Black sticky rice* from Indonesia and the Philippines makes a *luscious nutty dessert*. (*Australian Gourmet*)
d)   The *ancient Chinese confectionery* of *young stem ginger* in syrup adds an exotic touch to a *simple ice-cream dessert*. Packed in *elaborately decorated glazed ceramic jars*, it also makes an unusual gift. (*Australian Gourmet*)

What is the order of participles and noun modifiers? Where do the determiners go?

Note that long adjective strings are peculiar only to certain specialised text types such as advertisements. Is there any point in teaching learners the rules of adjectival order? Is there any basic logic to the order?

6 Adverbs   In this extract from a novel, five of the adverbs have been underlined. There are ten more. Can you find them?

'I've thought about you all day,' she answered <u>simply</u>, laying her hand on his arm. 'Tommy knows you're innocent. I've <u>always</u> known that. And we're <u>here</u> together now. What else <u>really</u> matters at the heart of it?'…
She lifted a hand to his cheek, smiling fondly when she felt its heat.

At her gesture, he murmured, bent to her again...<u>Then</u> his mouth moved warmly against her bare throat and shoulders...
The telephone rang shrilly.
They jumped apart as if an intruder were present, staring at each other guiltily as the telephone went unanswered. It made its way through four jarring double rings before Lady Helen realised that Caroline, already two hours behind schedule on her free evening, had left the flat. They were entirely alone.

> (from *Payment in Blood* by E. George)

7 Adverbs Adverbs convey a wide range of meanings. Of the underlined adverbs in the previous text, can you find an example of each of the following types:

a) adverb of place
b) adverb of time
c) adverb of manner
d) adverb of degree
e) linking adverb

Now assign a category to the other ten adverbs.

8 Adverbials Notice that, in the text in Task 6 *all day*, and *to his cheek*, although not adverbs (one is a noun phrase and the other a prepositional phrase), function like adverbs of time and place respectively. Expressions that function like adverbs are called 'adverbials'.

Identify any adverbials of time or place in this extract (also from *Payment in Blood*):

Barbara Havers paused on the wide drive before going back into the house. Snow had fallen again during the night... Nonetheless, after a foully sleepless night, she had risen shortly after dawn and had set out through the snow...

What form does each adverbial take?

9 Adverbs and adverbials Devise the following:

a) an activity to introduce adverbs of frequency (*always, sometimes, never* etc.) at an elementary level
b) an activity to present and contrast *yet, still* and *already* at an intermediate level
c) an activity to test understanding of the difference between *for* and *since*, used with time adverbials, at an intermediate level

10 Comparison In the following extracts from student writing, correct the errors in the adjective or adverbial phrases, and explain the rule that has been broken:

a) He looks more younger than he really is.
b) It all happen when I was very younger.
c) He was polite, nice and more different that the boy I had live for fifteen years.

d) Now, my brother is most tall than before.
e) Pierre is same intelligent as me.
f) I was the person happier in all the world.
g) People doesn't work as hardly as they thinks.

11 **Noun phrase review**   Identify the noun phrase errors in this text. What 'rules' of noun, determiner, and adjective usage are being broken in each case?

COMPOSITION

—Advantages and disadvantages of Barcelona
They are the sames of the other important cities. Life's conditions offer good and bad things to the citizens. The firsts are, for instance, the good communication between people through telephone, fax, computer, radio, T.V. etc; the public services like bus, train, underground, etc.; the leisures as to do shopping in the supermarket, to go to the cinema or theatre, etc.

The seconds are typical, for instance, the pollution, which cause diseases or health's problems; the noises, which disturb the old people; to live together in the same built which cause noises, arguements between neighbours, etc.

Barcelona has advantages and disadvantages, the firsts are good and the seconds are bad. Is very difficult to find some city or village which hasn't problems. I prefer the villages for their calm and natural life, but I prefer the cities for their diversions and entertainments.

I think that there isn't some place where doesn't exist disadvantages.

25 Prepositions and phrasal verbs

Introduction

Prepositions – or, at least, the rules governing their use – are elusive. This unit addresses some of the issues before going on to look at how prepositions and adverbs combine with verbs to form 'multi-part verbs'.

Tasks

1 Prepositions   Identify the prepositions in this text.

Hillary, Sir Edmund Percival (1919–) New Zealand explorer and mountaineer who, in 1953 with the Sherpa mountaineer Tenzing Norgay (*c*. 1914–86), first climbed to the summit of Mount Everest. He received a knighthood in the same year...
Born in Auckland, Hillary spent two years at Auckland University College and worked on his father's farm before joining the Royal New Zealand Air Force in 1943. He served as a navigator aboard flying boats in the Pacific during the war...

(from *A Dictionary of 20th Century World Biography* edited by A. Briggs)

Can you classify the prepositions you have identified? For example, can you identify any prepositions of:

– place
– time
– accompaniment
– belonging

2 Prepositional phrases   Prepositions are followed by a noun phrase (the 'complement' of the preposition) to make up a 'prepositional phrase'. For example: *in Auckland*; *as a navigator*.

Underline all the prepositional phrases in the above text.

3 Prepositions of place   Can you complete this chart, by putting a common preposition in each box?

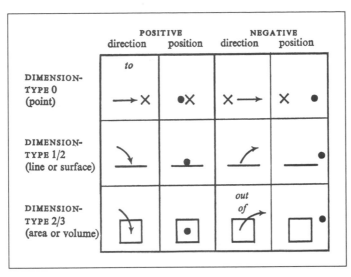

(from *A University Grammar of English* by R. Quirk and S. Greenbaum. Reprinted by permission of Addison Wesley Longman Limited)

4 Prepositions   Look at this exercise. What kind of prepositions does it practise? What other vocabulary would learners need to know in order to be able to do the exercise?

Look at the three pictures below, and say:

1 exactly where the road goes
2 exactly where the burglar went, from the evidence of his footprints in the snow
3 exactly what the soldier has to do to complete the assault course

(from *Meanings Into Words Intermediate* by A. Doff, C. Jones and K. Mitchell)

5 Error analysis   Correct these preposition mistakes and explain what rule the learner has broken:

a) This island would be located on the Caribbean Sea.
b) And at 25 of December I used to have a big surprise.
c) I remember going at school every day.
d) She arrives at home to the one o'clock and watches TV till at two o'clock.
e) They have travelled during a lot of years.
f) I walked until the job.
g) When I was a child my life was a little different of my actual life.
h) They spend the money in buy one house and give the rest at the poor people.

6 Dependent prepositions   Notice that in the last two examples above, specific prepositions depend on the preceding adjective (*different from*), or verb (*spend...on*).

Identify any dependent prepositions in this transcript of a listening text. How could you use this material to highlight this particular feature?

ANN: Hello, it's me. You haven't phoned me for weeks. I was getting a bit worried about you.

CLARE: Sorry, Mum. I'm fine. In fact, I'm feeling very proud of myself at the moment.

ANN: Proud? Why?

CLARE: I had my first scuba-diving lesson last week.

ANN: Weren't you frightened of being under water?

CLARE: Yes, I was absolutely terrified at first. But then I was O.K. In fact I'm quite pleased with myself.

ANN: Do you think you're going to be good at it?

CLARE: I hope so.

ANN: Good. Well, I'm glad you weren't disappointed with your first lesson.

CLARE: Disappointed? No, it was a great experience.

ANN: Anyway, I'm pleased to hear you're well. I'll speak to you again soon. Bye!

CLARE: Bye!

(from *Blueprint 2 Teacher's Book* by B. Abbs and I. Freebairn)

---

7 Prepositions and adverbs   There are a number of prepositions that are also adverbs. Unlike prepositions, however, adverbs can stand on their own, without a complementary noun phrase. For example:

– He served as a navigator *aboard* flying boats.
– When the ship arrived they went *aboard*.

In the first sentence *aboard* is a preposition and in the second it is an adverb.

In the following text, which of the underlined words are prepositions and which are adverbs?

TAURUS
APRIL 21–MAY 20

Career matters are slow but financial opportunities pop <u>up</u> everywhere, enabling you to excel <u>at</u> your natural talent <u>for</u> money management...Old friends could turn <u>up</u> again...

LEO
JULY 23 – AUGUST 22

Spring energy means you're ready to forge <u>ahead</u> <u>with</u> major projects...Your earning potential remains strong but you would be wise to cut <u>back</u> <u>on</u> your casual spending in order to plan <u>for</u> essentials...

SCORPIO
OCTOBER 23 – NOVEMBER 21

You will be full <u>of</u> energy when your planets Mars and Pluto line <u>up</u> <u>together</u> <u>on</u> the 11th. Use this dynamic impetus to carry important matters <u>through</u> <u>to</u> a successful conclusion. You can impress people <u>at</u> work <u>by</u> clearing <u>up</u> various loose ends...

(from *Options*)

8 Multi-word verbs   Many verbs consist of two or more parts: *forge ahead*, *plan for*, *clear* things *up*. The second part (or 'particle') is either a preposition (e.g. *for*) or an adverb (e.g. *ahead*).

Identify the multi-word verbs in these extracts (from *Death on the Nile* by Agatha Christie). In each case, is it a *prepositional verb* or a *phrasal verb*, i.e. is the particle a preposition or an adverb?

a) I don't think that Simon would agree to run away.
b) 'That's enough. I'm through.' He made for the door.
c) Miss de Bellefort is on the line. Shall I put her through?
d) Pennington is Linnet's American trustee. We ran across him by chance in Cairo.
e) 'About time to turn in,' said Colonel Race.
f) I've been looking after Miss Van Schuyler for over two years now.
g) Joanna picked up a string of pearls from the dressing table.
h) It is *intolerable* that I should have to put up with this!

9 Multi-word verbs   Phrasal verbs may be either intransitive or transitive, i.e. there are phrasal verbs that don't take an object, and phrasal verbs that do. For example:

Type 1:   About time to turn in.
Type 2:   Joanna picked up *a string of pearls*.

Prepositional verbs, on the other hand, are always transitive – they always have an object: the complement of the preposition. For example:

Type 3:   He made for *the door*.

Three-part verbs – verb + adverb + preposition – are also always transitive for the same reason. For example:

Type 4:   It is intolerable that I should have to *put up with* this!

In these further extracts from *Death on the Nile*, classify the multi-part verbs according to the four categories above:

– After a bit I saw that he'd made up his mind. And I was terrified – simply terrified. Because, you see, I realized that he'd never pull it off.

– So I had to come into it, too, to look after him...

– I thought and I thought – trying to work out a plan.

– We worked everything out carefully. Even then, Simon went and wrote a J in blood which was a silly melodramatic thing to do.

– But it went off all right.

– Jacqueline looked at the sternness of his face.
She said gently: 'Don't mind so much for me, Monsieur Poirot. After all, I've lived hard always, you know. If we'd won out, I'd have been very happy and enjoyed things and probably should never have regretted anything. As it is – well, one goes through with it.'

(all extracts from *Death on the Nile* by A. Christie)

10 **Phrasal verbs**   'The most important thing you have to discover when you meet a new phrasal verb is whether it is possible to separate the verb and the particle.' (Naunton) Look at the transitive multi-part verbs in the previous extract. Find examples of these patterns:

a)   verb + particle + object
b)   verb + object + particle

Can you work out the rules that govern the choice of position?

11 **Teaching multi-word verbs**   There are a number of approaches to the organisation of this complex area for teaching purposes. What, for example, is the difference in approach between these two exercise types? Which approach do you think your learners would find more memorable?

1

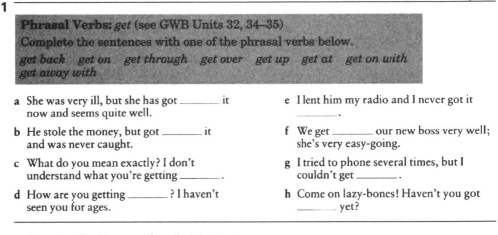

Phrasal Verbs: *get* (see GWB Units 32, 34–35)
Complete the sentences with one of the phrasal verbs below.

*get back   get on   get through   get over   get up   get at   get on with
get away with*

a She was very ill, but she has got _____ it now and seems quite well.

b He stole the money, but got _____ it and was never caught.

c What do you mean exactly? I don't understand what you're getting _____ .

d How are you getting _____ ? I haven't seen you for ages.

e I lent him my radio and I never got it _____ .

f We get _____ our new boss very well; she's very easy-going.

g I tried to phone several times, but I couldn't get _____ .

h Come on lazy-bones! Haven't you got _____ yet?

(from *Excel at First Certificate* by M. Vince)

2

Phrasal verbs

Up and *down* often combine with verbs to form what are called phrasal verbs. In phrasal verbs *up* often expresses the idea of 'increase' and *down* the idea of 'decrease'. Example:
The television wasn't loud enough so I turned it up.
The radio was too loud so I turned it down.

1   Match the phrasal verbs in column A with their definitions in column B. (Note that some of these phrasal verbs have more than one meaning.)

A	B
1 grow up	a) do less of something
2 heat up	b) become happier
3 wind down	c) be quicker
4 cheer up	d) make slower
5 bring up	e) make less loud/hot/ noisy, etc.
6 turn down	f) rear/educate
7 cut down	g) relax
8 hurry up	h) go from childhood to adulthood
9 slow down	i) make hotter

(from *Intermediate Matters* by J. Bell and R. Gower)

26 Cohesion

Introduction

So far we have looked at language from the point of view of several different levels of analysis – from isolated sounds to whole sentences. Traditionally, language analysis stopped at the sentence. More recently, the focus has expanded to take in whole texts, in order to see, among other things, if there is such a thing as a 'grammar of texts', that is, rules that give both structure and meaning to units of discourse beyond the sentence level.

Tasks

1 Texts   Do texts have a 'grammar'? Are there rules that determine their structure? Try putting the following jumbled text in the correct order. *Note:* there is an extra sentence that does not belong.

a) Inside its round fruits, called bolls, are masses of white fibres.
b) But, in the cotton fields, the bolls are picked before this can happen.
c) Pure copper is very soft
d) Cotton grows best in warm, wet lands, including Asia, the southern United States, India, China, Egypt and Brazil.
e) Cotton is a very useful plant.
f) When the fruits ripen, they split and the fibres are blown away.

What clues did you use to help you unjumble the text?

2 Cohesion   Look at the following two texts. What binds each one together as a text? Can you find examples of the following?

Lexical cohesion:

– Repetition of words: *cotton...cotton*; *fruits...fruits*
– Chains of words belonging to the same lexical set: *...grows...ripens...are picked*; *...plant...fruits...bolls...fibres...*

Grammatical cohesion:

– Tense agreement: *...is...are...ripen...split...are blown...*
– Pronoun reference: *...cotton...its...*
– Article reference: *...white fibres...the fibres...*
– Substitution: *The fruits ripen. When they <u>do</u>, the fibres are blown away.*
– Ellipsis: *The fibres are blown away. Before they are [blown away] they are picked...*
– Conjuncts (or linkers): *But, in the cotton fields...*

1

Fotedar visits hospital

By A Staff Reporter

NEW DELHI, September 25: It was Safdarjang Hospital's turn for 'spring cleaning'. The minister for health and family welfare, Mr M. L. Fotedar, kept his appointment with the hospital today. With a team of officials he went about inspecting the place, this morning.

'The casualty has never looked so clean before,' says a doctor.

(from the *Times of India*)

2

Using it is a piece of cake

The MT-20 offers you the most effortless way to operate a GSM mobile phone.

The revolutionary four-way rocker switch makes scrolling and controlling it as easy as pie. And it's helped the MT-20 win universal approval. Apart from the easy controls, it has all the functions you'd expect from the most advanced digital phone. And several you wouldn't. Like taking memos, receiving text messages, keeping your diary and recognising callers.

They make the MT-20 seem more like a complete communications centre than a mobile phone.

No wonder reviewers have singled it out for special acclaim. Pick one up at your nearest Mitsubishi dealer right away. You'd have to be half-baked not to.

(reprinted by permission of *Mitsubishi Electric Europe B.V.* and *CPS Golley Slater*)

3 Linkers Here are some common sentence linkers. Can you categorise them according to their logical function by putting them into the chart below?

However   Even so   Therefore   Also   Meanwhile   As a result
Then   On the other hand   Later   Moreover   So   Hence   First

Addition	Contrast	Cause/effect	Time sequence
Also			

Can you think of two others to add to each list?

4 Linkers The assumption that the liberal use of linkers automatically produces cohesive text has been questioned recently, as, for example, in this passage (adapted from Crewe 1990).

Logical connectors are frequently misused by EFL writers. They are either used erroneously or they are over-used. Over-use clutters up the text unnecessarily. It can cause the thread of the argument to zigzag about, each connector pointing in a different direction. Non-use is always preferable to misuse. If the sentences themselves are logically ordered, readers can always work out logical links that are not explicit. Misuse can lead them up the wrong track entirely.

How many sentence linkers are used in the above passage? What linkers *could* you insert at each sentence juncture? To what extent would the addition of linkers improve the text?

5 Reference to co-text In this extract identify where possible the 'referent' (i.e. the thing referred to) of each of the words underlined. What kinds of words are they?

> Hale knew, before <u>he</u> had been in Brighton three hours, that <u>they</u> meant to murder him…<u>That</u>, as it happens, is the opening of *Brighton Rock*; but turn up the opening lines of the rest of <u>his</u> books and <u>they</u> won't disappoint you. Graham Greene, <u>who</u> died yesterday, rich in years and rich in honour, was first of all a storyteller…

(from 'Odd genius out' in *The Bedside Guardian 1991*)

Which of the references are backward references, and which are forward references?

Do you think this kind of exercise – identifying referents – is of value to learners of English?

6 Deixis: reference to context   Notice the use of the word *yesterday* in the preceding text. When is *yesterday*? The question is not answered by consulting the text. The reference is beyond the text, to the real world – the *context* in which the text was written.

In this extract from Ayckbourn's *A Small Family Business*, identify all the 'deictic' expressions, that is, references to the 'here and now' in which the language is situated. The first two are done for you.

BENEDICT   Now, my [*my*: reference to speaker] guess is, it's somewhere in here [*here*: reference to place]. (*switches on the bedroom light*) Am I right?

POPPY   Look, I'm afraid I must ask you to leave now, Mr Hough...

BENEDICT   (*looks towards cupboard*) What about in here?...

POPPY   My other daughter is here as well, you know. Just along there...

BENEDICT   (*examining the cupboard*) No, nothing in here.

POPPY   I think that was my husband's car.

What clues has the writer provided to help you, the reader, identify the reference, in each case?

7 Deixis   Look at this exercise. What is it designed to practise?

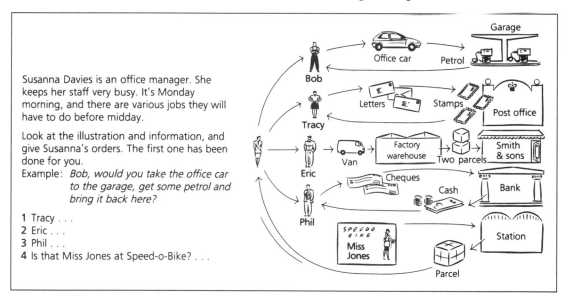

Susanna Davies is an office manager. She keeps her staff very busy. It's Monday morning, and there are various jobs they will have to do before midday.

Look at the illustration and information, and give Susanna's orders. The first one has been done for you.

Example: *Bob, would you take the office car to the garage, get some petrol and bring it back here?*

1 Tracy . . .
2 Eric . . .
3 Phil . . .
4 Is that Miss Jones at Speed-o-Bike? . . .

(from *The Sourcebook* by J. Shepherd and F. Cox)

Does deixis operate in a similar way in another language that you know? Some languages, for example, have a three-way spatial distinction where English only has two

– *here* and *there*.

8 Reported speech Deictic expressions are particularly problematic when we re-situate text, i.e. when we move text in either space or time, as we often do when we report things.

Can you do this exercise?

Change these sentences from reported into direct speech. Think carefully how you are going to deal with the words in **bold**.

A She said she was going to leave **the following day.**

B He said that **that** was the record he had bought **two days earlier.**

C They said the parcel would arrive **in two days' time.**

D He asked if anyone had come on **the previous day.**

E We told them their flat would be ready **the following month.**

F He said he had called **earlier** but nobody had answered the door.

G She asked him if **that day** was his birthday.

(from *Think First Certificate* by J. Naunton)

Transpose the direct speech *back* into reported speech. In what circumstances would it *not* be appropriate to change the time expressions?

What does this suggest with regard to helping learners with the 'rules' of reported speech?

9 Lexical cohesion   How does the writer of this text use words to connect each sentence to the one immediately preceding it?

TELEVISION

'Television' means 'pictures from a distance'. Television can show us live pictures of events on the other side of the world.

Two important pieces of television equipment are the *camera* and the *receiver*. The camera records an image of the scene it views on an electrically charged plate. A beam of electrons then sweeps back and forth across this plate. The result is electric signals which represent the brightness in different parts of the scene. These signals are combined with a radio wave and sent out by a transmitter.

The aerial of the television set picks up the wave. Circuits in the set separate the signal from the wave. These signals then go to the picture tube where a 'gun' fires a beam of electrons at the screen causing a spot of light. The television signals alter the strength of the beam and thereby the brightness of the spot. They also make the beam sweep back and forth in a series of lines of spots of varying brightness. The lines are very close together, and our eyes see them as a complete picture.

(from *Pocket Encyclopedia* by A. Jack)

What implications might this task have for the teaching of writing?

10 Lexical patterns   Each of the underlined words or phrases in this transcript of spoken language is repeated, either directly or indirectly, throughout the text. Identify these repetitions. What do they suggest about the way the text – and spoken language in general – is structured?

A. Oh and one <u>pig</u> <u>died</u> because it <u>ate too much</u>. Oh it was revolting. Oh they were terrible the pigs. They made a dreadful row in the morning when it was feeding time and one pig it was erm a young pig about that size you know – middling – and erm it was dead and it was lying there. I'd never seen a dead pig before – absolutely stiff.

B. Di...the <u>children</u> saw it did they?

A. Oh they were <u>engrossed</u> you know – it was marvellous erm they thought this was wonderful and erm they asked why it was dead and er the farmer apparently didn't want his wife to know because he'd overfed them before and she'd been furious and of course he was trying to keep it from her but all the kids were agog about the dead pig and *** was telling them not to tell the farmer's wife and all this. So this pig was absolutely dead so they put it on – they have a sort of smouldering heap that smoulders all the time so they went to burn the pig and all the kids hanging over the gate watching this pig and they were very er very taken that the pig had died because it had eaten too much.

B. What a marvellous death!

(from *Advanced Conversational English* by D. Crystal and D. Davy)

125

27 Texts

Introduction

So far we have looked at texts from the point of view of the surface features that bind them together. This unit looks at the 'deep structure' of texts and considers how different types of texts, with different communicative purposes, are characteristically organised.

Tasks

1 Cohesion and coherence The following text is invented. In fact, it is made up of sentences from different texts in the previous unit. Yet it has some superficial features of cohesion. Can you identify these? Do the texts cohere?

> Hale knew, before he had been in Brighton three hours, that they meant to murder him. They made a dreadful row in the morning when it was feeding time. With a team of officials he went about inspecting the place this morning. No wonder reviewers have singled it out for special acclaim.

2 Coherence Cohesion alone is not enough to make a text coherent. Texts have an internal logic, which the reader recognises even without the aid of explicit cohesive devices.

For example, the two columns below contain a number of short (two-sentence) authentic texts. There are no sentence linkers connecting the two sentences. Nevertheless, there *is* a connection. Can you match each sentence in the first column with the appropriate sentence in the second column to make a complete text?

1 Police discovered two 12ft tall cannabis plants in a greenhouse when they raided a house at Wokingham, Berkshire.	a) He is married to Antonia Fraser.
2 Memory allocation error.	b) There are mulberries being trod over the floors.
3 Harold Pinter was born in London in 1930.	c) Chew thoroughly before swallowing.
4 Please write firmly.	d) Cannot load COMMAND, system halted.

5 There's nothing worse than coming home to find plants in the greenhouse dead from the cold.

e) Two people were taken into custody.

6 Take one to four tablets daily.

f) This sturdy British-made paraffin heater will safely keep the chill off your garage or greenhouse for up to 14 days.

7 Please wipe your shoes clean on the mat.

g) You are making six copies.

Using the following categories, drawn from *Cohesion in English* by Halliday and Hasan, can you decide the sense relation between the first and second sentence in each case? Is it:

– Additive, i.e. an *and* relation?
– Adversative, i.e. a *but* or *however* relation?
– Causal, i.e. a *because* or *so* relation?
– Temporal, i.e. a *before* or *later* relation?

3   Text structure   What kind of text is each of the texts in Task 2? Is it an advertisement, a public notice, etc.? What purpose does each one serve? That is, is it designed to inform, to persuade, to warn, etc.? How is this purpose reflected in the way it is organised?

4   Text structure   Look at the following texts. Which of the 'mini-texts' in Task 2 do they most resemble, in terms of both function and structure?

a)

Folding bedboard firms up your mattress, home and away

Back pain is often exacerbated by soft, saggy beds. However, the Anatomia Bed Board could provide instant relief. It slips under any mattress to give firm 'orthopaedic' support for your back and hips – and because it folds up to only 25" x 7¼" x 2¼", it can also accompany you when you sleep away from home, especially useful for over-soft hotel beds.

b)

For left-handers only...

Life can be difficult for left-handers in a predominantly right-handed world. Scissors, for example, don't work properly the 'wrong' way, round, and right-handed vegetable peelers cut towards you, not away from you. Therefore in defence of the 'dextrously-challenged minority' we're offering high-quality scissors and peeler, purpose designed for left-handers! The Scissors have stainless steel blades (approx 4" long) with ergonomic plastic handles. The Vegetable Peeler features a fixed stainless blade set in a dishwasher-safe plastic handle.

c)

German precision scales

The trouble with most bathroom scales is that they can be very inaccurate.
But these German Seca Scales are precision engineered to meet the exacting
standards expected by the German medical profession. Used for accuracy in
surgeries, clinics and gyms throughout the world, they'll let you monitor
weight precisely in your own home. The
large dial is easy to read and the mat is
slip-proof for safety.

d)

Sinus Pillow helps relieve sinus problems

An estimated 8 million of us Brits suffer from recurring catarrh, sinusitis and
blocked-up noses. Now relief may be at hand with this specially designed
Herbal Pillow. The pillow contains a selection of natural aromatic herbs that
give off a soothing vapour while you sleep to help clear blocked sinuses and
relieve congestion. It can also provide relief for cold symptoms. Measures
approx. 27″ x 17″ to fit standard pillow cases (not supplied).

(from '*Self Care*' by *Innovations*)

What is the relation between the first and second sentences in Text (**a**)? How
is this signalled? What is the purpose of the third sentence? Can you find
equivalent sentences in Texts (**b**), (**c**) and (**d**)? Are there any variations in the
ways the texts are structured? What is the overall purpose of this kind of
text? How is this purpose reflected in the language used – for example, the
choice of vocabulary, use of personal pronouns, etc.?

5 Genre analysis   Having analysed the above 'genre', you should now be able
to attempt to reproduce it. Try writing a similar text for the following item:

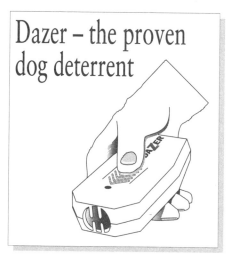

Dazer – the proven
dog deterrent

(from '*Self Care*' by *Innovations*)

6 Text structures   Consider the following text types. How are they usually organised? Can you think of any particular linguistic features (grammatical, lexical, etc.) that are typical of each?

a) recipes
b) answerphone messages
c) holiday postcards
d) newspaper reports

7 News reports   Compare a student's attempt to write a news report with an actual report from a newspaper. What are the differences in terms of the way the two are structured? Can you account for these differences?

PLANE CRASH

At 7.30, the Boeing 747 of Air France took off from the airport Paris to New York. When the plane was flying the passengers were reading, listening to music and sleeping – also the air hostesses were serving dinner, when suddenly a bomb exploded and the plane crashed.

JET CRASH KILLS 160

A CHINESE airliner crashed yesterday, killing all 160 people on board, following a mid-air explosion.

The Russian-built Tupolev-154, with 146 passengers and a crew of 14, plunged to the ground just after take-off from the tourist resort of Xian. According to witnesses there was a huge blast.

(from *Today*)

8 Paragraphs   Beyond the sentence level, the unit of discourse most easy to recognise in texts is the paragraph. However, the 'grammar' of the paragraph is not easily described. What are the rules that govern the internal structure of the paragraph?

Read this paragraph on the paragraph. Is it a good example of its own principles?

> Well-organised paragraphs generally begin with a topic sentence, which introduces the subject. This topic is then developed in a variety of ways: by extending the exposition, by using examples, making examples, indicating a contrast, etc. Subsequently, the writer frequently needs a transitional sentence or two to prepare for the conclusion. The organisation of paragraphs in this way enables the writer to express his thoughts in an ordered manner.

(from *New Proficiency English Book 1* by W. S. Fowler and J. Pidcock)

How useful is this kind of formula? What sort of activities would help familiarise learner writers with the formula?

28 Conversations

Introduction

In the last two units we have been concerned almost exclusively with written texts. Now it is time to look, briefly, at the analysis of examples of naturally occurring spoken language, particularly in its most common and informal variety, conversation.

Tasks

1 Spoken language   First of all, what distinguishes spoken and written language? Look at this extract. How do you know it is probably a transcription of spoken language, rather than a text designed to be read?

> And then he ran over to that place where you can get the water and he started screaming and she thought he was very clever and she thought he was thirsty and she pressed the button and that's all he wanted to know was how the hell do you get water out and she pressed the button to give him a drink and you could see his little face and he went whack with the button and filled the bucket, wet his clothes, got a smack, went back, for some more water.
> (Author's data)

2 Turns   The basic unit of conversation is the 'turn' (or 'on record speaking'). In the following extract (of a dinner-party conversation among friends), are the turns equally distributed? Who has the most turns? How do the speakers get their turns? Why do you think some turns overlap? Who holds the 'floor' in this conversation?

Note that in transcribing the conversation a number of conventions are used:

- Where utterances overlap, the point of overlap is marked by a single vertical line at the beginning of the overlap.
- Simultaneous utterances are linked together with double vertical lines.

(A and E have been explaining to B what junket is.)

(1) A: Junket, I mean |you have junket and stewed rhubarb

(2) B: |Oh I'm going to have to try it sometime

(3) C: It's one of those ridiculously old fashioned dishes that they make you cook in domestic science

(4) D: This is really nice this Rioja

(5) B: Well why don't you try making |some? Might be great

(6) C: |like kedgeree

(7) E: Spotted dick.

(8) C: Kedgeree, I remember saying to my mum

(9) A: Toad-in-the-hole

(10) C: I've got to take a pound of fish next week we're making kedgeree 'n she said (*mock accent*) 'you don't want to be making kedgeree' (*laughter*) 'n she said 'we don't like it' And I had to take a note to my domestic science taitch teacher saying 'Kathleen can't make kedgeree because we don't like it' (*laughter*). Awful. So I couldn't make it. I had to sit there while everybody else did (*laughter*).

(11) D: I would just make egg and bacon

(12) C: But kedgeree. This was a sort of comprehensive school the first year of. Nobody knew what kedgeree was. It was sort of kedgeree and junket (*laughter*)

(13) E: ||I love kedgeree

(14) C: ||I mean for God's sake

(15) E: Have you ever eaten kedgeree since?

(16) C: ||Oh yes I love kedgeree

(17) B: ||Didn't you say you could get hold of a decent bloody

(18) C: It's a sort of old colonial dish

(19) E: It is yes it's Indian

(20) C: like junket is but it was so |inappropriate

(21) B: |oh is it like galub jalum?

(22) C: for the first year comprehensive school kid to be making (*laughs*).
        (Author's data)

3 Cohesion   To what extent is this kind of discourse cohesive, in the way that written texts are cohesive? What examples can you find of lexical or grammatical cohesion across utterances?

4 Adjacency pairs   In looking for regularities in this kind of talk, discourse analysts have identified regular two-turn exchanges that follow predictable patterns, such as:

(15) E: Have you ever eaten kedgeree since? [question]
(16) C: ||Oh yes I love kedgeree [answer]

These exchanges are called 'adjacency pairs'. How many adjacency pairs are there in the following conversation?

(from *The New Cambridge English Course 1* by M. Swan and C. Walter)

Can you think of other common two-turn sequences that you might teach learners at an early stage? For example, how do speakers open and close telephone conversations in English? Does this differ from other cultures that you are familiar with?

5 Scripts/schemata   Certain kinds of talk have patterns beyond simple two-turn exchanges. Look at this 'model' for a shopping transaction. Can you map a conversation on to it? Which elements of the model are obligatory and which are optional?

A: Greet the shopkeeper.

B: Greet the customer. Offer service.

A: Ask for something.

B: Respond affirmatively or negatively; make another offer.

A: Decline offer.

B: Give total price.

A: Make payment and thank shopkeeper.

B: Respond and take leave.

A: Take leave.

How useful do you think these kinds of models are for learners?

Can you design a conversation model for the following situations:

a)   asking street directions
b)   phoning a restaurant to make a booking
c)   phoning a friend to invite him/her round for a meal

6 Politeness Look at this exercise. What is it designed to practise? How effective do you think it is?

Polite requests

Polite and friendly
Do you think you could come and look at it?

Polite but formal
Would you mind signing your name here please?

---

1. In pairs, practise making the two different types of requests.

Informally to a friend:
you think the TV is on too loud
you want a lift to the station
you want the window open a little
you want your letter posted

Formally to a stranger:
you would like him/her to move his/her car
you would like him/her to sign the visitor's book
you want to know the way to the main entrance of a building
you want a passer-by to be a witness to a car accident you have just had.

(from *Developing Strategies* by B. Abbs and I. Freebairn)

7 Topics Go back to the original dinner-table conversation. How many topics are introduced? How are the topics initiated?

Can you think of some typical conversational formulae for introducing new topics into conversations?

What classroom activities might be helpful in training learners to recognise topic shifts and to produce them?

8 Stories and jokes Look again at C's story in the extract in Task 2 (beginning at turn 8). What characteristics does it share with A's story in this extract (also from a dinner conversation)?

(They are talking about young children getting dirty)

(1) A: Yeah, I know. They take them to the park, the other day when Mum, we were we were they take them to the park

(2) B: ||They get a smack if they fall over

(3) A: ||this mother took her child to the park and he had a, she gave him a bucket of water so he had like sand and making a mush and she said (*high pitched voice*) 'No t'embrutis! Prou!'* but what

(4) B: he got a smack

(5) A: if you give if you give a two-year-old a bucket of water what do you want, no?

*'Don't get dirty! Stop it!' (Catalan) (Author's data)

Story-telling (including joke telling) is an important conversational skill in many cultures. Do you think it can be developed in the classroom? If so, how?

Examine a published EFL course. What examples of conversation (e.g. telephone conversations) does it include? How natural do these seem? Do they provide useful models for learners?

9 **Teaching conversation** Look at these exercises. How do you think each might help prepare learners for the skills involved in informal conversation in English?

a)

Speech features: Interrupting

Listen to T43 and make a note of the ways in which the speakers interrupt each other to say something and to change the subject.
In pairs, practise using these speech features, by discussing the advantages and disadvantages of different types of accommodation.

(from *Workout Advanced* by P. Radley and K. Burke)

b) **Some ways to start and continue a conversation:**

1 In England, talk about the weather.
2 Smile.
3 Sound friendly. Sound interested.
4 Look at the other person. Listen to them.
5 Don't stop the conversation. Answer.
    Then ask questions.
6 Give more information.

(from *Grapevine 1* by P. Viney and K. Viney)

c) **Work with four or five other students. You are all in the same compartment on a long train journey. Act out a conversation in which you get to know one another.**

(from *The Cambridge English Course 2* by M. Swan and C. Walter)

d)

Which of the following are answers to good news and which to bad news? Put a tick (✔) for good news and a cross (✗) for bad news. (Two of them could be good or bad.)

Thank goodness! ◯

That's terrible! ◯

Don't worry! ◯

Great! ◯

What a shame! ◯

Incredible! ◯

Try not to worry! ◯

I am sorry! ◯

Never mind! ◯

It'll be all right! ◯

Well done! ◯

That's marvellous! ◯

Oh dear! ◯

How awful! ◯

Oh no! ◯

What a pity! ◯

Congratulations! ◯

Really? ◯

Work in pairs. You are A or B. Cover up your partner's card. Your partner will tell you some news. Reply with one of the phrases in *D3*.

A Tell your partner that . . .

---

1 Your cat has just died.
2 You've passed your driving test.
3 You're worried about the exam tomorrow.
4 You've lost your passport and all your money.
5 You've won a free trip to Los Angeles.

B Tell your partner that . . .

---

1 You saw a UFO last night.
2 You've crashed your car.
3 You've just got engaged.
4 You've just got a new job.
5 You've scratched your partner's favourite record.

(from *Fast Forward 1* by V. Black *et al.*)

Key and commentaries

Introductory unit

1 Some of these issues have been dealt with in the Introduction, but, very briefly, the main arguments could be summarised thus:

a) Knowing about grammar – knowing *what* a verb is, *what* the past tense is – is of limited use unless you know *how* to put this knowledge to work. Moreover, grammar is just one area of what is called 'linguistic competence', other areas being, for example, knowledge of vocabulary and of phonology (and there is a lot of overlap in these areas). Linguistic competence, in turn, is just one of a number of competences that contribute to overall communicative competence, others being discourse competence (knowledge of how texts are put together) and sociolinguistic competence (knowledge of what is appropriate in different contexts). In short, there is a lot more to learning to speak a language proficiently than learning the rules of grammar (and there is plenty of anecdotal evidence to support this).

Nevertheless, the grammar of a language is highly generative: it is the basis from which it is possible to construct an infinite number of sentences. There are plenty of documented case histories of learners with 'no grammar', who rely mainly on vocabulary, and who have 'fossilised' at a very primitive stage of communicative competence. Grammatical knowledge (whether explicitly taught or picked up unconsciously) is probably therefore a necessary – though not sufficient – condition for language acquisition.

b) Regardless of the approach a teacher decides to adopt towards the teaching of grammar – such as whether to make it overt through explicit reference to rules, or to make it covert, for example by setting learners tasks at successive levels of difficulty – some understanding of linguistic systems is useful in terms of informing choices about the rules to be taught and the tasks to be set. Moreover, when it comes to making decisions about a learner's performance, in terms of providing useful feedback on errors, or measuring progress through tests, knowledge of the language systems is essential. It follows that the deeper the understanding on the part of the teacher, the greater the likelihood of making the wisest choices. It does not follow, however, that an exhaustive knowledge of grammar is *all* that is required in order to teach language effectively.

c) Deductive learning – studying rules and then applying them to examples – is contrasted with inductive learning – studying examples and (either consciously or unconsciously) working out the rules. Both approaches have been shown to work in language learning. Some methods, such as grammar-translation, favour a deductive approach; others, like audiolingualism, are wholly inductive. Different types of students also favour one approach over another: research suggests that some students are cognitively predisposed to 'rule-learning', while others are 'data-gatherers'. The level and the age of the student and the complexity of the rule will determine to a large extent which approach is the more appropriate: beginners are perhaps not ready to tackle the rules of article use, for example, and children under the age of ten are unlikely to grasp concepts such as 'indefinite past time'. It would seem, therefore, that a methodology that was either exclusively inductive or exclusively deductive might fail with at least some learners some of the time.

d) For reasons pointed out above, there are some students who are either not ready for, or not disposed to, heavy doses of grammatical terminology. Nevertheless, terminology can have its uses in terms of facilitating classroom communication: if a student knows what a verb is, it may be easier and less time-consuming to correct a tense error by saying 'wrong tense' than by any other means. Furthermore, some basic terminology will be an aid to those students who are resourceful enough to continue their learning in their own time, through the use of grammars and dictionaries, for example.

e) Having once decided to give explicit rules, the teacher is then faced with the dilemma as to which rules to give. Some rules – perhaps the vast majority – are in fact very complex and difficult to articulate. Even grammarians do not always agree as to the correct formulation of a rule (and the language is in a state of continual change, anyway). It is important to remember that the value of rules for learners is that they provide the means to generate original utterances, and that if they are so exhaustive as to be unwieldy, they are no longer functional. A good 'rule of thumb' (even if somewhat simplistic) is probably of more use than a rule that is comprehensive, but dense.

f) Since language is used in context, it follows that it should be learned in context: this, at least, is the thrust of an argument that has gained favour with the advent of discourse analysis and pragmatics. How, for example, can you explain (or learn) the meaning of a word like 'actually' without seeing examples of it in context – and, preferably, in an authentic context, not one that has been contrived by the writer of a coursebook? There will be times, however – just as in the study of anatomy, for example – when it may help the learner to understand how language works (and to notice naturally occurring examples) when it undergoes some kind of 'dissection' and analysis.

g) English is not a highly inflected language. In other words, it does not have a complex system of verb or noun endings, unlike, for example, Turkish or German. Nor are English nouns marked for gender; nor does English have the equivalent of *tu* and *vous* forms, i.e. familiar and polite pronoun forms. All this suggests that there is not much grammar in English, and, therefore, not much difficulty – but of course this assumes that grammar is (a) largely a matter of endings and (b) difficult. There is of course more to grammar than endings, especially if syntax is taken into account: a quick glance at *A Comprehensive Grammar of the English Language* (Quirk *et al.* 1985) suggests that there is a lot more to grammar than morphology, i.e. endings. In short, there is no satisfactory way of comparing the grammatical complexity of different languages, although artificial languages have been designed with a view to eliminating unnecessary complexity. The fact is, children take more or less the same time to learn their mother tongue, whatever it is, which suggests that – to children at least – all languages are equal.

h) The point has just been made that there is more to grammar than verbs, but a glance at most coursebook contents would suggest otherwise. The importance that materials writers and programme designers place on the verb system may not be entirely unjustified, however. Every sentence, after all, must contain at least one verb. Verbs unpack a great deal of information: they tell us about states, events, processes, and habits; they can tell us very generally when these things occurred, and if they were completed. They are also marked for person (*I go*, *he goes*) and number (*I am*, *we are*). However, to teach only the verb phrase would be to deprive learners of other crucial areas of grammar, not least the noun phrase. The complaint 'I've taught them all the tenses: there's nothing left to teach' is a sad reflection of this 'verb's eye view' of grammar.

2   Text type

These questions focus on the features that identify this text as belonging to a distinctive genre.

a) This text is from a newspaper: the headline is typical of newspaper news stories, especially those in the 'tabloids' or popular newspapers such as the *Daily Mirror*.

b) The purpose of the text is to inform, but in such a way as to engage the attention of the reader, however uninterested initially.

c) Among the features that are typical of tabloid newspaper reporting are: one sentence paragraphs; long, information-packed, noun phrases (*a plan...Evita, Angry...Rice, Walt...picture*); use of direct speech; special newspaper expressions: *dumped, clashed, vetoed*; simple linking devices: *And..., but..., now...*; idiomatic and colloquial language, especially when quoting; a non-chronological sequence (see below).

Text organisation

The way the information in a text is organised by the writer is an important factor not only in maintaining the reader's interest, but in helping the reader to make sense of it. As readers, we assume that the organisation of the text is not arbitrary, but that it serves to convey the writer's intention – that it makes the writer's intention coherent. (Coherence is dealt with in Unit 26.)

The chronological order is (**b**), (**e**), (**c**), (**a**), (**f**), (**d**). The actual order has probably been chosen in order to present the most newsworthy information first (although not necessarily the most recent), with background information added later. Note that the implication of the last paragraph, i.e. that Oliver Stone played some part in rejecting Madonna, is not mentioned anywhere else, and its connection with the rest of the text is tenuous.

Cohesion

There are a number of linguistic devices that affect the extent to which a collection of sentences holds together as a complete and cohesive text. (Cohesion will be covered in Unit 26.)

a) The references are as follows: *his* / Webber's; *they* / Disney; *their* / Madonna's and Webber's. Reference is deducible from the overall sense of the text, in conjunction with grammatical markers such as number and gender.

b) The references are all to the same person. Different ways are chosen for variety; also to supply additional information (*Composer*); and – in the case of *Andrew* in line 24 – to mark familiarity.

c) (1) Words connected with cinema: *star* (x2); *film version*; *play*; *part* (x2); *makers*; *picture*; *director*.

   (2) Words connected with music: *pop queen*; *composer*; *co-wrote*; *stage blockbuster*; *rewrite*; *songs* (x2); *award-winning score*; *music*; *writing*.

   (3) Words connected with argument: *vetoed*; *angry*; *vowed*; *demanded*; *insisting*; *sort out*; *differences*; *clashed*; *pain in the butt*.
   Note that these words, along with the proper names, comprise over a third of the text, and supply an important element of cohesion.

d) The references are: *now*: around the time of writing the article; *this* (week): the week in which the article was published; *last* (year): the year before that in which the article was written; *then*: at that time, i.e. last year, when she was offered the part. These are all examples of 'deixis', which is the way speakers or writers anchor their discourse to the context in which they are speaking or writing.

e) Pronouns and possessive adjectives are used to refer back to people already mentioned: this helps bind the text together; so does repetition of names; and so do lexical 'chains' or 'sets'; expressions that 'point' to the time and place (*here*, *now*) anchor the text in the 'real world'.

Vocabulary

a) Words are formed in four main ways: by adding suffixes such as *re-* to the stem *write*, or *-(e)r* to the stem *compose*; by putting words together to make compounds, as in *award + winning*; by clipping or shortening existing words, as in *pop* from *popular*; and by converting words from one part of speech to another – thus the verb *to star* is derived from the noun *a star*.

b) Both *dumped* and *clashed* have violent connotations; they are also commonly used journalistic expressions, e.g. in headlines.

c) This is US slang.

Grammar

a) a: determiner (specifically, an article)
plan: noun
vetoed: verb (the past participle of the verb, in this case)
by: preposition
angry: adjective
who: pronoun (a relative pronoun, in this case)
after: conjunction
now: adverb

Note that these are the eight categories into which words are traditionally classified.

b) a noun phrase: a film version of Evita
a verb phrase: has been vetoed
an adverb phrase: then
an adjective phrase: interested in working with Andrew
a prepositional phrase: in the end

These represent the five ways in which words are grouped together to form elements in sentences. Note that phrases can consist of a single word or a number of words.

c) *Webber* is the subject of the headline; *blocks* is the verb; *'Evita' Madonna* is the object.

Most sentences have a subject and a verb. Other possible elements include objects, complements and adverbials (see Unit 12)

d) The analysis of the sentence is as follows: *Walt Disney, makers of the £30 million picture* is the subject; *are insisting* is the verb; *that she must star* is the object.

Note that *Now* is an adverbial, and that *that she must star* is a clause which, in turn, has a subject (*she*) and a verb (*must star*).

e) infinitive: *to star*; *to rewrite*; *to sort out*
present participle: *insisting*
past participle: *vetoed*; *called*; *offered*; *dumped*; *interested*
auxiliary verb: *has*; *been*; *should*; *are*; *must*; *have*; *was*
modal auxiliary: *should*; *must*

f) present tenses: *has been vetoed*; *are insisting*; *must star*; *have called*; *needs*
past tenses: *co-wrote*; *vowed*; *should play*; *demanded*; *was offered*; *was dumped*; *clashed*; *said*; *told*; *was interested*; *thought*; *was going to be*
perfect aspect: *has been vetoed*; *have called*
progressive aspect: *are insisting*; *was going to be*

g) transitive verbs: *star* (line 1); *veto*; *co-wrote*; *vow*; *play*; *demand*; *rewrite*; *insist*; *call*; *sort out*; *offer*; *dump*; *update*; *tell*; *interest*; *write*; *think*
intransitive verbs: *star* (line 11); *clash*; *work*
phrasal verb: *sort out* (*call for* is better classed as a prepositional verb: see Unit 25)

Discussion

Opinion differs widely over this issue. However, it is a basic assumption of this book that some familiarity with the metalanguage enables teachers to talk to each other, to make sense of much of the literature on language teaching, and – should they choose to – to talk to their students about the language that is the object of study. Of course, simply to talk *about* the language does not constitute *learning* the language, and the use of grammatical terminology should always be considered a means and not an end in itself.

1 Language standards and rules

1 Questions like the 'How do you do?' one may be answered by recourse to one of the following:

- A prescriptive grammar, i.e. a grammar that tells you what you *should* say.
- A descriptive grammar, i.e. a grammar that tells you what people *do* say. This may be based on some kind of corpus data, i.e. a data-base of actual utterances, which – in the case of this particular problem – could be sifted through to find out what is the most frequently occurring response.
- A pedagogical grammar, or a students' grammar, i.e. a grammar designed to help language learners with 'rules of thumb', and not necessarily as comprehensive as a descriptive grammar.
- Asking other speakers of the language what they themselves say; or setting up situations in which they respond naturally.
- One's own intuitions.

All of these – except perhaps the first – have a certain validity, although it would be dangerous, given the wide number of speakers of English, and the rate at which languages change, to make a hard and fast 'rule'. It is probably only possible to suggest a *tendency*, as in this pedagogical grammar:

Note that *How do you do?* does not mean the same as *How are you?* It is used when one is introduced to a stranger. The normal answer is to use the same expression – *How do you do?* (Swan 1980)

2 This is how the other questions have been dealt with by various authorities on the subject:

a) In British English…the normal sequence for a call to a private residence is as follows:
   - Telephone rings.
   - Answerer gives number.
   - Caller asks for intended addressee.
   (Crystal 1987)

In American phone conversations, the most frequent response is *hello*. If the person answering knows ahead of time to expect a call, the response may be a *hi* or even *yeah?* Self-identification responses such as *Acme Computers* or *Dr Jones's office* more often mark the communication as business rather than personal. (Hatch 1992)

b) Most of these verbs have the preferred ending *-ize* with *-ise* as an acceptable variant in British English (but not in American English)… Exceptions include *advertise, compromise, improvise, supervise*. (*The Penguin Spelling Dictionary* 1990)

c) *Must* has no past tense form. For the Past Simple, use *had to...* (meaning *was/were obliged to*). (Leech 1989)

d) You use emphasizing adverbs to modify adjectives such as *astonishing*, *furious* and *wonderful*, which express extreme qualities. (*Collins COBUILD Student's Grammar* 1991)

e) Although *different to* (BrE) and *different than* (AmE) are commonly used, teachers prefer *different from*. (*Longman Active Study Dictionary of English* 1983)

f) There is very little consensus on this, usage depending on factors such as age, sex, sexuality, and the degree of formality imposed by the situation, but 'my partner' seems to have a fairly wide currency.

g) Of *usedn't to, Collins COBUILD English Grammar* advises that 'this form is now rarely used, and thought to be very old-fashioned'.

3 'Prescriptive' grammars are designed to tell us what we *should* say. 'Descriptive' grammars, on the other hand, aim to describe the language as it is spoken and written, without placing any particular value on it. 'Pedagogical' grammars are those designed for teaching and learning purposes, and their rules are often simplifications of descriptive rules. Good pedagogical rules should be easily applicable, have a wide coverage and few exceptions, as well as being short and memorable.

The 'rules' are categorised as follows:

a) pedagogical   b) prescriptive   c) descriptive   d) prescriptive
e) pedagogical   f) descriptive   g) pedagogical (or descriptive)
h) prescriptive   i) pedagogical

Of the pedagogical rules (a) is helpful, but only if it is understood that for 'vowels' and 'consonants' you should read 'vowel sounds' and 'consonant sounds'. Otherwise *an university* and *a heir* would be correct, according to the rule.

Likewise (e) is a good 'rule of thumb', especially if we add '...when the sound is pronounced *ee*'. Exceptions include *seize* and *weird*.

Rule (g) is largely true, although it doesn't take account of certain spelling problems such as verbs ending in *-e* (*arrived*), or *-y* (*married*), and verbs such as *pat* and *beg* (*patted, begged*).

Rule (i) is more problematic, although it is still widely propounded. It does not account for such perfectly acceptable sentences as 'Would you like some cake?' and 'Any fool knows that'.

4 **a)** One of the problems, even with descriptive grammars, is the fact that language is constantly undergoing change. Usage has changed from Jane Austen's day (the author of this extract): standard English would have *He has come*. There must have been a time in the past when purists objected to the change from *he is...* to *he has....* Most language change, however, tends to ignore all attempts to halt it.

b) Changes are going on 'as we speak': extract (**b**) was said by a native speaker, and although purists might complain that 'correct' English demands *If I'd thought...*, there is a lot of evidence that *If I'd have thought...* is widely used (see MacAndrew 1991). At what point does a variant form become 'the rule'?

c) One problem with most grammars, whether prescriptive or descriptive, is that they are usually based on the written form of the language and tend to ignore spoken English. Recently attempts have been made to describe the 'rules' of spoken English. This extract comes from a native speaker and is quoted verbatim (Crystal and Davy 1975). It demonstrates the 'ungrammaticality' of spoken English – its repetitions, false starts, use of 'fillers' (*I mean*) and shortened forms (*'cause*). Yet this is normal conversational style. Is it ungrammatical because it does not obey written norms?

d) As well as tending to focus on the written form, most grammars choose what is called 'standard' English as their model. This raises the question as to *whose* standard? Since the majority of English-speakers speak some form of 'non-standard' English, who is to say that one is 'more grammatical' than another? This extract comes from an interview with Shabba Ranks, a Jamaican and a native speaker of English. On the streets of Kingston *ain't* would be considered 'standard' (hence grammatical) and *is not* would seem deviant.

e) The final two extracts are both from learners of English. This should be clear from the obvious 'ungrammaticality' of the first – lack of subject (*it*), reversed word order (*village beautiful*), and lack of agreement between subject and verb (*the peoples is...*). Note, however, that even 'standard' English allows these 'deviations' in some contexts:
  – in a diary, subject omission is common (*Went to see Rob Roy's grave.*);
  – certain adjectives can follow the noun they qualify (*the person responsible*);
  – some plural nouns take singular verbs (*the news is bad*).

f) While there are no obvious 'grammatical' errors here (e.g. lack of agreement) the extract sounds odd simply because of the way the words are combined. A *smile* is usually *broad* in English; *remembering* is not something one gets *used to*. However, if challenged, a teacher might find it difficult to articulate a 'rule'. 'That's just what we say' is probably not far from the truth.

5 **a)** This is legal English: this extract comes from a National Insurance Act schedule. Legal language is distinguished by long and complex sentences, out of the wish to avoid any ambiguity that might provide 'loophole'. The assumption is that only members of the same 'discourse community', i.e. those in the legal profession, will read such texts, hence no concessions are made to the lay reader. The effect is often both pompous and extremely impenetrable.

b) These are instructions from a computer manual (MS-DOS 3.30 Operating System Manual): these kinds of instructions are characterised by a specialised vocabulary, often involving quite common words, like *drive*, taking on new and technical meanings; the use of commands, such as the imperative *Do not...*, and *you must....* Again, clarity and unambiguity are important: the reader is prepared to waive social niceties in the interest of directness.

(MS-DOS® is a registered trademark of Microsoft Corporation)

c) This is advertising language: the aim is to persuade but to do so in as familiar a way as possible, even when talking about technical or medical subjects. The vocabulary is non-technical and often idiomatic (*hard to get at places*), and hyperbolic language, including the liberal use of superlatives, is common. Note also the use of non-standard verbless sentences, a simplified syntax that contrasts strikingly with legalese – an attempt, perhaps, to imitate some of the characteristics of spoken language.

d) This is an extreme example of the poetic use of language. It comes from a poem by E. E. Cummings, whose experiments with syntax and punctuation pushed to the limit the bounds of what is commonly called 'poetic licence'. Poetry, unlike scientific language or legalese, for example, tolerates a high degree of ambiguity and imprecision. It derives its effect from the creative, idiosyncratic, and often playful use of language, as evidenced in songs and nursery rhymes, and in some advertising copy.

e) This extract comes from a work of fiction (*Once Were Warriors* by Alan Duff). It attempts to reflect the vernacular of its subjects, the urban Maori population of New Zealand, to the extent that features of the accent are transcribed in non-standard spellings *fulla* for *fellow*, *n the line toem* for *in the line to them*, etc. Use of slang (*jack their ideas up*) and Maori words (*Heke, Pakeha*) reflect local usage.

f) This comes from an English language teaching course, where the language is being used, not for any communicative purpose, but purely for the purposes of displaying certain grammatical and lexical forms. This kind of language has been criticised for not reflecting 'real-life' language use, although it has also been argued that it *is* authentic in its context (i.e. language classrooms), just as the language of the church is authentic in a church, and so on. Nevertheless, students exposed only to a diet of this kind of language may not be best prepared to handle the more communicative uses of language.

g) This is part of a composition written by a young learner of English as a foreign language, in response to the task: 'Write about the best day in your life'. It is non-standard in terms of grammar (*borned*, etc.), punctuation (lower-case *i*), and spelling (*mutch*, etc.), as well as in its choice of vocabulary (*bowels*, *going out*, etc.), all of which features reflect the learner's developing grasp of the target language systems (his 'interlanguage'). Nevertheless, it manages to convey, in an idiosyncratic way, a sense of the drama and excitement of the occasion, as well as the writer's sense of humour. To re-cast it in standard English might in fact diminish its overall effect.

6 Tests (**a–c**) are designed to elicit ways of refusing and making excuses, the situations differing according to whether the speakers know each other ('social distance') and their relative status ('social dominance'). Thus, in (**a**) there is no social distance or status difference; in (**b**) there is social distance but no apparent status difference; and in (**c**) while there is no marked social distance (assuming the speakers know each other), the person doing the refusing has social dominance (in most cultures). Possible (but by no means the only) responses might be:

a) Oh, we'd love to. But I'm afraid we've arranged to go to the country this weekend.
b) Well, actually, I'm expecting someone.
c) That's very kind of you, Etsuko, but Bob told me he doesn't want to be disturbed. I'm sure you'll understand.

In a study of refusals made by Beebe *et al.* (1990), using discourse completion tests, it was found that native speakers of English began with an empathetic statement (*We'd love to…*) then a regret statement (*I'm afraid…*) and then the excuse. However, Japanese speakers – both in English and Japanese – omitted the empathetic statement. It is studies like this that are of interest to language teachers, not least for what they reveal about our own language. Whether discourse completion tests are the best way of accessing this kind of information is still a matter of debate.

7 The dialogue from *Fast Forward* offers two alternative greeting sequences, according to the degree of formality – a function of social dominance (see the preceding task). It is suggested that *How do you do?* should be used in formal situations and that an appropriate response is to return the question. The extract from *Opening Strategies* suggests the same, but implies that British speakers of English are more formal than American speakers, and hence use *How do you do?* in situations where Americans would use *Hi. Pleased to meet you.* Note that the traveller in India (in fact J.R. Ackerley, in his book *Hindoo Holiday*, first published in 1932) adopts the 'British' strategy.

2   Language systems and syllabuses

1 The alternative versions of 'You heard a seal bark' all fail to achieve an accurate realisation of the speaker's intention, but each for different reasons.

   a) *You heard a sill berk*: this does not work because it is pronounced wrongly.
   b) *You heard a seal moo*: seals don't moo, they bark.
   c) *You heard bark a seal*: rules of English syntax do not allow a change of word order here.
   d) *You've heard a seal barking*: wrong choice of verb forms – or inflexions.
   e) *Would you like to hear a seal bark?*: the form does not match the intended function, since the speaker's intention is not to make an offer.
   f) *Dear Albert…*: the conventions of letter writing are inappropriate to what is clearly a spoken piece of language.
   g) *A marine pinniped…*: the sense of the original utterance is maintained, but the language chosen is inappropriate, given the context and the relation between the speakers.

2 Vocabulary – **b**   Syntax – **c**   Appropriacy and style – **g**   Phonology – **a**   Grammar and morphology – **d**   Discourse competence – **f**   Pragmatic competence – **e**

   The fact that the original speaker has not made any of the above 'mistakes' suggests that she/he has an expert user's knowledge of the above language systems.

3 The writer of this text is not yet an expert user of the lexical system (*millionary* for *million-dollar*, *compositor* for *composer*, *argues* for *arguments*, *to be the main star* for *to star*, etc.); the syntactical system (for example, *refuse somebody* can be followed only by a noun phrase); and there are one or two stylistic errors (e.g. *Miss Madonna, I don't know why*). Also, at the level of discourse, the overall organisation of the text, and its generally chronological account of events, is not how most newspaper reports are organised. News reports tend to start with the most newsworthy information (usually announced in the headline) and then they sketch in the background later on. Notice how the discourse organisation affects grammar. The present perfect (*has been chosen*) in the first sentence, while appropriate to the first line of a news article, incorrectly suggests that this is a recent event – *was chosen* would be more accurate.

4 The extracts provide examples of the following: (**1**) comes from a vocabulary course, and is a semantic syllabus, i.e. a syllabus of meanings, organised around specific themes; (**2**) is from a writing course, and is a checklist of different text (or discourse) types; (**3**) is a syllabus of language functions, i.e. the communicative uses to which the language systems are put; (**4**) represents a way of organising the teaching of pronunciation; (**5**) is a grammatical syllabus.

5 a 3 b 1 c 5 d 4 e 3 (also 1, or even 4?) f 2 g 4 h 1 i 5 j 2 k 3 l 5

6 Some factors that might influence the choice of items in a syllabus are:
   - Frequency: for example, how often does the item occur in natural contexts?
   - Range and coverage: the item may have a high frequency of occurrence, but is it used in a wide range of contexts and does it express a number of different meanings as well?
   - Usefulness: to what extent (and how soon) does the learner need the item?
   - Complexity: for example, does learning the item involve learning a number of components and manipulations?
   - Teachability: how easy is it to present, practise and test the item?
   - Learnability: for example, how memorable is the item, how similar is it to its equivalent in the learner's mother tongue, how easily is it acquired?

   Taking these factors into account, a beginners' syllabus might include (among other items) the following: describing places and describing people; entertainment; going to do; and, possibly, writing a story.

7 a) The grammatical complexity of the verb phrase is a function of the number of auxiliaries and word endings that comprise it. So, *she works* and *she worked* are equally complex; more complex are *she is working* and *she has worked*; *she has been working* is more complex still, but less complex than *she will have been working*.
   b) Questions (involving a change of word order and the use of the 'dummy operator' *do/does*) and negatives (involving the addition of *not* and the dummy operator again) complicate the picture further. In order of complexity, according to the number of operations involved, we have:

   she works
   does she work/she doesn't work
   where does she work?
   doesn't she work?

8 The main difference seems to be the order in which the past is acquired (irregular before regular; past before present simple). Note also that the present participle (-*ing*) form seems to be acquired ahead of the verb *to be* auxiliary, suggesting that forms like the present progressive are acquired piecemeal. Possessive *'s* appears to be relatively 'late acquired', compared with traditional syllabuses.

The significance of there being a 'natural order' of acquisition of grammatical items is still being hotly debated, but the basic positions can be summarised thus:
   - *Teaching syllabuses should try to replicate the natural order*: this is probably unwise, given how little is still known about the natural order. Nor does it follow that an item-by-item approach is necessarily the best, since natural language acquisition seems to take place seemingly irrespective of how the input is organised.

- *Language instruction should not attempt to follow an item-by-item syllabus at all, but rather expose learners to lots of natural input, since acquisition seems to take place in spite of formal syllabuses, not because of them*: this is the principle underlying the 'Natural approach' (Krashen and Terrell 1983), for example. Research suggests, however, that some focus on form does help language acquisition – which, again, raises the question of *which* forms.
- *Language instruction can still be organised around traditional syllabuses, but teachers should not expect instant 'learning', and should not be insistent, therefore, on immediate accuracy. Teaching should allow for plenty of recycling, as well as exposing students to language that may be beyond their productive means, so that they have an opportunity to 'pick up' new forms which they are 'ready' for*: this is a compromise position, and is probably the one that many experienced teachers (often unconsciously) have adopted.

9 Factors that might determine the selection of vocabulary items for teaching include:

- Frequency: Is the word (and this meaning of it) common?
- Coverage: Can you use the word in a wide range of contexts, or does it have a very narrow coverage? For example, is its meaning very specific, is it only used regionally, or is it jargon or slang?
- Usefulness: How relevant is it to the students' needs? (Sometimes relatively infrequent items with a narrow coverage might nevertheless be very useful.)
- Use: Will the learner need only to recognise the item (i.e. while listening or reading) or will it be needed for production (speaking and writing)?
- Learnability/teachability: Is it easy to learn and remember? Is it easy to convey the meaning and form of it to learners?

It is difficult to make generalisations about usefulness or even learnability and teachability, especially with regard to vocabulary. On the basis of frequency and coverage, however, a possible selection might be:

Beginners	*Intermediate*	*Advanced*
angry	mad	cross
	annoyed	be in a temper
	furious	pissed off*
		pissed*
		be worked up*
		irate
		incensed
		livid*
		seething*
		be on the warpath*

*recognition only, possibly

3   Forms, functions, notions, texts

1 a) The literal meaning of the two sentences is represented in picture 2. This picture best reflects the semantic meaning of the words and structures that make up the text.

 b) The writer's probable intention was to warn against opening the windows. This is because in its context of use – a sign in a bus – we are unlikely to assume that the text has been displayed for any other purpose. Notice, however, that there is no explicit warning-type language: 'you are warned' or 'it is forbidden'. The writer's intention is inferred from the context of use. This is the 'pragmatic' meaning.

2 Notice that the same sentence can take on different pragmatic meanings in different contexts. For example:

'Coffee?'

 – Said to a shop-assistant in a large supermarket, this might be a request for directions.
 – Said by a host to his or her dinner party guests, it would probably be construed as an offer.

Thus, the function of an utterance is context–dependent. For utterances (**a–f**) there are many possible contexts and related functions. Likely ones might be:

 a) Context: the phone is ringing. Function: a request, i.e. *Can you get it?*
 b) Context: thieves are robbing a flat, one is watching from the window. Function: a warning.
 c) Context: people still waiting for 4.30 bus. Function: expressing indignation, complaint.
 d) Context: classroom, teacher is checking pupils' knowledge of numbers. Function: eliciting.
 e) Context: in a cinema, a late arrival is about to sit down. Function: prohibiting.
 f) Context: one thief to another (armed) thief, both cornered by a policeman. Function: command i.e. *Give him the gun!* (A celebrated court case in Britain did in fact hinge on the ambiguity of this statement: the prosecution successfully argued that *Let him have it!* meant *Shoot him!*)

3 Texts can be analysed and described in terms of both their structure (beginning, middle, end, etc.), and their purpose, or 'function'. (Text *structures* will be looked at in more detail in Unit 27.)

The study of the functions of texts has been a concern of '*genre analysis*'. '*Genre*' is a term used to refer to the way social processes – such as thanking a guest speaker, or writing a note for your child's teacher – are realised in language. Factors that will influence language choices when realising a genre are:

- what is being talked (or written) about
- who is being addressed, and by whom
- whether the text is written or spoken

These three factors (sometimes called 'field', 'tenor', and 'mode') determine language choices such as style and organisation, as well as the individual words and structures chosen.

a)   The first text constitutes the author's acknowledgements in a reference book, and its function is to give thanks.

b)   This is a postcard. It is used to convey short messages, usually between friends: in this case the main function is to give thanks.

c)   This is a Valentine's Day message, published in a national newspaper, and its function is to make a declaration of love.

d)   This is a recorded message on an answerphone. It is for the use of friends calling a private residence and specifically excludes certain kinds of callers. It functions as a request.

e)   This is a recorded announcement on an underground train, relayed to passengers, and it functions as a warning.

f)   This is a written sign or notice, and, in this particular case, was addressed by the owner of a taxi cab to his passengers. It functions as a request.

4   The 'function' of an utterance or of a text is the effect it is intended to have on the listener (or reader). The term 'notion', on the other hand, is used to refer to the semantic meaning – or concept – expressed by a grammatical or lexical item.

a) notion   b) function   c) grammatical form   d) function   e) text type
f) function   g) notion   h) function   i) grammatical form   j) notion
k) text type   l) grammatical form   m) notion   n) notion   o) function
p) text type   q) grammatical form

5   The 'functional' approach to language teaching encouraged course designers to identify common ways that different functions are realised at the sentence level. One problem, however, is that there doesn't appear to be a one-to-one relation between (grammatical) form and (communicative) function.

a)   The requests in this task use the following structures:
   1 modal verb *could*
   2 modal verb *can*
   3 past progressive + reporting clause, which is in turn a conditional construction (*Would you mind if...?*)
   4 modal verb *may*
   5 imperative
   6 present simple negative question

b)   The second set of examples all use the imperative form, but each one realises a different function:
   1 offer   2 order   3 request   4 threat   5 warning   6 advice

c) Possible functions of the first conditional include:

- Threats: *If you do that again, I'll call the police.*
- Promises: *I'll buy you an ice cream if you're a good girl.*
- Instructions/directions: *If you take the left fork, you'll end up in Dover.*
- Advice: *If you have an aspirin, you'll feel better.*
- Offers: *I'll do the dishes if you like.*

6 The contents page looks like this:

Unit number	Main language point	Notions/Functions
1	*Have got*	Identifying Describing
2	Prepositions of place	Asking and saying where things are
3	Imperatives	Understanding and giving instructions
4	Simple Present tense	Personal habit and routine Describing how things work Asking for information
5	*Will*: future Simple Present tense	Describing a process Predicting
6	*Can*	Ability Polite requests Possibility Understanding messages
7	*Let's* *Could*	Making suggestions Stating intentions Understanding instructions
8	Comparatives and superlatives of adjectives	Making comparisons Stating opinions Agreeing and disagreeing
9	Countable and uncountable nouns – *much, many, some, any*	Expressing quantity

(from *English in Perspective* by S. Dalzell and I. Edgar)

7 The dialogue contextualises the functions of inviting, refusing (plus giving excuses) and accepting. The material is designed for beginners/elementary learners, and a certain lack of naturalness is perhaps inevitable, given the need to simplify the language. In 'real' phone invitations there are usually many more exchanges in the opening and closing stages, and the refusals would probably be more elaborated. It is unlikely, for example, that the excuse 'I'm washing my hair' would be stated in such a matter-of-fact way. Compare 'Well, actually, I was planning to wash my hair on Saturday evening, and, you know, it takes so long to dry…, etc.'

One way of using the material might be to play it once and ask the students to identify the gist of the conversations: who is speaking, to whom, about what? They could then listen again, and fill in Sue and Val's 'diaries' respectively. Having now established the 'meaning' of the text, students' attention could be directed to the forms used to express the functions of inviting, refusing, and accepting. This could be done by playing the tape through again, pausing it at strategic points, getting the students to predict what is to follow, and then resuming the tape in order to check if they were right. At the same time, key expressions could be written on to the board.

4 An introduction to phonology

1 a) It is certainly the case that few adult learners of a foreign language 'lose their accent', and various theories have been proposed as to why this is so. The physiological argument is that after a certain age – probably the onset of puberty – the vocal apparatus loses its malleability and becomes 'set' and resistant to change. The psychological argument proposes that, because our accent is one way we signal our identification with a group, changing accent is tantamount to changing identity. So, at the stage of our development where our identity becomes fixed, the same thing happens to our accent. It may be that a combination of both factors are involved. Nevertheless, there are plenty of cases of adults who *have* achieved a native-like accent, even if they are the exception rather than the rule.

b) There is no 'best model'. The fact is, however, that RP, while spoken by a very small minority of native speakers, is still generally regarded as a 'standard' variety of British English for global communication and educational purposes. Native speakers are less likely to be surprised by a foreigner speaking with an RP accent than, say, a Glaswegian or broad Australian accent. And it may be the case that two non-native speakers having to speak English together are more likely to be mutually intelligible if they have each learned to speak with the same accent. Nevertheless, for comprehension purposes it is obviously better if learners have been exposed to a wide variety of English accents. And, as was pointed out in (a) above, it is unlikely that an adult non-native speaker is going to completely lose his or her original accent in favour of RP.

c) Discussion of the preceding two points should suggest that a realistic (and less controversial) objective in terms of teaching spoken English might be simply: is the speaker intelligible? This raises difficult questions, however, not least being: who is to be the judge? Intelligibility is a subjective assessment and will vary widely from listener to listener, and from context to context. Moreover, purists might object that any lowering of expectations may discourage learners who really *do* want to aim higher. Some writers prefer the term 'comfortable intelligibility': that is, speech which is not only intelligible, but which also has no intrusive features likely to distract the listener. Again, the notion of 'comfortableness' is also subjective, and is difficult to identify in classroom conditions.

d) There is a general consensus that the features of spoken English most likely to impede intelligibility are those that are called 'suprasegmental'. These are those features which operate over larger stretches of speech – stress, rhythm, intonation – as opposed to 'segmentals', which refer to individual sounds. A word with the stress on the wrong syllable is more likely to be misunderstood than a word in which the vowel sound is mispronounced, for example. This is in large part because the suprasegmentals influence the way individual sounds are pronounced, rather than the other way round. Nevertheless, the general context will play a large part in determining the ease with which the listener can reconstruct the message.

e) The 'integrative' view derives support from the fact that, in real speech, pronunciation interacts with all the other systems – grammatical, lexical and discoursal. It is very rare that meaning is conveyed simply by a feature of pronunciation in complete isolation (although consider how the otherwise meaningless 'Mm' can be given different shades of meaning depending on the intonation). Moreover, individual sounds vary widely according to their phonetic environment and hence are best practised in these environments. The 'segregationists' argue that it is easier to learn and practise an item of pronunciation in isolation before re-integrating it into the general stream of speech. (A similar case is made for segregated grammar.) Perhaps a compromise position is best, with the two approaches working in tandem.

f) It is reasonable to suppose that it might be easier to produce a new and possibly strange sound if you have first listened to it a few times, distinguished it from similar sounds, and learned to recognise it in contexts of use. This belief underpins an approach to pronunciation teaching that begins with recognition and discrimination activities, before moving to production activities – that is, listening before speaking. There is a counter-argument, however, that the effort involved in trying to produce a new sound may make the learner more alert to naturally-occurring examples, which in turn will have positive feedback on production – that is, speaking, then listening, then speaking again. Again, neither view is conclusively proven, and it would be as well to experiment with both approaches.

g) Those who argue in favour of teaching learners to read the phonemic script cite the irregularity of English sound–spelling relationships. They argue that a knowledge of phonemic symbols is not only a useful classroom tool, for example, when teaching new vocabulary, but that it also allows learners to make productive use of dictionaries and is thus an aid for autonomous learning. Those who argue against might claim that the sound–spelling relationship is not as irregular as is often made out (see section **h**) and that the learning of a somewhat esoteric set of symbols may take place at the expense of discovering useful regularities in the spelling: native speakers, after all, learn to make reliable guesses about pronunciation when confronted with new words.

h) The ability both to deduce the pronunciation of a word from its written form and to make a reasonable guess as to how a word, once heard, is written, is what we mean when we talk about the learning of sound–spelling relationships. Native speakers learn these relationships, by memorising rules (*i* before *e* except after *c*, etc.), by trial and error, and by recognising certain patterns in written English. While English does have some quirky features (*cough*, *bough*, *through*, etc.) it is claimed that in fact around 75 per cent of the words in English are regular in terms of their spelling. This would suggest that not only is spelling teachable, but that it should play an important part in the teaching of pronunciation.

2 *phonology*: the study of how speech sounds are produced, used and distinguished in a specific language

phonetics: the study of speech sounds and sound production in general

phoneme: the smallest element of sound in a language which is recognised by a native speaker as making a difference in meaning

stress: the greater emphasis of some syllables or words over others during speech

vowel: a vocal sound made without the audible stopping of breath

rhythm: the regular repetition of stress in time

sound system: the different phonemes that make up a language's phonology

intonation: the rise and fall of the voice when speaking

3 tongue: 6   soft palate: 5   alveolar ridge: 7
lips: 2   teeth:3   nasal cavity: 1
hard palate: 4   vocal cords and glottis: 9   larynx: 8

5   The consonants

1 a) /p/ as in *pip* – if the vocal cords were to vibrate, the sound would be /b/; the point of obstruction is the lips.

b) /θ/) as in *thin* – /ð/ with vibration; obstruction at teeth.

c) /n/ as in *nose* – obstruction at alveolar ridge.

2 PLACE
bilabial: formed at the two lips
labiodental: formed at the lips and teeth
dental: formed at the teeth
alveolar: formed at the tooth ridge
palatal: formed at the hard palate
velar: formed at the soft palate
glottal: formed in the gap between the vocal cords

MANNER
plosive (or stop): by explosion
fricative: by friction
affricate: by explosion ending in friction
semi-vowel: with little or no interruption or friction
nasal: through the nose

a) /p/: bilabial plosive
b) /θ/: dental fricative
c) /n/: alveolar nasal

3 m: voiced   b: voiced   t: voiceless   d: voiced   g: voiced   th (*thy*): voiced th (*thigh*): voiceless

A voiced bilabial nasal is /m/.

A voiceless alveolar stop is /t/.

4

Manner of articulation	Place of articulation							
	Bilabial	Labiodental	Dental	Alveolar	Palato-alveolar (Post-alveolar)	Palatal	Velar	Glottal
Plosive	p b			t d			k g	
Fricative		f v	θ ð	s z	ʃ ʒ			h
Affricate					tʃ dʒ			
Nasal	m			n			ŋ	
Lateral				l				
Approximant (or semi-vowel)	w				r	j		

(after *English Phonetics and Phonology* by P. Roach)

5 The text reads as follows:

- 'Next lets check Jen's fresh breath then says Jeff'
- The phonemic transcription is: /ðɪs θɪŋ ɪz tɪnd fɪʃ mɪkst wɪð dʒɪn/

6 *Learner English* by Swan and Smith is a good source of information on comparative phonology.

7 The exercise is designed to contrast /s/ and /θ/. One possible exploitation might be as a discrimination exercise – the words in the exercise are read aloud in a random order and the learners simply have to indicate if the word they hear contains /s/ or /θ/ by saying (or writing) 'one' or 'two'. (This is often called a 'minimal pairs test'.) Once learners seem familiar with the distinction, they could then practise the exercise in pairs, one saying the word and the other identifying the sound.

8 These exercises target sounds that are spelt 'th' – /θ/ and /ð/. These are contrasted in exercises 2 and 3 with easily confused sounds such as /s/, /t/, /d/ and /z/. Exercises 2 and 3 focus on recognition, whereas 1 is a production exercise. Given that production probably presupposes the ability to recognise and discriminate, a logical order might be 2, 3, 1.

9 This exercise is designed to contrast /t/ and /d/. In contrast to Task 8, Exercise 3, where minimal pair discrimination is practised using isolated words, this exercise, somewhat ingeniously, puts the words into sentence-length contexts.

10 The objective of the exercise is to practise a common set of English 'consonant clusters', i.e. groups of two or more consonants. These can be problematic for some learners both to recognise and to produce. Final consonant clusters are even more problematic, given that they contain important grammatical information – plurals, possessive *'s*, past tense markers, etc.

One way of highlighting the way final consonants encode grammatical meaning might be to read minimal pair sentences, such as *I walk a lot/I walked a lot*, and get the learners to identify whether each sentence is either present or past.

6 The vowels

1 a) In many Scottish accents there is no distinction in the pronunciation of *look* and *Luke*. In other words, where RP has two phonemes, /ʊ/ and /uː/, these accents have only one.

b) In many American accents /ɑː/ and /ɒ/ are not distinguished, so that *calm* rhymes with *bomb*.

c) The distinction between the diphthongs /eə/ and /ɪə/ is disappearing in New Zealand English, so that *three little bears* and *three little beers* sound the same.

d) In Northern England many words such as *pass*, *laugh* and *bath* are pronounced with /æ/. However, the /ɑː/ sound is retained in other words, for example, *father*. Unlike the previous examples, where an RP distinction between two phonemes has been collapsed into one phoneme, the distinction between /æ/ and /ɑː/ has been retained in Northern England, but is simply applied to different words.

e) Most RP speakers would be happy with this rhyme, since RP is 'non-rhotic' – *r* is not usually pronounced if it comes after a vowel. 'Rhotic' accents, like those spoken in the United States, Scotland, Ireland, and the west of England, on the other hand, pronounce final *r*. If you pronounce final *r*, you may have fewer diphthongs in your accent, since words like *beer* will be pronounced like *bee + r* – /biːr/ and not /bɪə/ as in RP.

2 The couplet is as follows:

He clasps the crag with crooked hands
Close to the sun in lonely lands

The point of the incomplete couplet is to demonstrate that consonants play a more important role than vowels when it comes to distinguishing the meaning of words. It should have been easier to reconstruct the couplet from the second version than from the first. The exercise is slightly skewed by the fact that the written realisation of vowel sounds is less consistent than that of consonant sounds – how do you pronounce *oo* or *u*, for example? Nevertheless, the exercise makes the same point if transcribed into phonemic script. This suggests that consonants carry a greater burden in terms of intelligibility. This fact, and the fact that even within the native speaker population there is a wide diversity in the pronunciation of vowel sounds (see Task 1), suggests that accurate pronunciation of vowel sounds is less a priority than perhaps some teaching materials have led us to believe. Well-worn distinctions between, for example, *ship* and *sheep* are seldom problematic, given contextual factors, and, theoretically, at least, have no greater potential for confusion than a Scots person's *look* and an RP speaker's *Luke*.

4 Diagram 1 shows /uː/; Diagram 2 shows /ɑː/; Diagram 3 shows /iː/.

In the first diagram the back of the tongue is 'close' to the top of the mouth; in the second diagram the mouth is 'open'; in the third the front of the tongue is close to the top of the mouth. The combinations of close or open, and front or back, tongue positions are used to describe the formation of vowels.

5 'Schwa' is the shorter version of the vowel sound in *bird* /ɜː/ and is generally plotted in alongside.

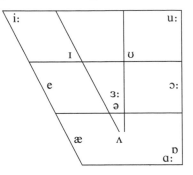

Remember that this chart, which was devised by the phonetician Daniel Jones, represents the distribution of vowels in an idealised RP speaker. Your own accent may have a slightly different distribution, but the number of vowels, give or take one or two, and the approximate distance between them will be much the same.

6 – The reason we say 'Cheese' when having our photograph taken is that the production of the sound /iː/ involves lip-spreading, conducive to smiling!
   – When saying /ɑː/, the tongue is at its flattest, and the jaw at its most open, thus allowing a good view of the larynx – and beyond.
   – If caught off guard, it is likely that a sudden expulsion of air will produce an /ɜː/ sound, since this central position is the position the tongue takes when at rest – its 'neutral' position, if you like.

7 The diphthongs are not so much combinations of two vowels, as a glide from one vowel in the direction of another. The eight diphthongs in RP English are these:

I	fear	no	boy	may	cure	their	cow.
/aɪ/	/fɪə/	/nəʊ/	/bɔɪ/	/meɪ/	/kjʊə/	/ðeə/	/kaʊ/

They are divided into two groups:
   – the centring diphthongs, which glide towards the central vowel /ə/: (ɪə), (eə), (ʊə).
   – the closing diphthongs which glide towards a close vowel. These divide into those that glide towards /ɪ/: /eɪ/, /aɪ/, /ɔɪ/; and those that glide towards /ʊ/: /əʊ/, /aʊ/.

8 The arrangement of vowels follows more or less that of Daniel Jones' vowel chart (see Task 5) with the vowels distributed according to tongue position (front versus back; close versus open). The diphthongs are organised (vertically) according to the direction of glide (to /ə/, to /ɪ/ and to /ʊ/ respectively). The first two rows of consonants are organised in pairs, unvoiced and voiced respectively, and from left to right according to the place of articulation: from sounds formed at the front of the mouth (e.g. /p/, /f/ on the far left to sounds formed at the back of the mouth (e.g. /g/) on the far right. The top row comprises the plosive (and affricate) sounds; the second row the fricatives. The bottom row groups together first the three nasal sounds and then the sounds produced with minimal interruption of the airflow, including the 'semi-vowels' /r/, /w/ and /j/.

9   The sentences are:

   a) Come live with me and be my love.
   b) Sweet, be not proud of those two eyes.
   c) Slow, slow, fresh fount: keep time with my salt tears.
   d) I am, yet what I am none cares or knows.

10   The phonemic transcriptions are as follows:

/fəʊniːm/	/dɪfθɒŋ/
/vaʊl/	/ʃwɑː/
/kɒnsənənt/	/fənɒlədʒiː/
/prənʌnsiːeɪʃən/	/sɪləbəl/

11   Note that these communication breakdowns are unlikely to occur where there is sufficient context for the listener to be able to work out what is intended. The pronunciation problem is often only a problem when compounded with other grammatical and lexical difficulties.

   a) Many languages, e.g. Arabic, have no equivalent to the /ɒ/ and /ʌ/ distinction, so that an intermediate vowel is used for both.
   b) *Are you living here?* sounded like *Are you leaving here?*, since in French, Italian or Spanish, for example, there is no distinction between /ɪ/ and /iː/.
   c) *Rug* not *rag* was understood. Many languages, for example, Latin languages, have no /æ/ sound, and the nearest equivalent may sound more like /ʌ/.
   d) This is a common mistake with speakers of languages that either do not have the /ɜː/ vowel, or for learners who have learned that -or- is pronounced /ɔː/ (as in *walked*).

12 The aim of the sequence is to sensitise learners to, and have them produce correctly, the difference between the sounds /æ/ and /ʌ/. (This is the problem identified in Task 11 (c) above.)

The original, and probably most logical, sequence was:

- Exercise 4: Ear-training, or receptive discrimination practice, at the same time sensitising learners to the effect of the vowel difference on meaning. Note that the words chosen are meaningful, as opposed to nonsense words, or vowels in isolation.
- Exercise 5: Presentation – Having learned to discriminate the two sounds, the learner is shown how to produce them.
- Exercise 2: Initial production – an imitation drill of 'minimal pairs', i.e. words that differ only with respect to one phoneme – in this case the target phonemes. The exercise involves further ear-training, as pairs of students attempt to co-ordinate the spoken form and the way it is perceived.
- Exercise 1: Further ear-training, this time in larger contexts (whole sentences).
- Exercise 3: Practice in larger contexts.

7 Stress, rhythm and connected speech

1 b) You probably found that, with the emphasis as marked, B's responses in the dialogue sounded very unnatural, not to say deranged. A more natural placement of emphasis would be:

A: What's on telly?

B: I thought you wanted to go <u>out</u>.

A: Well, let's go to the movies then.

B: We <u>always</u> go to the movies.

A: There's a new Clint Eastwood on.

B: I thought you <u>hated</u> westerns.

A: Speaking of which, have you ever been to Hollywood?

B: Yes, but I didn't go to Hollywood because of the <u>westerns</u>.

The way we emphasise certain words in utterances is called sentence stress. Usually, in any one utterance one word carries the main (or primary) stress. Note that in the last sentence *Hollywood* is also stressed, but not to the extent that *westerns* is: *Hollywood* carries the secondary stress. Note, too, that we usually only stress one syllable of the word: in this case *HOL-lywood*.

2 A theory has been proposed that stress is used to signal the introduction of *new* information in spoken discourse. The new information is highlighted to contrast it with what is 'given', i.e. what has just been mentioned or implied, or is taken for granted by the speaker.

So, in the first exchange of the dialogue, B stresses *out*, since *going out* is a new idea, in contrast to the implication of A's statement, i.e. watching telly means staying in. In the second exchange *always* is added to the existing information (you and me – go to the movies). In the third exchange B picks up on the implication that A likes westerns (A having suggested a Clint Eastwood movie, and Clint Eastwood often starring in westerns) and therefore stresses *hated* as the new idea, in contrast to implied *liked*.

The last exchange is a little more complicated and the difference in meaning between these two sentences has as much to do with intonation (see unit 8) as with stress:

i) | I didn't *go* to Hollywood | because of the *westerns*. |
   – The westerns were the reason I didn't go to Hollywood.
ii) | I didn't go to Hollywood because of the *westerns*. |
   – It wasn't because of the westerns that I went to Hollywood (it was for some other reason).

Note that in (i) it is possible to drop the pitch and pause after *Hollywood*. In fact, (i) consists of two distinct tone groups, whereas (ii) consists of one, with no change of pitch on *Hollywood*. The given information, then, is *I went to Hollywood*; the new information is *not because of the westerns*, of which the key word – *westerns* – is stressed.

3 It is important to remember that stress in utterances is context-sensitive, and that one of the commonest contexts for spoken language is conversation. So, in the example 'You've got <u>two</u> sisters, haven't you?' by stressing *two* the speaker is signalling that he or she knows (or assumes) that the hearer has got sisters, but simply wants to check how many. This constrains the hearer to formulate a response that takes account of this assumption, for example, 'No, as a matter of fact, I haven't got any. Perhaps you're thinking of..., etc.'

The writers of *The Cambridge English Course* suggest the following responses:

(3) No, I live there – I work outside London.
(4) No, it's Ann's father.
(5) No, a white one.
(6) No, French.
(7) a) No, not you.　b) No, write.　c) No, just Peter.

The exercise could possibly be made more interesting by asking the learners questions about themselves that you know not to be true, and showing them how to contradict you using stress:

You're from Thailand, aren't you?

No. I'm from Tai<u>WAN</u>.

The students could then try the same thing on each other.

4 These are probably the words and syllables that carried the beat:

a) '<u>Ab</u>ercrombie <u>arg</u>ues that <u>speech</u> is in<u>her</u>ently <u>rhyth</u>mical.' (Brazil *et al.*)
b) 'The charac<u>ter</u>istic <u>rhyth</u>m of <u>one</u> language may <u>dif</u>fer con<u>sid</u>erably from that of a<u>noth</u>er.' (Brown)
c) 'The re<u>cur</u>rence of <u>stressed</u> <u>syll</u>ables at <u>reg</u>ular <u>int</u>ervals gives <u>speech</u> its <u>rhyth</u>mical <u>qual</u>ities.' (Wells and Colson)
d) 'It is <u>plain</u> that this regu<u>lar</u>ity is the <u>case</u> only under certain con<u>di</u>tions.' (Crystal 1980)

Notice that these would not normally be all stressed equally: there is usually one primary stress in an utterance, and one or more secondary stresses. The intervening syllables are unstressed, and the alternating pattern of stressed and unstressed syllables (or beats) is what gives the impression of rhythm.

Such claims for the rhythmicality of English have been contested recently, but the notion that English is a 'stress-timed' language (like German and Arabic) has a wide currency. 'Stress-timed' means that the stressed syllables in an utterance fall at regular intervals and that intervening syllables are accommodated to fit the rhythm, so that different syllables have different lengths. This contrasts with 'syllable-timed' languages (such as French, or Spanish), where all syllables, whether stressed or not, are the same length.

Notice that the stressed words tend to be nouns, verbs and adjectives, i.e. words that carry the burden of the meaning, as opposed to grammatical words, like articles and auxiliaries. These are accommodated into the rhythm by some form of reduction, usually the replacement of the vowel with a 'schwa' (see Task 6 below).

5 The text is designed to practise English rhythm, using simple, short utterances, in a relatively natural context. It is a type of activity known as a 'jazz chant', since the point is to produce the dialogue in time to a regular beat, accommodating any unstressed words into the rhythm. Thus:

<u>Are</u> you <u>rea</u>dy

<u>Are</u> you <u>rea</u>dy?

<u>Not</u> <u>quite</u>. <u>Just</u> a <u>mi</u>nute.

Note that *Just a minute* (four syllables) is expected to be said in the same time as it takes to say *Not quite* (two syllables).

This kind of activity lends itself to choral practice, with, for example, one half of the class taking the role of A and the other taking the role of B. The teacher (or all the students) can beat or clap the rhythm. Students can then practise in pairs.

6 Other words that have both strong and weak forms include:

and   but

a   the

him   her   your   us

for   from   at   to

do   does   did   have   has   had   were   been   could   should   must

They tend to be 'function' words – that is, words which play a grammatical role in the sentence: conjunctions, articles, pronouns, prepositions or auxiliary verbs.

In the extract, the probable weak forms are in italics.

DISSON   How *do you* do, Miss Dodd? Nice *of* you *to* come. Please sit down.
That's right.
Well now, I've had *a* look *at your* references. They seem *to* be excellent.
You've had quite *a* bit *of* experience.
WENDY   Yes, sir.
DISSON   Not *in* my line, *of* course. We manufacture sanitary ware...*but* I suppose *you* know that?
WENDY   Yes, *of* course I do, Mr Disson.
DISSON   You've heard *of* us, have you?
WENDY   Oh yes.

Auxiliary verbs are *not* reduced when in final position (*of course I do*), and when in questions tags (*have you?*) They are not reduced in their negative forms, either, although there are no examples in this text.

7 A: What do you think we should do this evening?

B: I can try and book some seats for a movie.

A: What's on?

B: There's 'Rain Man' or 'The Night Porter' or 'Batman 2' at the Odeon.

A: Let's go and see 'Batman'. Where's my handbag?

what do you	/wɒt duː juː/	/wɒdʒʊ/
should	/ʃʊd/	/ʃəd/
can	/kæn/	/kən/
try and book	/traɪ ænd bʊk/	/traɪm bʊk/
some	/sʌm/	/səm/
for	/fɔː/	/fə(r)/
a	/ʌ/ or /eɪ/	/ə/
Rain Man	/reɪn mæn/	/reɪm mæn/
Night Porter	/naɪt pɔːtə/	/naɪp pɔːtə/
Batman	/bætmæn/	/bæʔ mæn/
two at	/tuː æt/	/tuː wæt/
the Odeon	/ðə əʊdəjɪn/	/ðɪjəʊdəjɪn/
go and see	/gəʊ ænd siː/	/gəʊwənsiː/
handbag	/hændbæg/	/hæmbæg/

8 **a)** Assimilation: what do you   try and book   Rain Man
handbag

b) Elision: Night Porter   Batman

c) Liaison: two at   the Odeon   go and see

9 Exercise 1:   Contractions and weak forms (recognition).

Exercise 2:   Contrasting weak forms and strong forms (production).

Exercise 3:   Assimilation and elision (recognition).

Exercise 4:   Weak forms and elision (recognition).

8 Intonation

1 **a)** The implication in the first utterance is that the speaker likes Elizabethan drama *and* Elizabethan poetry, while in the second the speaker likes Elizabethan drama, and poetry in general.

   b) In the first utterance, only the passengers who didn't have tickets were fined. In the second *all* the passengers were fined. We are also told that they didn't have tickets. (This is the difference between a defining and a non-defining relative clause.)

   c) In the first utterance, the way she went to answer the phone was hopeful. *Hopefully* is an adverb qualifying the verb went. In the second utterance, the speaker is expressing the hope that she went to answer the phone. *Hopefully* is a disjunct, expressing the speaker's opinion about the whole sentence it is attached to.

   d) In the first utterance, dancing, with music playing in the background, is preferred – rather than dancing *without* music. In the second, dancing is preferred, rather than music.

   e) In the first utterance, I married him, but for reasons other than his looks. In the second, I didn't marry him at all, the reason being his looks.

You may have noticed that there was a perceptible change of pitch before the marked pauses. Technically, the tone unit consists of a prominent stress (its 'nucleus'). It is here that there is a change in pitch. The tone unit may also have a 'head' and a 'tail'. So, in the first utterance of (a), which consists of a single tone unit, the nucleus would normally be the first syllable of *poetry*. The head consists of everything from the first stressed syllable (*like*) to – but not including – the nucleus. (Unstressed *I* is the 'pre-head'.) The unstressed syllables of *poetry* form the tail.

In the second utterance, which consists of two tone units, there are two nuclei – *I like Elizabethan drama | and poetry* – *dra* forms the nucleus of the first tone unit, after which there is a rise in pitch; *po-* is the nucleus of the second.

In the other examples the nucleus is marked by a small box.

b) – The passengers who didn't have ti◻ckets | were fi◻ned.

   – The pa◻ssengers | who didn't have ti◻ckets | were fi◻ned.

c) – She went to answer the phone ho◻pefully.

   – She went to answer the pho◻ne | ho◻pefully.

d) – We prefer dancing to mu◻sic.

   – We prefer da◻ncing | to mu◻sic.

e) – I didn't marry him because of his lo◻oks.

   – I didn't ma◻rry him | because of his lo◻oks.

2 If we were to represent *Hi* as if on a simplified musical scale, it is likely that each dialogue would look like this:

a)

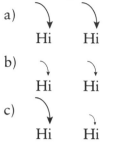

Hi   Hi

b)

Hi   Hi

c)

Hi   Hi

These examples demonstrate a theory of intonation that attempts to relate differences in the extent and direction of pitch change to attitudes. Thus, a wide pitch range, as in the case of (**a**) denotes high involvement, typically excitement or surprise. By contrast, a very narrow pitch range suggests distance, boredom, even hostility, as in the case of person B in (**c**). By extension, politeness and rudeness are thought to be linked to wide and narrow pitch ranges respectively. Example (**b**) is supposedly neutral, both in terms of the range of pitch and also the starting point, or key.

This theory has given rise to a repertoire of classroom activities designed to encourage learners to broaden their pitch range, and learners are often cautioned that 'if your intonation is flat you can sound bored' (*Headway Intermediate Pronunciation*). The theory seems to work well for such obvious signals of involvement as greetings and short responses – *Did you? Really!* – but attempts to rate particular intonation contours to specific emotions have not been convincing.

3 A possible rendering of the dialogue (and one that allows all the standard tone contours apart from the level tone) might be:

A: Tea?   (rise)

B: No.   (fall)

A: No?   (rise)

B: Well...   (fall–rise)

A: Here.   (fall)

B: Ta.   (fall)

A: Well!   (rise–fall)

Practise the dialogue again, trying to use these tones.

4 Assigning tones to written text is highly conjectural, although it is something that actors have to do all the time. One possible interpretation:

POPPY: What's that? [↘]

JACK: What's what? [↘]

POPPY: That. [↘] What's that? [↘]

JACK: That? [↗] That's a – that's a briefcase. [↘]

POPPY: Is it yours? [↗]

JACK No. [↘]

POPPY: Oh. [↘] What's in it, then? [↘]

JACK: Nothing. [↘] Just paper. [↘] Bits – bits of paper. [↘]

The conventional view on the relation between intonation and sentence structures claims that:

– statements and *wh*-questions have falling tones
– *yes-no* questions have rising tones

This is consistent with the interpretation above. However, the following tone contours are equally plausible:

POPPY: What's that? [↗]

JACK: What's what? [↘]

POPPY: That. [↗] What's that? [↗]

JACK: That? [↗] That's a – that's a briefcase. [↘]

POPPY: Is it yours? [↗]

JACK No. [↗]

POPPY: Oh. [↗] What's in it, then? [↗]

JACK: Nothing. [↗] Just paper. [↗] Bits – bits of paper. [↗]

Clearly, the conventional rules need to be qualified if they are to be of any use. Attempts have been made to elaborate on them. O'Connor (1980), for example, comes up with 24 rules, including:

– Use the Glide–Down for statements which are *complete* and *definite*.
– If the statement is intended *as a question* use the Glide–Up.
– If the statement is a *correction* of what someone else has said, use the Dive.
– For *short questions* used as responses, like *Did you?*, *Has she?*, etc. use the Glide–Down.
– For all other *yes-no* questions use the Glide–Up.

5 a) This activity focuses on the choice of intonation contour in tag questions: a rise for genuine questions; a fall when the question is simply to confirm what the speaker already knows. This is arguably one of the more reliable rules when it comes to assigning intonation patterns to specific grammatical forms. The activity is a production one. Learners could be prepared for this by first listening to a selection of tag questions and identifying those which rise and those which fall.

b) This exercise is a receptive one, designed to sensitise learners to the attitudinal function of intonation, specifically the broader pitch range associated with high involvement, in this case interest.

c) This is a tone unit exercise. It requires the learners to recognise and produce the appropriate phrasing so that the information is packaged correctly. A similar activity involves learners listening to and reading out telephone numbers.

d) This production exercise aims to practise what is sometimes called the 'discourse' function of intonation: the way intonation – in conjunction with sentence stress – is used to organise information in conversation. Brazil *et al.* (1980) make a basic distinction between 'open-ended' rising tones and 'closed' falling tones, the former being used to 'refer' and the latter to 'proclaim'. Speakers use referring tones to refer to what is 'common ground' between speaker and listener. Proclaiming tones meanwhile indicate the speaker's intention to enlarge the common ground, by either adding or soliciting some new information.

So, in each of these examples, B reminds A of things they both know, and uses a referring tone (fall–rise ⤻). In the second part of each example B introduces a new idea, and therefore uses a proclaiming tone (fall ⟍).

9 Word formation, spelling and word stress

The study of the structure and formation of words is called 'morphology' and the basic units of meaning that make up words are called 'morphemes'. Thus, the word *formation* consists of two morphemes: *form-* and *-ation*. *The Concise Oxford Dictionary* tells us that *form* means 'shape, arrangement of parts…' and that *-ation* is a 'verbal action, or the result of this'. *Formation*, therefore, consists of a stem to which a suffix (*-ation*) had been attached. (Notice here that, as is often the case, the stem can stand on its own – *form* – whereas the suffix *-ation*, like most affixes, cannot.)

1 These word-formation processes occur in most languages although to a greater or lesser extent, depending on the language. For example, word compounding is a common means of forming words in German; Latin-based languages such as Italian and Portuguese employ affixation.

2 successfully: affixation (*success + -ful + -ly*)
research: affixation (*re- + search*)
interface: affixation (*inter- + face*) and conversion (noun -> verb)
CD: 'shortening' (*compact disc*)
workstations: combining (*work + station*)
recorders: affixation (*record + -er + -s*)
networked: combining (*net + work*) and conversion (noun -> verb)
DAT: 'shortening'

3 The multi-word units in the extract are:

How can I help you?: formula
more or less: binomial
a friend of mine: semi-fixed phrase
helping her out: phrasal verb
a sticky spot: idiom
was up before: phrasal verb
under a cloud: idiom
I don't know where to begin: discourse marker
at my wit's end: idiom
Take your time: formula
you see: discourse marker
means all the world to me: idiom
Against my better judgement: discourse marker
you'll never know…: sentence builder
I've been through: phrasal verb
these last few weeks: semi-fixed phrase

4 The exercises are designed to practise the following:
Exercise 1 – converting nouns to verbs
Exercise 2 – affixation
Exercise 3 – word combination

5 English spelling is commonly thought of as being highly irregular, and therefore virtually impossible to teach. Examples such as *cough, through*, etc. are cited as proof of this. However, it is probably more regular (at least 75 per cent regular, according to one study) – and hence more teachable – than is generally supposed. It is important, therefore, to be able to convey its regularities (as opposed to only its irregularities) to the learner.

O'Connor and Fletcher have devised the following spelling boxes for /dʒ/ and /ɑː/:

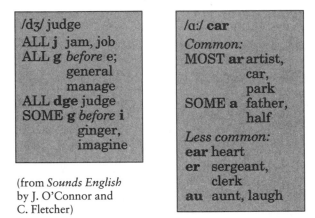

/dʒ/ judge
ALL **j** jam, job
ALL **g** *before* e;
general
manage
ALL **dge** judge
SOME **g** *before* **i**
ginger,
imagine

(from *Sounds English* by J. O'Connor and C. Fletcher)

/ɑː/ **car**
Common:
MOST **ar** artist,
car,
park
SOME **a** father,
half

Less common:
ear heart
er sergeant,
clerk
au aunt, laugh

6 a) *stin* /stɪn/: If a single vowel is followed by a single consonant (consonant–vowel–consonant, or CVC), the vowel is generally a short form. Compare this with *stine* /staɪn/: If a single vowel is followed by a consonant and the letter *e*, the vowel is lengthened or turned into a diphthong. (Children are taught the rule: if you add an *e*, the vowel in front says its name.)
b) *stinning*: In CVC combinations, the final consonant is doubled when a suffix beginning with a vowel is added – *tapped; hopping; wetter*; etc.
c) *stiner*: Add *er* unless the word already ends with a silent *e*.
d) *gimmies*: Final *y* changes to *ie* if *s* is added; or to *i* if a suffix beginning with *e* is added – *funnier; happiest*.
e) /ɡreɪk/: Probably spelled *grake*, which is the most common way of spelling this diphthong (90 per cent of cases, in some estimates).
f) *sploes*: Final *o* takes *e* before *s* – *goes; echoes*.

7 The placing of stress in words in English, like spelling, at first appears to be rather arbitrary, compared to some languages, where the stress always falls on the same syllable. However, certain patterns do recur.

a)

Stress on first syllable	Stress on second syllable
teacher	repeat
student	begin
English	explain
listen	discuss
written	describe
study	complete
reading	
phoneme	
grammar	

In two-syllable words, the tendency is to stress the first syllable, unless it is a prefix.

b)

Stress on first syllable	Stress on second syllable
all the nouns	all the verbs

Where the form of a two-syllable word is the same for both nouns and verbs, the stress is on the first syllable in the noun, and on the second in the verb.

c)

Stress on fourth to last syllable	Stress on third to last syllable	Stress on second to last syllable
dictionary	syllable	syllabic
vocabulary	lexical	comprehension
	grammatical	phonemic
	lexicography	authentic
		dictation
		linguistic

Certain endings determine where the stress is placed, for example:

 – The suffix *-ary* (along with one or two others) causes the stress to fall on the 4th to last syllable.
 – The suffixes *-ical*, *-ic*, *-ion*, and *-graphy* (among several others) cause the stress to fall on the syllable immediately preceding the suffix.

d) The stress falls on the first word of each compound:

hómework, fláshcard. This is the tendency in most compound words.

8 The first exercise is designed to sensitise learners to the existence of different stress patterns in polysyllabic words, and to demonstrate that, within 'word families' (e.g. *generous*, *generosity*) the stress can shift according to the suffix. As a sensitising exercise it is probably useful, but there is not enough data for learners to work out the rules for different suffixes – something which at this level would be rather ambitious.

The second exercise is designed to guide learners to the rule for stress on words that can be both nouns and verbs. Perhaps more examples are needed for learners meeting this distinction for the first time to work out the rule. Part (b) encourages learners to demonstrate understanding both of the stress rule as well as the meaning of the word.

10 Lexical meaning

1 The corrections to the errors and their explanations are as follows:

    a) *trees, with*: Wrong forms. These are probably spelling mistakes rather than confusion between different meanings.

    b) *some bad news* or *a piece of bad news*: Wrong form. The learner is not aware that *news* is one of a small set of words that have singular meaning but plural form. It is also uncountable, so cannot take the indefinite article *a*.

    c) *sang a song*: Wrong forms.

    d) *working hard*: Wrong form. The learner has overgeneralised the *-ly* adverb ending. In fact, the adverb form of the adjective *hard* is the same – *hard*.

    e) *She made films like 'Gentlemen prefer blondes'*: This is a case of the wrong words. The error probably derives from a mistranslation. The use of *did* for *made* is a common mistake where the learner's own language may use only one verb for both sets of meanings.

    f) *a famous scientist*: The learner has chosen the wrong words. The meaning is roughly the same but, in the case of *notorious*, there is a different (negative) connotation (see Tasks 3–5).

    g) *double-decker bus...top floor* (or *top/upper deck*): The wrong words, or, rather the wrong collocations (see Task 7 below).

    h) *I was speechless*: There is no equivalent expression in English.

2 **b)** homonyms

    c) antonyms

    d) polysemes – although there is a difference in meaning, they are related since they share the meaning 'something that transports a person from one place or level to another'

    e) co-hyponyms – members of the same lexical field, in this case, household cleaning equipment

    f) antonyms

    g) synonyms

    h) *birds* is the superordinate term to the co-hyponyms *quails* and *fieldfares*

    i) polysemes

3 The answers to the task are:
holiday travellers – holidaymakers
delays – were held up
dispute – row
failure – breakdown
chaos – confusion
unable to leave – stranded

Texts, especially authentic ones, are excellent sources for vocabulary development since any text, if it is coherent, will contain networks or chains of words that are semantically related. Another way of highlighting this is simply to blank out one of each of the synonym pairs and ask students to fill in the blanks, using dictionaries if necessary. You can also create artificial texts that have a high frequency of repeated words and ask students to rewrite them using synonyms: 'I woke up. It was a *nice* day. I went for a *nice* walk and had a *nice* cup of coffee...', etc.

Combing texts for all the words related to a specific topic is a useful activity, especially if the students are then asked to create their own texts using some of the words or expressions they have extracted.

Comparing similar texts, for example a news report in two different newspapers, is also useful. Not only can this help sensitise learners to synonyms, but it is useful for highlighting how vocabulary choices are related to style.

4 The dictionary categorises the words as:

knackered: slang
whacked: infml dated
fatigued: fml
buggered: slightly taboo slang
ennervated: literary
dog-tired: infml

Few language learners will have a degree of sociolinguistic sophistication sufficient to be able to do this task. Most will need either to see the language in typical contexts of use or have access to a dictionary. There are teachers who believe that it is ill-advised, even irresponsible, to introduce learners to language considered taboo. They argue that, without the strong social and cultural conditioning that native speakers are exposed to, learners may underestimate the unacceptableness of this language in certain contexts. On the other hand, it could be argued that it is exactly this sort of exercise that helps raise learners' awareness of what is or is not acceptable.

5 The *Collins COBUILD English Language Dictionary* in fact has sixteen different meanings under the entry *fair*, including such fixed collocations as *fair enough*, *fair's fair*, *fair and square* and *to play fair*. The *Longman Active Study Dictionary*, a dictionary for intermediate students, reduces the number to six. There is a completely separate entry for meanings (k) and (l), suggesting that there are two different words with the form *fair*: one an adjective and one a noun.

The meanings given are:

– free from dishonesty or injustice: (a – d)
– fairly good, large, fine, etc.: (e) and (f)
– (having skin or hair that is) light in colour: (h)
– having a good clean clear appearance or quality: (i)

– beautiful, attractive: (**i**)
– (of weather) fine; clear: (**j**)

and

– a market: (**k**)
– a very large show of goods: (**l**)

Notice that *COBUILD* example (**g**) is not covered in the *Active Study* definitions, while the latter has two meanings for what is only one entry in *COBUILD* (example **i**). This is not to suggest that either dictionary is unsatisfactory, only to point out the problem of delineating the boundaries of the meaning.

6

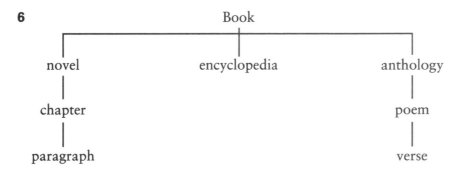

A similar diagram for *transport* might look like this:

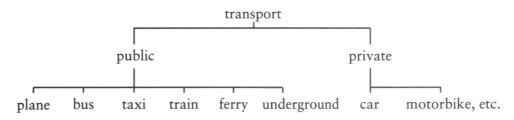

The use of tree-diagrams and 'spidergrams' (word association networks radiating out from a central topic like a cobweb) are analogous to the ways in which it is believed vocabulary items are stored in the memory. Hence their use in the classroom as devices for helping the learning of vocabulary, and for helping activate existing vocabulary in advance of production activities such as writing.

Some techniques promoted in EFL materials include doing exactly what Task 6 asked you to do. This can be made easier by providing the 'tree' – without the words – or with some key words marked in. Students can be encouraged to construct their own trees by building up a bank of words in dictionaries and/or texts, and elaborating these as they encounter new items.

7 The verb–noun collocational pairs are: *give notice*; *withdraw money*; *issue cheques*; *draw cash*; *make a charge*.

8 The following would probably qualify for idiom status, according to McCarthy's definition: *wind up*; *up to*; *hang around*; *upped sticks*; *shies away from* (although, if you know the meaning of *to shy*, the meaning is fairly transparent); *bunks off school* (again, transparent if you know the colloquial expression *do a bunk*); *window shopping*; *face the music*; *has in store*.
Note that assigning idiomaticity to a phrase is quite subjective. *Window shopping* may seem perfectly obvious to a native speaker, but not to a learner of English.

9 The vocabulary problems are as follows:

a) *view* does not collocate with *CV*; *own experience* is the wrong collocation.
b) *gave birth to techniques* is a problem of collocation.
c) *envisage*, *excellency* and *establishment* all have very formal, somewhat old-fashioned connotations.
d) *desire* is perhaps too strong (connotation) and *collaborate* has a slightly negative connotation; *particular professor* (for *private teacher*) does not collocate in English, and professor is the wrong word anyway: a case of denotation rather than connotation.
e) *get rid of* has a rather informal connotation, and does not collocate with *job*; *real and favourite task* sounds distinctly un-English: a problem, again of collocation.

11 Word classes and phrases

1 **a)** adverb   **b)** pronoun   **c)** determiner   **d)** noun   **e)** preposition
f) conjunction   **g)** verb   **h)** adjective

2 Nouns   summer; 1993; walking; tour; grandfather's; house;
                           Henfield; Sussex; evening; river; aunt; way

Pronouns   I; me; she

Determiners   the; my; first; one

Adjectives   early; pleased; rid

Verbs   started; left; walked; seemed; to be; speeded

Adverbs   out; rather; too; gaily; quickly

Prepositions   in; of; for; at; towards; on

Conjunctions   and

Note: Words like *my* are sometimes classified as possessive pronouns or
possessive adjectives. Words like *first* are sometimes classified separately as
ordinals. Words like *pleased* and *rid* originated as verb participles, but are
used here adjectivally. *To* as in *to be* is not a preposition, since it is followed
by a verb, not a noun, and is best classified as part of the verb. In short, none
of the conventional categories is completely 'watertight': it is the nature of
language – essentially a fluid object – to elude tight categorisation. Hence,
there are many words that can be classified as different parts of speech,
according to context.

3 This is the subdivision that best represents the phrase structure of the
sentence:

c) In the early summer of 1933 | I | started out | for my first walking tour |

4 **a)** *pleased to be rid of me*: AdjP
    b) *rather too gaily*: AdvP
    c) *my grandfather's house at Henfield in Sussex*: NP
    d) *started out*: VP
    e) *towards the river*: PP

Note that phrases can be embedded in other phrases. So *at Henfield* is a
prepositional phrase embedded in a noun phrase, and *Henfield* is a noun
phrase embedded in a prepositional phrase. Note also that phrases can
consist of only one word: *I* in the sentence that begins the extract is a noun
phrase consisting of a single pronoun.

5 – *a little unhappy* is an adjective phrase with *unhappy* as its head
   – *had not started out* is a verb phrase with *started* as its head
   – *the river banks* is a noun phrase with *banks* as its head
   – *still* is an adverb phrase consisting of one adverb
   – *high* is an adjective phrase consisting of one adjective
   – *was turning* is a verb phrase with *turning* as its head
   – *an old man who was smoking his pipe near the water* is a noun phrase
     with *man* as its head
   – *could see* is a verb phrase with *see* as its head
   – *the other bank* is a noun phrase with *bank* as its head

6

PRE	HEAD	POST
the	edge	of Dartmoor
yet another	great-aunt	in view
my next night's	bed	
the	sister-in-law	of the uncle I had stayed with at Petersfield
not very	far	from Okehampton

Note that the first four phrases are noun phrases; the last is an adjective
phrase.

7 The prepositional phrases in the extract are: *in the evening*; *to the river
banks*; *to an old man who was smoking his pipe near the water*; *near the
water*; *on the other bank*.

Note again that phrases can be embedded in other phrases.

8 The activities practise the following:

   – Activity 1 practises prepositional phrases. Note, however, that *last
     Monday* is a noun phrase. Nevertheless, many time expressions take the
     form of preposition phrases: *in 1984*; *on Thursday*; *at five o'clock*; etc.
   – Activity 2 practises adjective phrases, specifically the pattern with the
     adverbs *too* and *not…enough* plus postmodification using non-finite
     clauses beginning with *to*: *too big to put in the car*.
   – Activity 3 practises noun phrases, specifically premodifications of the
     head noun using the correct order of adjectives and noun modifiers (see
     Unit 22).

12 Sentence structure: the simple sentence

1 Defining such a basic unit of grammar as the sentence is notoriously problematic, the fact that we do not speak in 'sentences' being just one of the difficulties. This definition, from *Collins COBUILD Grammar*, will serve for the purposes of this unit and the next:

sentence: a group of words which express a statement, question or command. A sentence usually has a verb and a subject, and may be a simple sentence, consisting of one clause, or a complex sentence, consisting of two or more clauses. A sentence in writing has a capital letter at the beginning and a full-stop, question mark, or exclamation mark at the end.

a) This extract contains the following sentences:

- We appear to be...executive-type estate. (complex)
- Ours is a rear view. (simple)
- Downstairs...sitting room. (simple)
- It is a fairly...into one. (complex)

The other groups are verbless, consisting of noun phrases. They function as items in a list.

b) This extract contains these sentences:

- How did it go, then?
- I'm not that late, am I?

As for the other groups of words:

- *All right*: This is a perfectly well-formed answer to the question, but its subject and verb (*It went...*) are omitted (or 'ellipted') since they are redundant. It does not qualify as a grammatical sentence, therefore.
- *You know*: Grammatically speaking, this is a well-formed sentence since it has both subject and verb. However, it is not really a statement, question or command. It is a discourse marker – a way of linking two sets of ideas, and signalling their relationship.
- *Fond farewells. Usual thing*: Two noun phrases, as examples of how 'it went well'.
- *We shall miss...at last*: This consists of two sentences juxtaposed to form one, but there is no formal linking device (such as *and*) so, technically, it is not grammatically well-formed. The effect is to replicate spoken English by the absence of any pause after *...miss you forever*.
- *Only a little*: Ellipsis for 'You are only a little late'. (See the comment above on *All right*.)

This task demonstrates some of the difficulties in deciding what is a well-formed sentence, since none of the above 'non-sentences' are 'wrong'. In the context of their situation and text-type they are perfectly appropriate. They also obey rules, and a comprehensive descriptive grammar needs to be able to describe these rules. However, our concern is going to be largely with the 'well-formed' sentence, since, like it or not, this is still the basic unit of most English teaching materials.

2 The groupings in (**b**) best represent the three components which form the 'deep structure' of this sentence, which can be reduced to these three ideas: PLAN | VETOED | BY WEBBER.

Similarly, the other sentences are best segmented thus:

d) Australia's most senior female politician | has resigned.

e) The All Black side to play the British Lions in the first test in Christchurch on Saturday | was | predictable.

f) Hundreds of angry Afghans | sacked | the Pakistan embassy.

g) The counting of votes from thousands of expatriates | gave | the Prime Minister | a majority of one seat.

h) A Pakistani court | cleared | Asif Ali Zardari, husband of the Prime Minister, Benazir Bhutto, | of bank fraud charges.

3 *subject*: identifies what or who is the topic of the clause and/or the agent of the verb

verb: the clause element that typically expresses an event, action or state

object: identifies who or what is affected by an action

complement: gives further information (or completes what is said) about some other element

adverbial: adds extra information about the time, manner, or place, etc. of the situation

Note that these are the categories of traditional sentence analysis. They are sometimes labelled differently (e.g. 'predicator' for 'verb'; 'adjunct' for 'adverbial'), and further distinctions are sometimes made (e.g. between optional and obligatory adverbials, the latter being called 'verb/predicator complements'). For our purposes, the traditional categories are probably sufficient.

4 The subjects in these sentences are:

b) *Your Mum*. Also, *she*, which is the subject of the tag question.

c) *I*

d) *Tina* (Note the inversion of subject and verb in this type of construction)

e) *this family*

f) *a small gin with just a dab of tonic*

g) *Someone*

h) *Who*

i) *what*

j) *you* (Note that *what* is the object in this question, which could be reformulated as 'You are saying what?')

k) *I* (Note the inversion of subject and verb in the question.)

l) *the expert* (Note the inversion of subject and verb in this kind of construction.)

m) *I* and *we* are the subjects of the respective clauses that make up this complex sentence; *what I'm saying* is the subject of the sentence as a whole (see Unit 13).

5 Whereas the object is something acted upon or affected by the subject, the complement provides further information about the subject (or, in the case of object complements, the object). Complements are generally realised by noun phrases or adjective phrases. The underlined phrases are as follows:

c) object
d) complement (even though an object pronoun is used)
e) complement
f) Traditionally, this would be classified as an adverbial, since it tells us 'where', and is formed by a prepositional phrase. Some grammars now classify this as a 'circumstantial complement'.
g) object
h) complement
i) object – in this case a direct object. Some verbs, like *give*, have two objects: a direct and an indirect one.
j) object – in this case an indirect object.
k) complement – This last is an example of an object complement since it complements the object of the verb. All other examples of complements in this exercise are subject complements.

6 Generally speaking, adverbials provide circumstantial information, such as manner, place and time. Some verbs (e.g. *put, go*) require adverbials, whereas for many verbs adverbials are optional.

b) *always* (AdvP); *to Tina* (PP) *Note:* An alternative analysis has *listens to* as a prepositional verb, with *Tina* as its object (see Unit 25).
c) *there* (AdvP); *all day*(NP)
d) *privately* (AdvP); *in Dorset* (PP)
e) *perfectly well* (AdvP)
f) *in here* (PP); *for a moment* (PP); *first* (AdvP)
g) *in our spare room* (PP); *these days*(NP)
h) *Perhaps* (AdvP); *somewhere* (AdvP)

7

S	V	O
I	can't do	that.

S	V	C
It	's	a match.

S	V	C
It	's	Jack.

S	V	O
He	knows	everything.

S	V	A
He	knows	about you.

S	V	
Jack	does?	

S	V	A	C	A
It	's	probably	him	at the door.

S	V	O_i	O_d	
I	pay	him	the money	

(In this example the first object is an *indirect* object, the second is *direct*.)

A	S	V	C
Then	that	's	it.

S	V	C
It	's	my fault.

S	V	O	A
I	got	you	into this.

8 The analysis of the sentences is as follows:

a) It   's   a free country.

S	V	C
NP	VP	NP
pn	vb	det + adj + n

b) My friend   lent   them   to me.

S		V	O	A
NP		VP	NP	PP
poss.adj + noun		vb	pn	prep.+ pn

c) She   gave   me   a false name

S	V	O_i	O_d
NP	VP	NP	NP
pn	vb	pn	det + adj + n

d) I   was educated   privately   in Dorset.

S	V	A	A
NP	VP	AdvP	PP
pn	aux. + participle	adv	prep + n

e)

We	'll use	the front door	this time.
S	V	O	A
NP	VP	NP	NP
pn	aux. + inf.	det + adj + n	det + n

f)

Poppy	doesn't get on	too well	with Harriet.
S	V	A	A
NP	VP	AdvP	PP
n	aux. + not + phrasal verb	adv + adv	prep + n

Sentences (**d–h**) in Task 2 should be labelled as follows:

d) Australia's most senior female politician: S
   has resigned: V

e) The All Black side to play the British Lions in the first test in Christchurch on Saturday: S
   was: V
   predictable: C

f) Hundreds of angry Afghans: S
   sacked: V
   the Pakistan embassy: O

g) The counting of votes from thousands of expatriates: S
   gave: V
   the Prime Minister: O (indirect)
   a majority of one seat: O (direct)

h) A Pakistani court: S
   cleared: V
   Asif Ali Zardari, husband of the Prime Minister Benazir Bhutto: O
   of bank charges: A

9 a) In (classical) Arabic, the verb element often comes at the head of the clause, reversing the normal English order of subject–verb–object.
  b) In Hindi, the verb element comes last; the preposition follows the noun it qualifies.
  c) Spanish pronouns precede the verb, and Spanish allows a double negative (*no...nunca*).
  d) In Turkish, the verb element comes last, and (in this example at least) the adverbial of time precedes the adverbial of place. English tends to favour the reverse order. Note that prepositions follow nouns (postpositions).
  e) In German, the verb element takes final position in subordinate clauses, and, in main clauses, participles take final position.
  f) In French, adjective phrases tend to follow noun phrases.

13 Sentence structure: the complex sentence

1 suffered: finite
walking: non-finite (participle)
left: finite
walked: finite
had finished: finite
pulled: finite
receiving: non-finite
disconnected: finite
was taken: finite

Note: although *shaken* is the past participle of the verb *shake*, in this context it functions as an adjective.

2 – Simple sentence: The incident left staff as well as the man badly shaken.
– Multiple sentences: all the other sentences are multiple sentences, since they all contain more than one clause.
– Independent clauses: A young Dunedin man suffered a severe electrical shock in the Income Support Service office; The incident left staff as well as the man badly shaken; The young man walked out of the interview room; He pulled a wire from his clothing; (he) plugged it into a wall socket; a staff member swiftly disconnected the plug; the man was taken to hospital.
– Compound sentences: the last two sentences, each of which uses *and* to link two independent clauses.
– Dependent clauses: after walking out of an interview; before the interview had finished; receiving a severe shock.
– Complex sentences: sentence one, three and four. (Sentence four is an example of a compound–complex sentence, in that it is both compound and complex.)
– Finite clauses: A young Dunedin man suffered a severe electrical shock in the Income Support Service office; The incident left staff as well as the man badly shaken; The young man walked out of the interview room; before the interview had finished; He pulled a wire from his clothing; (he) plugged it into a wall socket; A staff member swiftly disconnected the plug; the man was taken to hospital.
– Non-finite clauses: after walking out of an interview; receiving a severe shock.

3 The noun clauses and their functions are as follows:

c) *I steal things*: object
d) *killing people*: object
e) *what she likes*; *what I like*: both objects
f) *All I did*: subject; *stand up to blackmail*: complement
g) *What I'm saying*: subject; *we're trying to keep this in the family*: complement
h) *what he wants*: object
i) *what you think*: object (of *know*); *you're doing*: object (of *think*)

4 A re-construction of the conversation might look something like this (although what is reported is usually only the gist of the conversation):

Charles: I'm doing nothing but think of you and the children ever since our troubles started.
Diana: I don't believe that. Stop being so self-centred...
Charles: Three days is hardly a lifetime.
Diana: What exactly do you mean by three days? Have you considered the implications of a custody battle over the children?
Charles: Don't be silly. I haven't.
Diana: This is what would happen. The boys would suffer...

Notice that a number of reporting verbs are used: *say, reply, ask, tell* and *warn*.

The choice of verb affects the syntax of the reporting clause. Thus *say, reply* and *warn* take *that*-clauses; *warn* takes a direct object (*him*) but *say* and *reply* do not; *tell* takes both a *that*-clause (with direct object) and a non-finite clause (a *to*-infinitive clause). The *to*-infinitive is used when *tell* has the meaning of 'command': *Charles tells her not to be silly and that he hasn't.*

When reporting questions (using *ask*, for example), there is no inversion of subject and verb as there is in direct questions: *Diana asks him exactly what he means by three days.*

When reporting a *yes-no* question, an *if*-clause is used: *Di asks him if he has considered the implications of a custody battle...*

Had the reporting verbs been in the past tense, it would have been necessary to change certain finite verbs in the reporting clauses into the past tense as well. For example:

Charles said he *was* doing nothing but think of Di and the children ever since their troubles started.

Di replied that she *didn't* believe that and told him to stop being so self-centred...

Di asked him if he *had* considered the implications of a custody battle over the children.

Notice that it is not necessary to change the tense of verbs in dependent clauses (*ever since their troubles started*), nor of modal verbs already in their 'past' form, such as *would*.

Di warned him that this is what would happen and that the boys would suffer.

5 It is difficult to design natural and productive speaking activities for practising reported speech, perhaps because reported speech forms are a feature of written rather than spoken language. The task at least attempts to inject interest into the activity by having students formulate (and report) their own opinions, rather than those of a coursebook writer, for example. Nevertheless, since only one sentence is reported at a time, it is not very language-productive; nor is it very authentic in its use of language since: (a) there is no particular reason supplied for students to produce unsolicited statements of opinion or to report them (other than practising the conventions of reported speech, of course); and (b) a native speaker would probably not report the opinion in the way suggested by the model, but would ignore the rules of sequence of tense and say 'Saima said that every mother *is* a working mother', since the opinion is a general truth that holds, not only for the time when it was first voiced, but for now.

6 a) Time clause: *When I come back*.... Generally, when the verb in the main clause refers to the future, the verb in the adverbial clause of time is in the present simple.
b) Purpose clause: *to look for a job*. This is the infinitive of purpose; *for* can only be followed by a noun.
c) Concessive clause: *In spite of the fact that you're less free...* or *In spite of (your) being less free...* *In spite of* can only be followed by a noun, or *-ing* form, not by a clause. A less complicated choice of conjunction is *although*.
d) Manner: *...as if they were stars.* Although *like* can be used as a conjunction with the clauses of manner, it cannot be combined with *if*.
e) Condition: *If you had worked harder...* For hypothetical past conditions the usual tense sequence is to use the past perfect in the conditional clause and *would have* in the main clause.

7 b) resented paying (*resent* + *-ing*)
c) seem to be (*seem* + *to*-infinitive)
d) stop doing (*stop* + *-ing*)
e) let me make (*let* + object + bare infinitive)
f) help me to stop (*help* + object + bare infinitive)
g) want to get...[want to] have (*want* + *to*-infinitive)
h) want him working (*want* + object + *-ing*)
i) like you and Anna to consider (*like* + object + *to*-infinitive); consider coming (*consider* + *ing* form)

8 The exercise is designed to test: it assumes previous knowledge. This is how the exercise is answered in *Think First Certificate Self-Study Guide* (Acklam 1990):

1 no difference
2 big difference – in the first sentence *remembering* came before *closing the window*.
3 no big difference here although with *I like to play tennis* we usually give more specific information as well, e.g. *I like to play tennis at the weekends*.
4 big difference – the first sentence is in the passive sense, the second active.
5 big difference – similar to (2)
6 quite a subtle difference – *learning Japanese* was her final goal. *Learning ten words a day* was the method she used.

9 Here are some examples of classroom instructions using chain verbs:

Remember to do your homework.
Try to use the present perfect.
Stop writing.
Try not to make any noise.
Let's have a break.
Try saying it without looking at your book.

10 b)

I	listen	in the mornings	when	I'm	'm jogging
S	V	A	A		
			conj.	S	V

(◄——— main clause ———►) (◄——adverbial clause——►)

c)

I	'll shout	if	I	need	you
S	V	A			
		conj.	S	V	O

(◄main clause►) (adverbial clause of condition)

d)

I	'm	at Des's	so	I	won't talk	for long
S	V	A	conj.	S	V	A

(◄—main clause—►) (◄———main clause———►)

e)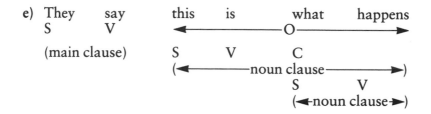

Here is an analysis of the sentences in the news article in Task 1:

A young Dunedin Man	S
suffered	V
a severe electrical shock	O
in the Income Support Service office	A
after walking out of an interview	A (adverbial clause of time: non-finite)
The incident	S
left	V
staff as well as the man	O
badly shaken	Object complement
The young man	S
walked	V
out of the interview room	A
before the interview had finished	A (adverbial clause of time: finite)
He	S
pulled	V
a wire	O
from his clothing	A
and	conjunction
[he]	S (ellipted)
plugged	V
it	O
into a wall socket	A
receiving a severe shock	A (adverbial clause of result: non-finite)

A staff member	S
swiftly	A
disconnected	V
the plug	O
and	conjunction
the man	S
was taken	V
to hospital	A

14 Negatives and questions

1 The seven examples of negation are: *not surprised*; *we don't get scurvy*; *she can't see anything*; *didn't close*; *Nobody knows*; *No sign*; *the dog hasn't come back*.

2 The examples of negation can be categorised as follows:

a) *not*-negation: not surprised; can't see; didn't close; hasn't come
b) dummy operator: don't get
c) negative pronoun: nobody
d) negative determiner: no sign
e) non-assertive form: anything; yet

3 A more complete rule might be:

'To make a negative statement in English, insert *not* after the first auxiliary verb, or, if the verb is *to be*, after the verb. If there is no auxiliary or no verb *to be*, insert the appropriate form of *do* before the verb, and add *not* after it.'

4 The non-assertive forms and their equivalent assertive forms are:

a) *any more money*; *hadn't any left*. Non-assertive forms are commonly found in negative statements like these. Assertive form: *some*.
b) *any help*. Non-assertive forms are used in *if*-clauses. Assertive form: *some*.
c) *ever*. Non-assertive forms are used in some comparative constructions. Assertive form: *sometimes*.
d) *any longer*. Verbs with a negative meaning, like *refused,* are commonly followed by non-assertive forms. Assertive form: *still, longer*.
e) *at all*. Similarly, they are used after *nothing*, since this conveys a negative meaning. The most approximate assertive form is *to some extent*.
f) *any work*. After *only* + NP. Assertive form: *some*.

5 The extract contains the following questions:

a) *yes-no* questions: Did you catch much? Did you have the good fortune…? Do you believe her?
b) *wh*-questions: What were you doing that day? Where? Whoever heard of catching salmon in a canal? What are you going to do? Why did you call her Maddy?
c) indirect question: Would you mind telling me…why you killed my brother?
d) subject question: Whoever heard of catching salmon in a canal?
e) object questions: What were you doing that day? Where? What are you going to do? Why did you call her Maddy?
f) intonation question: She told you that?
g) tag question: (There's) Nothing I can do, is there?

6 The rules for question formation in English are:

To make *yes-no* questions, invert the first auxiliary verb, or the verb *to be*, and the subject. If there is no auxiliary, use the appropriate form of *do* (the dummy operator): *Do you believe her?*

To make *wh*-questions, place the *wh*-word at the beginning of the sentence. If the *wh*-word stands for the object or adverbial of the sentence, the word order is as in *yes-no* questions (see above): *What were you doing that day? Why did you call her Maddy?*

7 Other popular classroom guessing games are described below:

- 'What's my line?': one student thinks of a job; the others have to guess what it is, asking *yes-no* questions.
- 'Alibis': two students construct a joint alibi for a specified period of time when a crime supposedly occurred. They are then interrogated separately, and their stories compared. This practises a variety of questions, particularly *wh*-forms.
- To practise *yes-no* questions using the present progressive, students choose to 'be' one person in a picture which includes lots of people doing different things. Their partner asks questions in order to guess who they are.

(Other ideas for question-based activities can be found in *The Q Book* by J. Morgan and M. Rinvolucri.)

8 The learners' questions involve the following errors:

a) lack of inversion
b) omission of subject pronoun *you*
c) failure to insert dummy auxiliary *do*
d) falsely assuming that *can* is a lexical verb, not an auxiliary, and therefore requires *do*
e) same problem as (d), this time with auxiliary *be*
f) failure to ensure question tag agrees with main verb of sentence

9 The activity practises the difference between subject and object questions, the former retaining SV word order, the latter requiring inversion of subject and first auxiliary (or, as in this case, the dummy operator *do*). To prepare students for this exercise it might be useful to establish the difference between subjects and objects, as well as to check understanding of the verbs used.

10 Some useful classroom questions at beginner/elementary level are:

What does X mean?
How do you spell Y?
How do you say Z in English?
How do you pronounce X?
What's the plural/past/infinitive/opposite, etc. of Y?

At higher levels the following questions can be useful:

What's this called in English?
What do you call a person/thing that...?
What's another way of saying Y?
Does X take a preposition/an infinitive, etc.?
What preposition does Y take?
Is there a *t* in *thistle*, etc.?
What's the verb/noun/adjective from...?
What does Y refer to?

15 The verb phrase

1 'The verb, or the verb phrase is often heavily packed with meaning. This is because we build into it a number of concepts and devices…' (Broughton 1990).

These concepts and devices include:

- events versus states
- time: past versus present
- aspect: progressive versus perfect
- voice: passive versus active
- mood: indicative, subjunctive, imperative (factual, non-factual, directive meanings)
- modality: attitude

2 a) Irregular verbs: *going*; *making*; *begin*; *known*. Compared to regular verbs, like *start*, they do not follow the pattern *start, started, started* in the formation of their infinitive, past form, and past participle respectively:

go	went	gone
make	made	made
begin	began	begun
know	knew	known

b) Auxiliaries: *is*; *are*; *must*. (*Must* is a modal auxiliary.) All the other verbs in the text are full verbs (or lexical verbs). Auxiliaries perform a grammatical function. The primary auxiliaries – *be*; *have*; *do* – are combined with lexical verbs to make different tenses. Modal auxiliaries – *must*; *can*; *should*; etc. – are used to form modal constructions (see Unit 19 for modality).

c) Participles: *going*; *making*; *testing*; *learning* (in *start the students learning…*); *known*. The -*ing* forms are traditionally called 'present participles'; *known* is an example of a 'past participle'.

Note that while *the learning* and *the beginning* are clearly noun phrases, and *going* and *making* are clearly components of verb phrases, it is not so clear whether *testing* and *learning* are more 'noun-like' or more 'verb-like'. (One way of testing the difference is to try substituting a pronoun, e.g. *it*. If you can, then the -*ing* form is noun-like – what is also called a 'gerund'.)

Infinitives: there are no infinitives on their own in the passage – *be known* is, technically, the simple passive infinitive, composed of the infinitive *be* plus the past participle *known*. In combination with *must* it forms a finite verb phrase: *must be known*. Non-finite verbs are not marked for tense, person or number: *to be* is non-finite; (*she*) *was* is finite – past, third person, singular.

Note: an 'unmarked' form of a verb is structurally the most simple form of the verb – the form you would expect to find in a dictionary – and is not 'marked' with any particular contrastive feature such as aspect or modality, tense, person or number.

d) Imperatives: *begin*; *start* (see Task 4 below).

e) Chain verbs: *begin…testing*; *start…learning*. Notice that the second verb in each pair is non-finite. Verbs that go together with non-finite verbs (participles or infinitives) are also called 'catenative' verbs: e.g. I *want to go*; *Stop complaining*.

f) Intransitive verbs: (*is*) *going*. All the other verbs are transitive. Intransitive verbs cannot take an object. Transitive verbs can be used to make passive constructions (*is learned*, *was begun*, etc.), whereas intransitive verbs cannot.

g) Passive constructions are those where the object of the verb becomes the subject of the sentence: *These must be known* (active form – *you must know these*).

h) Verbs that cannot normally be used to talk about events, but refer to states are called 'stative' verbs – for example, *be*; *belong*; *understand*. The only example in the text is *know*. The other verbs are dynamic. Dynamic verbs can be made progressive (e.g. *Students are making mistakes*), whereas stative verbs cannot normally be made progressive, unless they are being used dynamically (e.g. *She is being silly*). For this reason, it is better to talk about stative and dynamic *uses* of verbs. Compare the following:

   – The children *stood* up (dynamic)
   – The house *stood* on a hill (stative)

i) Aspect: verbs marked for progressive aspect are *is…going*; *are…making*. Aspect will be dealt with in more detail in Units 17 and 18.

j) Modality: the one example of a modal construction is *must be known*. Modality is dealt with in Unit 19.

3 Examples of each irregular verb pattern are:

a) bring; catch; think; seek
b) drive; ride
c) ring; drink; sing; spring
d) let; put; shut; set

Any kind of organisation is potentially helpful to learners – or at least, some learners. There is, however, evidence to suggest that irregular verb forms are acquired as individual lexical items, rather than through the application of rules or patterns.

Normally, learners first encounter past participles when they are introduced to the present perfect (*She has done her homework*) at pre–intermediate level. Past participles are also essential in passive constructions (*It was stolen*), which are often introduced at any early intermediate level.

4 The classroom instructions contain the following imperatives: *Look…*;
Pay…; *Try…*; *Don't look…*; *Be…*; *…listen…*; *Sit…*; *Don't move*; *…move…*;
Settle…; *…stay…*

  a) The imperative is formed from the base form of the verb, i.e. the present
     infinitive without *to*.
  b) The negative imperative is formed by placing *don't* (or *do not*) before the
     base form.
  c) Imperatives can have third person subjects, such as *everyone, everybody,
     somebody*; and, more informally, the second person subject pronoun
     you.
  d) Imperatives can be softened by the use of modals, for example, *Could
     you…? Can you…? Would you…?*, as well as the use of politeness
     markers such as *Excuse me*; *…please*.

5 The text includes the following examples of the passive:

  – *she was attacked*: This is the past simple. Jessica is the topic of the
    sentence, as well as of the article as a whole.
  – *was bitten*: This is the past simple. It is taken for granted that it was the
    dog that bit her.
  – *had become infected*: This is not technically a passive construction,
    although the sense is passive. The agent is not mentioned since it is
    obvious what infected the wounds (the microbes/bacteria).
  – *was admitted*: This is the past simple. The actual person who admitted her
    is not important, or not known.
  – *was discharged*: This is the past simple (see the preceding example for an
    explanation).
  – *was told*: This is the past simple. It is not important *who* told her and GP
    has already been mentioned anyway.
  – *is self-employed*: This is the present simple. This could be considered a
    passive construction, although there is no active form **to self-employ*.
  – *was affected*: This is the past simple. There is no particular agent, apart
    from Jessica's general situation, which is obvious and not worth
    mentioning.
  – *were ruined*: This is the past simple. Although bloodstains are mentioned,
    they are not sufficiently 'agentive' to merit placing in the role of subject.
    They did not really do anything.
  – *to be thrown away*: This is the present passive infinitive. It is not
    important, or not known, who threw them away.

     * indicates that this usage is ungrammatical

One way of using a text like this to focus on a language area such as the
passive is for the students first to read it and answer comprehension
questions to extract the gist of the story ('When did the dog attack her?'
'Where was she bitten?', etc.). Then, using word prompts such as *walk,
attack, bite, infect*, students re-write the story from memory. Comparison
with the original text should then show to what extent they can use the
passive appropriately.

6 The stative verbs in these texts are:

a) knows; states; contains
b) measures; weighs; is
c) loves; has; wants; are
d) looked; tasted

Note that with dynamic meanings the agent is actively involved in a specific action (*The man weighed the dog; the dog bit the man*). Stative meanings, on the other hand, identify processes or states of being in which no obvious action takes place (*The dog weighed 10 kilos; the man was angry*). One way of distinguishing between stative and dynamic phrases is to see if they fit into constructions beginning 'What the [subject] does (or did) is (or was)…':

What the man did was weigh the dog.
* What the dog did was weigh 10 kilos.
* What the man did was be angry.
? What the label does is state that each tablet contains 190 milligrams…

* indicates that this usage is ungrammatical
? indicates that this usage is doubtful or unlikely

Stative verbs are customarily divided into these categories:

– relational verbs: *be; belong; have; consist; weigh; measure; cost; state; own; possess*
– verbs of appearance: *seem; look; sound;* etc.
– verbs of involuntary perception: *see; hear; smell; taste; feel*
– verbs of cognition: *know; think; understand; recognise;* etc.
– verbs of liking and disliking: *like; dislike; hate; detest; love; want*

7 ACTIVE

	simple	*progressive*	*perfect*	*perfect progressive*
present	I watch	I am watching	I have watched	I have been watching
past	I watched	I was watching	I had watched	I had been watching
future	I will watch	I will be watching	I will have watched	I will have been watching

PASSIVE

	simple	*progressive*	*perfect*	*perfect progressive*
present	I am watched	I am being watched	I have been watched	——
past	I was watched	I was being watched	I had been watched	——
future	I will be watched	I will be being watched	I will have been watched	——

8 The verb forms are as follows:

've had: present perfect
bought: past simple
'd done: past perfect
've been doing: present perfect progressive
likes: present simple
've finished: present perfect
'll ditch: future simple

16 Time and tense

1 If *tense* is used to refer to the way the basic verb form changes in order to situate the event in a different time frame – past, present, or future – then English has only two tenses: present (*I work*) and past (*I worked*). This does not mean, of course, that future reference is not possible in English: only that the verb is not *inflected* for the future, that is, there is no future verb *ending*. Instead, auxiliary verbs are conscripted to do the job, as in *I will work* or *I am going to work*, etc.

For teaching purposes, however, there are a number of verb phrase combinations that are often loosely called 'tenses': the present progressive, the past perfect, and so on. These are, in fact, simply different combinations of the two basic tenses of English and its two *aspects*, i.e. progressive and perfect. There are eight in all, excluding modal auxiliaries, or sixteen if you count the passive forms.

2 The fact that there is no one-to-one relation between time and tense is, according to Broughton, 'the crux of much confusion about the English tense system. We have the concepts of time; past, present and future. We also use *past*, *present* and *future* to talk about tenses and thereby encourage the false assumption that the present tenses refer only to the present time, and the past tenses refer only to the past time etc. This, of course, is not so'.

(from *The Penguin English Grammar A–Z for Advanced Students* by G. Broughton)

The tense of the verb in both (**a**) and (**b**) is the present:

a) Present tense with future reference
b) Present tense with past reference

Below are some examples of the present tense that don't refer to present time and examples of the past tense that don't refer to past time.

c) Present tense with future reference:

- She's *flying* to Rome tomorrow. (present progressive)
- I'll phone you when I *get* home. (present simple)
- When you'*ve finished* that, how about doing the dishes? (present perfect)

d) Present tense with past reference:

- This man *walks* into a bar, and he *says* to the barman... (present simple)
- Pru *tells* me that you are thinking of retiring. (present simple)
- R.W. Johnson *writes* in a recent article in *The Observer* that... (present simple)
- *Have* you ever *been* to Hungary? (present perfect)

e)   Past tense with present reference:

   - I *was* interested in those earrings in the window. (past simple)
   - *Could* you open the window, please? (past form of *can*)
   - I didn't know you *were* engaged. (past simple)
   - It's time you *were going* to bed. (past progressive)

f)   Past tense with future reference:

   - If no-one *gave* you any presents next Christmas, what would you do? (past simple)

3 A distinction can be made between verbs which describe states (or static situations) and those which describe events (or dynamic situations). Events, in turn, can either be one-off or repeated: repeated events can loosely be called habits. (Verbs can also describe processes.)

a) and **b)** The examples of the present simple and their uses are as follows: *likes*: present state; *listens*: present habit; *knows*: present state; *has*: present state; *saunters*: present event; *tells*: present event; *listen*: present habit.

c)   The uses of the present simple represented by the time lines are as follows:

1   present event
2   present habit
3   present state

4 The concepts corresponding to each example are: 1 – E   2 – B   3 – F   4 – C   5 – A   6 – D

Typical contexts for uses **A–E** are: **A**: scientific facts (*Water boils at 100 degrees*, *Two and two makes four*); characteristics of different peoples, animals, etc. (*Hindus don't eat beef*, *Bears live in caves*); likes and dislikes, beliefs, knowledge, etc. (*Do you like jazz?*, *She still believes in Father Christmas*, *What do you know about cars?*). **B**: daily routine (*I get up round seven*, *We play bridge on Fridays*); habits (*He smokes a pack a day*). **C**: sports commentaries (*Jimmy pots the black*); demonstrating (*I chop the fruit and put it into the blender...*). **D**: anecdotes, jokes (*This man walks into a bar, and he orders...*); plot summaries (*Golaud finds Mélisande weeping beside a pool...*); newspaper headlines and captions (*SIR CHARLES GROVES DIES*). **E**: timetable information (*This bus leaves at 5.35*, *The film starts at 8.30*); itineraries (*We spend two days in Singapore...*).

Typically, learners encounter use **B** at beginner level when they describe their daily routines. Use **A** is also introduced early, for example to give personal information (*I live...*) and to talk about likes and dislikes. Use **E** features in many beginners' courses as well. Uses **C** and **D**, however, are reserved for much later, and are often not included in courses until an advanced level.

5 a) This is a transcribed spoken anecdote. In the present simple it has a timeless quality, befitting an urban legend. Transposed into the past, it sounds more like a specific, remembered incident.

b) This is a diary entry. Again, the present simple gives a sense of immediacy, as if the events are fresh in the writer's mind.

c) This is a biographical note. As it is written, it implies Baker is still alive. In the past, it implies the contrary.

The use of the past tense has the effect of 'distancing' the events, usually in time, although it could also be said that the use of the past for unreal or hypothetical events and states (*I wish I lived in the country*) is also a form of distancing. The past is also used to establish social distance, as in *I was wondering if you could...?* and *Could you...?*

Some writers on grammar argue, therefore, that the fundamental difference between the so-called present tense and the so-called past tense is nothing to do with time at all: the 'past tense' is simply the 'remote' form. According to this view, the so-called present simple is simply the unmarked form of the verb – the form of the verb used when no distancing is required.

The more conventional view is that the 'basic' meaning of the present tense is present time reference, and the 'basic' meaning of the past tense is past time reference. In other words, the cases where there is a mismatch between time and tense are simply exceptions to a general rule, or, examples of the 'secondary' meanings of these tenses.

6 The past simple verbs in the extract are: *hurried*: past habit; *seemed*: past state; *gave up*: past event; *accepted*: past event; *expected*: past state; *received*: past habit.

7 b) Joke: If it is a narrative, there will be a high frequency of past forms (including the past progressive to provide a background to the events), unless it is told in the present (see comment on Task 4 above). Sequencing devices (such as *And then ...*, *at which point...*) and cohesive ties (such as *so...*, *but...*) are likely to co-occur.

c) Weather report: Where the weather of the past day or night is being reported, the past simple may be used (*Rain fell over Scotland during much of the day*). Of course, the forecast will use future verb forms. Associated language might include time expressions (*this morning, during the night*) and place expressions (*in the north-east, on the coast*).

d) Complaint: The past tense is likely when establishing the circumstances both of the purchase (*I bought this pullover here last week...*) and of the problem (*...and when I washed it, it shrank*). Logical connectors, such as *but* and *however* are likely to occur in this context, as well as time clauses (*When..., as soon as...*).

e) Holiday postcard: Past forms are likely, in conjunction with time adverbials (*Yesterday we went to see the Olympic stadium*). Other verb structures that might occur are the present progressive (*We're having a lovely time*) and the present perfect (*I've met some interesting people...*).

f)   Film review: The plot of the film is likely to be related in the present simple, not the past. Some biographical or background information might be written using the past, but this is not a context in which you would expect a high frequency of past forms.

g)   News broadcast: This is likely to have a high frequency of past forms, in conjunction with expressions of time and place. Note, however, that news is often introduced using the present perfect (*There has been a military coup in...*) before the details are elaborated in sequence, and in the past.

h)   Insurance claim: Any account of an accident or incident that prompted the claim would be written in the past, including the past perfect to relate events retrospective to the main event. Sequencing devices and other cohesive ties would co-occur (*I had just parked my car and was crossing the road, when...*).

The fact that there are certain text types in which there is likely to be a high frequency of past simple verb phrases suggests that such texts might be a useful vehicle for introducing and practising this structure. It would also be helpful to draw the learners' attention to those linguistic items that tend to co-occur with the past, including other past verb structures, sequencing and linking devices and time adverbials. By these means, learners could be encouraged to produce original texts of the same type.

8   The examples of the past perfect are: *We'd bought; hadn't got round; I'd been nagging; Ian had put.*

9   All three explanations apply satisfactorily to the examples, but the first two do not necessarily explain why the past perfect is used in preference to the past simple. The *COBUILD* explanation leaves it unclear what 'a particular time in the past' is, i.e. the point of orientation of the story – in this case *installed*. Close is perhaps nearer the mark when he suggests that the past perfect is used only where *not* to use it would result in ambiguity. However, this suggests that the use of the past perfect in *After Ian had put...* is redundant, since the past simple (*After Ian put...*) would not be ambiguous. Lewis captures the retrospective nature of the past perfect, but none of these explanations makes it very clear how the past perfect and past simple inter-relate in texts, i.e. beyond the level of the single sentence (see Task 10).

10   The verb phrases that refer to past time are: *was working; discovered; had...trained; had (a degree); had...used; heard; realised; was something; fitted; enrolled; completed; was...hired.*

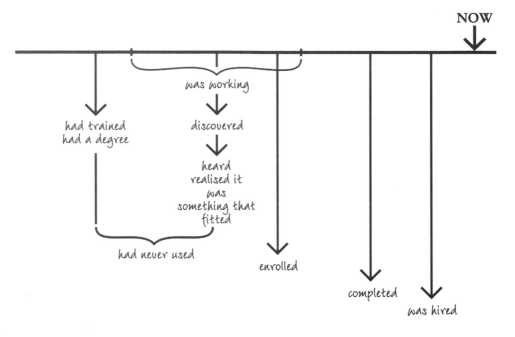

11 The corrections and their explanations are:

a) *When we arrived home and I opened the door some other friends were already inside. They had prepared a party and I was surprised.* The writer has used the passive where the active was required (*had been prepared*) and the active where the passive was required (*I was surprising*).

b) *I didn't realise it was so late and the underground had stopped working* (or:…*was no longer working*). What is best here is either a past perfect, to refer to a point further back in time, or the progressive to describe a temporary (non-) state that existed around the time of the 'realisation'. It's also probable that the context requires *I hadn't realised….*

c) *When we arrived, the train had left the station and we waited three long hours before the next train arrived.* The past perfect is obligatory, to denote which event preceded which.

d) *My mother told me that my boyfriend, Andrew, had had an accident and he was in the General Hospital.* As (c) above. This is also an example of reported speech, which often requires 'backshift' of tenses, in order to make it clear whether the events reported precede the reporting or co-occur with it.

e) *It seems difficult to believe that I arrived here two weeks ago.* This is active, not passive; the past perfect is not necessary (unless the verb in the main clause is supposed to be *seemed*).

f) *That afternoon my cousin killed his mother's cat because the cat was in the road and my cousin wasn't looking* (or …*didn't see it*). This is active, not passive (*was killed*). If the dynamic verb *look* is used, the past progressive is necessary, since it was an action in progress at the time of the killing; if the stative verb *see* is used, the past simple is required.

17 Progressive aspect

1 The interview contains the following examples of progressive and perfect aspect: *has…been published*: present perfect; *I've had*: present perfect; *have read*: present perfect; *are you working*: present progressive; *I've been working*: present perfect progressive.

2 Perhaps the single common concept – and, hence, primary meaning of the progressive – is that of something being 'in progress'. Notions of 'temporariness', 'incompleteness' and 'limited duration' may be secondary meanings, or implications, of this primary meaning. In other words, when we talk about things 'in progress' it is often the fact that these things *are* temporary and/or incomplete, but it is not *necessarily* the case. For instance, does example (**d**) refer to an incomplete situation; does example (**e**) refer to a temporary situation?

3 The difference in meaning is as follows:

In (**a**) there remains the possibility that the woman didn't complete the crossing of the road: *I saw the woman crossing the road but she was knocked down by a bus before she could reach the other side.*

Sentence (**b**) suggests that the 'crossing' was seen in its entirety. The following is unlikely: *I saw the woman cross the road but she was knocked down by a bus before she could reach the other side.*

These examples suggest that aspect relates to non-finite verb forms too, in the sense that a distinction is maintained between events seen in their entirety and which are indivisible (base form: *cross*), and events seen as being in progress and having successive stages (*-ing* form: *crossing*).

4 1 situations in progress at the moment of speaking: **g**
    2 temporary situations in the present: **b**
    3 changing or developing situations: **a**
    4 repeated events or situations: **h**
    5 background to an event: **f**
    6 a present arrangement for a future event: **j**

All these uses share the basic notion of a situation in progress in the present, if the present is considered very generally as 'not the past'. Example (**j**) is perhaps the hardest to fit in to the pattern, unless we consider an arrangement as an event that has already been set in progress, and remains in progress until it is executed.

5 Typical situations or contexts for these uses include:

    1 Situations in progress at the moment of speaking: describing on-going events to someone not present, e.g. in a postcard or over the phone; interrupting activities in progress, e.g. bursting in on a party; complaining to neighbours about the noise they are making: *What are you doing?*

2 Temporary situations in the present e.g. studying or reading habits: *What are you reading at the moment/these days?*; preparations for a major event, e.g. the Olympic Games or an election: *I'm doing research into…*

3 Changing or developing situations: similar to (2), but with an emphasis on trends, developments, e.g. rising prices, environmental change, marketing and fashion trends, using figures or graphs.

4 Repeated events or situations e.g. irritating habits: *He's always/forever complaining…* (Note that, contrary to what some teaching materials suggest, this use of the present progressive is not restricted to irritating habits.)

6 The sentences, with past progressive verbs converted to past simple are:

a) *In December 1989, 208 English hotels were built, extended or refurbished*. This suggests that the building, etc. was completed in the month in question.

b) *I put the milk bottles out when I heard the planes*. This suggests that the person first heard the planes, and then put the milk bottles out, perhaps as a result of hearing the planes. This reverses the actual order of events. It could also be interpreted – in the absence of context as a habitual activity: read *whenever* for *when*.

c) *Everyone around me cried and screamed*. This suggests they did this just once, or intermittently, rather then continuously as implied in the progressive.

These examples demonstrate some of the implications of describing events 'in progress': incompleteness and (limited) duration, as well as showing the discourse function of the progressive to provide a background to events, as in example (**b**).

7 The past progressive, as noted above, is used in narrative to provide the background to the events that constitute the story itself. In this sense, the participle is used almost adjectivally – compare the difference between *It was wet* and *It was raining*; or the difference between *I was asleep* and *I was sleeping*.

This is generally not a difficult use for learners to understand, especially if they are introduced to the term 'background'. It is probably easier to introduce and practise the past progressive in this kind of narrative context, than to practise it in isolation as if it were a separate 'tense'. Some EFL materials introduce the concept of 'interrupted past' to explain the past progressive, but it should be clear that the background situation is not always interrupted (in the sense of unfinished): *I was having a bath when the phone rang, so I didn't bother answering it*.

An activity that lends itself to the practising past progressive (as well as the past simple) is the game 'Alibis', when two or more students are quizzed separately about a crime that they allegedly committed at a clearly established time. Any discrepancy in their story (which they have jointly prepared) proves them guilty.

18 Perfect aspect

1 The sentences contain the following perfect verb structures:

  a) I've had: present perfect simple active
  b) will have increased: future perfect simple active
  c) I have experienced: present perfect simple
  d) she has been rehearsing: present perfect progressive active
  e) had been issued: past perfect passive

The common aspectual feature is that the event or state is viewed as occurring in a period of time up to and including the point of orientation – the present moment (present perfect), or a past point of time (past perfect), or a future point of time (future perfect). Some writers talk about the period of time as being *retrospective* or *anterior* to the point of orientation.

2 and 3 The examples of the present perfect and their categorisation are as follows: *I've found*: Swan's category B; *I've had*: B; *They've (already) arranged*: B; *have you worked*: A; *I've been*: A; *we've (never) met*: B; *I've (always) entered*: could be A or B; *we have met*: B; *I've offended*: B.

(Note that *How strange we've never met* is a finished event that *didn't* happen in the period from then until now.)

I've always entered by number fifteen could be interpreted as a number of finished past events (A), or actions continuing up to the present (B). This demonstrates that even Swan's very clear distinction can get blurred. But all examples are consistent with the definition of the present perfect as events and situations occurring in a period of time and up to and including the present.

4 Perfect of result: **d**
Experiential perfect: **b**
Perfect of persistent situation: **c**
Perfect of recent past: **a**

5 The following sentences are unacceptable:

*She's been here last year.
*She's been here two weeks ago.
*She's been here at three o'clock.
*She's been here yesterday morning.

None of these is acceptable since the use of the present perfect does not allow time expressions that situate the event in a definite time in the past. Note that *She's been here this morning* is only acceptable if it is still morning at the time of speaking.

6 The tenses are as follows:

survives: present simple. This is typically used in headlines to state facts and give immediacy.

has been attacked: present perfect. This is used to announce a past event that is still thought to be relevant to the present, hence newsworthy. There is no time adverbial to situate the event in the definite past.

lived: past simple. This is used, perhaps, because there is an implied time sequence – the 'living' took place *after* the attack, and therefore not at an indefinite time.

suffered, attacked: past simple. This is used to narrate the events of the incident, now fixed definitely in the past by use of the time expression *on Tuesday*.

7 Some example situations for presenting the four uses of the present perfect are:

- Perfect of result: e.g. a person who has changed (*You've lost weight, You've cut your hair*); or a place that has changed (*They've pulled down the old post office*); talking about jobs or chores done (*I've typed those letters*).
- Experiential perfect: e.g. talking about travel experiences; job interviews/talking about work experience.
- Perfect of persistent situation: e.g. personal information (*I've lived here all my life, How long have you been married?*); talking about possessions (*I've had this watch since I was little*).
- Perfect of recent past: e.g. news commentaries (*The Queen has just stepped out of her car*); the day's activities (*I've been to the gym, I've bathed the baby*).

8 The exercise focuses on the use of the present perfect progressive (*I've been getting ready*) to suggest the incompleteness of activities that started in the past and continued to the present. This contrasts with the present perfect (*I've packed the cases*) which is used when the activity is seen in its entirety, hence completed.

Note that the implication of incompleteness is *only* an implication and that it is possible to think of examples where the present perfect progressive is used for actions that are clearly completed, as in *I've been sleeping*. The primary meaning of the present perfect progressive, as opposed to the present perfect simple, is that the activity is viewed as having been in progress, as being a process (its progressive meaning) and that it occurred in a period of time leading up to, and including, the present (its perfect meaning).

9 Here are some comments on each rule:

1 This is true (e.g. *I've lived here all my life*). As a rule it is incomplete, however, since the present perfect can also be used to talk about finished events (e.g. *I've been to Japan*).

2 This is not true (e.g. *We've met before*).

3 This is generally a good rule of thumb. When referring to past events, if the time is specified, either explicitly or by context, the past simple is preferred: (*I've written two songs* – time is not specified; *I wrote two songs last week* – time is specified). One 'exception' to the rule is when the specified time is also the time of speaking (e.g. *I've written two songs this week* means it is *this week* at the time of speaking). In spoken English *I've written two songs last week* may occur, with a short pause between the two propositions:*I've written two songs – last week*.

4 This contains an element of truth but is misleading. The present perfect is often used for recent actions, but can equally well be used for actions which happened in the distant past (e.g. *Mt Egmont has erupted only once in the last 10,000 years*).

5 This is true – especially when *announcing* news, as opposed to detailing it.

6 This is true – but, again, not when the time or sequence is being specified.

19 Modality

The 'pure' modals are considered to be those that fulfil all the conditions in the left-hand column of the chart in 2 below. They are nine in number: *will, shall, can, may*; their respective 'past' forms: *would, should, could, might*; and *must*.

1 Of the nine true modals, the following appear in the text: *can, may, will, must, should*. The marginal modal *need* also appears, as does the form *be able*, which has modal meaning.

2 The completed chart looks like this:

	can	must	need	want
It takes the infinitive without '*to*'	✔	✔	✔ and ✘	✘
There is no special third person form	✔	✔	✔ and ✘	✘
The negative is formed simply by adding '*not*'	✔	✔	✔ and ✘	✘
The question is formed by inversion	✔	✔	✔ and ✘	✘
It cannot be preceded by other auxiliaries	✔	✔	✔ and ✘	✘
There is a past form	✔	✘	✔	✔

In the case of *need*, the features apply when it functions as a modal auxiliary verb, but usually only in questions and negatives (e.g. *Need he...? You needn't...*). By contrast, in the sentence *You will need to complete an application form, need* is preceded by an auxiliary and takes the infinitive with *to. Need* is, therefore, classified as a semi-modal, since it sometimes behaves like a modal auxiliary, and sometimes like a lexical verb.

Must has all the features of a modal verb, but it lacks a past form. There are, then, nine modal operators, ten, if we add *ought*, which only differs from the others in taking the infinitive with *to*.

3 Even in English there are a number of ways of expressing modality apart from using modal verbs. For example:

adverbs: probably; perhaps; maybe
adjectives: it's likely that; it's possible that
participles: you're allowed to; it's forbidden to
lexical verbs: I advise you to; I suggest that you

(Note that some of these alternatives are characteristic of more formal or written English.) Learners whose mother tongue relies less on modal auxiliaries than, for example, lexical verbs, or conditional or subjunctive constructions, may have difficulties both with the syntax and the meaning of modal verbs in English.

4 The corrections and their explanations are as follows:

a) *don't have to* instead of *shouldn't*: *Should* and *have to* share the sense of 'obligation' in their affirmative forms. Their negatives are quite different in meaning, however, 'no obligation' being realised by *don't have to*, not *shouldn't*.

b) *had to* instead of *must*: There is no past form of *must* – *had to* is used instead.

c) *had to* instead of *should to*: *Should* expresses obligation in the present only, not in the past and *should* does not take the infinitive with *to*.

d) *Was able to* (or *managed to*) instead of *could*: In the past *could* refers to general ability (*I could ski when I was younger*), but for ability on a single occasion, *was able to* (or *managed to*) is used.

e) *can* or *will be able to* instead of *will can*: There is no future form of *can*.

f) *I'll have to* instead of *I'll be able to*: Obligation, not ability, is indicated here.

5 The completed chart looks like this:

	can can't	could couldn't	may may not	might mightn't	should shouldn't	must mustn't
likelihood/ probability	✔(1)	✔(2)	✔(3)	✔(4)	✔(5)	✔(6)
ability	✔(7)	✔(8)	✗	✗	✗	✗
permission	✔(9)	✔(10)	✔(11)	✔(12)	✗	✗
prohibition	✔(13)	✔(14)	✔(15)	✗	✔(16)	✔(17)
obligation/ duty	✗	✗	✗	✗	✔(18)	✔(19)

The numbers in brackets refer to the example sentences in the following list.

Example sentences:

1 It can't be five o'clock! Can he really be 70?
2 It could rain tomorrow.
3 She may have been held up in the traffic.
4 You might be right.
5 They should be there by now.
6 It must have been the fish.
7 Can you touch your toes?
8 She could speak three languages by the time she was six.
9 Can I leave early today?
10 He asked me if he could smoke in here.
11 You may sit if you wish.
12 Might I have a look at your photos?
13 I'm sorry, you can't eat in here.
14 They told her she couldn't take photos.
15 Dictionaries may not be used in the examination.
16 You shouldn't really do that, you know.
17 You mustn't tell a soul.
18 We should write and apologise.
19 I must get a move on.

The text in Task 1 contains the following examples of modals:

probability: *should (expect)*; *may*
ability: *can*; **be able*
prohibition: *cannot*
obligation/duty: *must*; **need*; *should (be directed to)*

*these are not full modals.

6 b) *could*: extrinsic (probability)
  c) *must*: intrinsic (obligation)
  d) *should*: extrinsic (probability)
  e) *can*: intrinsic (ability)
  f) *can't*: extrinsic (probability)
  g) *may*: extrinsic (probability)
  h) *should*: intrinsic (obligation)
  i) *cannot*: intrinsic (prohibition)
  j) *could (have given)*: extrinsic (probability); *couldn't*: intrinsic (ability)

7 The answers to the exercise are:

you aren't allowed to: you mustn't
you are required to: you must/you have to
it isn't necessary to: you don't have to
you are obliged to: you must/you have to
you don't need to: you don't have to
it's forbidden to: you mustn't

Notice that, for the purposes of this exercise, no distinction is made between *must* and *have to*. The difference is subtle: *have to* is used for obligation that is externally imposed (e.g. by some person or organisation), while *must* is used for obligation that is subjective, or self-imposed.

All the above expressions are alternative ways of expressing obligation (or lack of obligation) and prohibition.

8 a) Here are some examples of making a request using modal verbs: *Can you / could you / will you / would you...open the window? Can I / could I / may I / might I...borrow your pen? I would like to / should like to leave early, please.*

b) Here is a list of functions using *can*: asking and giving permission; making requests; offering; and, in the negative, refusing permission/prohibiting; refusing a request. To these functions could be added notional areas, such as talking about ability; talking about theoretical possibility.

c) Here is an example of a functional syllabus for beginners that uses only modal verbs:

asking permission:	Can I...?
making requests:	Can you...?
inviting:	Can you...?
refusing:	I can't...
recommending/advising:	You should / You must...
expressing obligation:	I have to...
offering:	I'll...
ordering (food):	I'll have...
suggesting:	What shall we do?
expressing possibility:	I may be...
expressing certainty:	It must be... / It can't be...
expressing general ability:	I can... / I could...
predicting:	It will...

9 According to data in the Birmingham Corpus (quoted in Carter and McCarthy 1988), these are the modals ranked in frequency of occurrence. The number represents the position each word occupies in a ranking order of frequency. Thus *would*, which is 44, is the 44th most frequent word in the corpus. (The corpus consists of some 20 million words of text, both spoken and written, although predominantly the latter.)

would	44
can	60
could	71
will	77
may	118
should	133
must	141
might	155
shall	(does not occur in the first 200 words)

The high frequency of *would* may seem surprising, but perhaps reflects the wide range of important meanings it conveys (see Unit 21). The relative low frequency of *shall* should not be surprising, since it has a very restricted usage (mainly for asking and for making suggestions) and in some varieties of English it is virtually non-existent.

Unfortunately, the corpus data does not specify which meanings of each modal are most frequent, so it is of only limited use in assigning priorities for teaching. Nevertheless, the fact that auxiliaries like *will* and *could* are more frequently occurring in English than, say, *did* (95), or the fact that *may* and *should* are more frequent than *does* (188), suggest that all the modals (apart from *shall*) deserve a place on a beginners' syllabus, not least because of the important meanings they convey.

20 Futurity

1 Grammarians differ as to whether *will* represents the English future or not (see below), but clearly there is no verb form marked for the future in the way *they walked* is marked for the past, hence the claim that there is no future tense in English. Instead, there are a variety of verb structures that can, in certain contexts, have future reference. In the extracts they are:

   a) *is getting married*: present progressive; *will tie*: sometimes called the future simple.
   b) *going to stay*: marginal modal *going to*; *may change*: modal *may*; *will have to* : future simple.
   c) *returns*: present simple; *will be conducting*: future progressive; *plays*: present simple.

Not included in these extracts, but also exponents of futurity, are:

to be: *The Queen is to open parliament next week.*

future perfect: *100,000 people in Britain will have died from AIDS by the year 2000.*

2 Some grammarians (e.g. Comrie 1985) take the line that, since *will* can make clear predictions about the future without a hint of modal 'colour', as in *Edward will be 32 tomorrow*, it is possible to talk about a 'future tense'. Others (e.g. Palmer 1988) argue that the 'pure future' use of *will* is relatively rare, and that *going to* has as much, if not more, claim to be considered a tense. *Will*, according to this view, is simply another modal auxiliary that, like *may*, can have future reference, but can just as well have present reference – in fact, in its sense of 'is willing', *always* has present reference.

Will/won't is used in the following ways in the examples:

   a) *Will* is used here with present reference, not future. This is the extrinsic use of *will* (see Unit 19, Task 5 for an explanation of extrinsic and intrinsic), meaning predictability, or high probability.
   b) *Will* is used here with future reference to make a prediction – extrinsic use.
   c) There is no future reference here. This is the intrinsic use of *won't*, referring to the volition of the subject and meaning 'is not willing to', i.e. she refuses to.
   d) There is no future reference here. This example is like example (**a**). This use of *will* for predictable routines is common in English, as is the past form *would* for talking about past habits.
   e) This is like example (**b**).
   f) Like (**a**), this is the extrinsic use, referring to predictability or high probability. Notice that the reference is to the past.
   g) There is no future reference. This is the intrinsic use of *will*, expressing the speaker's volition, and can be paraphrased as 'I intend to…' or 'I am deciding to…'. Note that the intention is coincident with the time of speaking, even if the intended action is in the future. (Compare this with the sentence *It will rain tomorrow*.)

h) There is no future reference. *Will not* is used here in the intrinsic sense to refer to volition ('is not willing to'), although an argument could be made for the extrinsic use, meaning 'it's not likely/predictable that...' This demonstrates that there is some overlap of meaning between prediction and volition.

i) There is no future reference. The stressed form of *will* denotes strong volition, or insistence.

j) This is a prediction with future reference, retrospective to a future point in time (the year 2000). This form is commonly called the future perfect. (Compare this example with (f), which has the same form, but which has past reference.)

To summarise, then, *will*, like the other modal auxiliaries (whose syntactic features it shares) has two main areas of meaning: extrinsic (predictability and prediction) and intrinsic (strong and weak volition). It is only in the 'prediction' sense that *will* has purely future reference. There is some crossover, however, between futurity and volition, especially in first person uses, such as *I'll phone you tomorrow* which could be read as 'My phoning you tomorrow is a predicted event', or 'It is my intention, now, to phone you tomorrow'.

3 Extract (**b**) comes from a magazine horoscope, and (**e**) from a newspaper weather forecast. Other likely contexts for *will* used for prediction are: on the sports pages of newspapers, in advance of sporting events; in news reports in advance of political events such as elections and summits; on the diary page of newspapers when, for example, royal engagements are announced; forecasts of economic trends, such as some publications produce at the beginning of each year.

4 The first three examples all use *will*, but suggest different degrees of certainty. The speaker's attitude is conveyed not by the choice of verb structure, but by associated adverbials (*of course, probably, perhaps*, etc.). Speakers also have the choice of using other modal constructions to convey degrees of probability (*may, might, could*). In spoken English uncertainty can be conveyed by prosodic features, such as hesitations and rising intonation. If, sometimes, certain verb structures seem to imply a greater degree of certainty, it is probably due more to pragmatic, i.e. contextual, reasons than to semantic ones. Thus, for example, *The Queen opens Parliament tomorrow* has more authority than *Bert is going to open the garage*. But, it is quite possible to say *All being well, the Queen opens Parliament tomorrow* and *Bert is going to open the garage if it's the last thing he does*.

Thus, certainty is conveyed by co-textual and contextual features, not by the choice of verb structure.

The other common misconception, that the choice of future structure is determined by how *soon* the future event is expected to take place, is not borne out by the examples in Task 4. Despite the variety of exponents used, the election had the same 'degree of nearness' for each of the respondents. Of course, there is a high probability that future events that are already 'in progress', e.g. plans and arrangements, will happen soon, since we don't normally make plans in the long term. But it is not wrong for a 25-year-old to say *I'm going to retire when I'm sixty*.

5   Future events can be seen as having a present connection if they form the end point of a process that is already 'in progress'. When talking about arrangements that have already been made, we use the present progressive as in examples (a) and (b). Where an intention has been made and is now being reported, as in example (c), *going to* is used. Similarly, where there is present evidence for a prediction, the use of *going to* suggests this connection with the present, as in examples (d) and (e).

6   a)   As we have just seen, people are likely to use progressive forms to report arrangements that are 'in progress': *I can't meet you on Thursday – I'm having lunch with my boss*. They may also use the future progressive for activities that will be in progress at a certain time: *At five o'clock I'll be driving home*. Assuming they find a mutually convenient time, they may then make the arrangement using *will* and/or *shall*: *Shall I meet you in front of Debenhams?*

   b)   Timetable information is often conveyed in the present simple, since it is seen as being generally true for past, present and future. Thus, we might ask: *When does the next train leave for Luton?*

   c)   In this situation the person will probably be reporting previously-made intentions/decisions, and hence use *going to*: *We're going to have this wall knocked out.*

Each of these situations might provide a suitable context in which to practise the items in question.

7   We have seen that neither certainty nor proximity can account for the choice of future exponent. What, then, *does* account for the choice?

The choice is determined by how the speaker 'sees' the future event and the circumstances that have brought it about. In other words, choosing the future verb form is like choosing between present simple and present perfect – it is a question of aspect. For example, if we see the future as being somehow tied to the present, we are likely to choose a present tense form to express it. We also choose a present tense form if the event is seen as having the status of a fact – because it is timetabled, for example – and is therefore generally true for past, present and future: *The train leaves at 6.15 (tomorrow)*.

The answers to the task are as follows:

a) 5   **b)** 3   c) 4   **d)** 1   e) 2   f) 7   g) 6

8 *Will* and *going to* can both be used to express intentionality. *Will* is generally used when *making* decisions, while *going to* is used to *report* decisions already made. This, at least, is the point underlying this particular activity. Of course, in real life the pools winners would probably not have waited until the celebratory dinner to make their plans: it might have been better to have shown them at the very moment of hearing their good news. Also, the fact that each person precedes their 'decision' with *I (don't) think…* suggests either that *I'll* collocates exclusively with *think*, or that *will* is used when the speaker is not sure – exactly the (wrong) hypothesis that many learners reach independently. It would have been less misleading to have had at least one of the speakers saying *I know! I'll…*

A practice situation might be to establish some group outing or party. In groups the students have to decide: where, when, who is bringing what; who they'll invite, etc. They must then report these decisions to the rest of the class.

9 This structure is often used to describe a future situation that is seen as a 'matter-of-course', i.e. independent of human volition. *I'll get the plaster off…* sounds as if the speaker is deciding at the moment of speaking, with the implication, perhaps, that he or she will take the plaster off. *I'll be getting the plaster off* implies that this event is pre-arranged and is happening in the normal course of events. The same applies to examples (**b**), (**e**) and (**f**) – this last being a decision *not* to do something, as opposed to a refusal, which would be the implication of the sentence: *The House of Love won't release 'Shake and Crawl' as a single.*

10 Activity 1 is a useful way of 'personalising' the future, and it is true that in this context *I expect* and *probably* collocate more comfortably with *will* than with *going to*. But there is the danger that the exercise reinforces the idea that the distinction between *will* and *going to* is solely one of degree of certainty.

Activity 2 also presents a useful 'rule of thumb', but, by presenting de-contextualised sentences that are either 'right' or 'wrong', it creates a false distinction. There are bound to be a number of grey areas: and it is not impossible to imagine contexts in which *I go to the theatre tomorrow* would be quite acceptable. Unfortunately, in order to isolate different semantic concepts, it often seems necessary to create artificial distinctions. Rather than making these very fine distinctions, it may be easier – and less questionable – to establish an association between different ways of expressing the future and different *contexts* and *texts*. Thus, the present simple with future reference is often found in travel itineraries, and the kinds of discourse associated with relaying travel plans. By highlighting and practising that association, it may not be necessary to provide exercises such as Activity 2.

21 Hypothetical meaning and conditionals

1 In the following utterances the speaker is hypothesising:

if we could go (line 2)
even if we could get there, we'd have to live (line 4)
we'd need food and fuel and things (lines 4–5)
We could find enough to keep us going for a time until we could grow things…It'd be hard (lines 6–7)
If it had only been something we could fight (lines 8–9)

The implication is that the situation will not occur because the opposite state of affairs is the case:

if we could go (but we can't)
even if we could get there (but we can't), *we'd have to live*
If it had only been something we could fight (but it wasn't)

The following also express a kind of hypothetical meaning, but the hypothetical situation is implied by means of an unstated *if*-clause:

I'd rather have to work night and day to keep alive (line 12) (if I were given the choice)
I'd rather die trying to get away (line 13) (if I were given the choice)

This is a way of expressing preferences.
On the other hand: *I shall go mad if I have to sit here doing nothing any longer* (lines 10–11) is what is called an 'open (or real) condition', because the situation is considered a real possibility: *I shall go mad if I have to sit here doing nothing any longer* (which I may or may not do).

2 A conditional clause states the condition on which a possible or hypothetical event depends. Conditional clauses often begin with *if*, and are subordinate clauses – although in speech and literature, as in the case of *If it had only been something we could fight*, they sometimes stand on their own:

…if we could go
…even if we could get there
If it had only been something we could fight.
…if I have to sit here doing nothing any longer

3 The text contains the following examples of a modal in the main clause:

even if we could get there, <u>we'd</u> (we would) have to live
I <u>shall</u> go mad if I have to sit here doing nothing any longer

4 The examples of *would* that express conditional meaning are:

b) *...would have meant coming to live in London*
c) *I would, of course, vote Conservative...*
f) *I would advise would-be patients...* (Conditional *would* is commonly used as a politeness marker: its hypothetical meaning makes it less direct. The *if*-clause *If I were asked...* or *If it were up to me...* is implicit.)
g) *...I hope someone would do the same...*

Note that, according to the *COBUILD* corpus, *would* is the most frequently used modal verb in English, and that in at least half of its occurrences *would* is used to talk of events which are of a hypothetical nature. (See Willis 1990.)

The other uses of *would* are as follows:

– to talk about predictable behaviour in the past or describe past habits:
a) *...we would do a gig...*
g) *Sometimes I would give them food...*

– to talk about past willingness (or unwillingness):
e) *Buckingham Palace would not be drawn...*

– to report what was said, i.e. the past form of *will*:
d) *Major Phillips said Mark would continue...*

– to talk about the future in the past, i.e. from a point of time in the past, talking about what was then the future:
h) *...I already knew I wouldn't see her...*

5 Some of these examples can be considered variants of the basic conditional types as described in the Stannard Allen extract. Others are not really classifiable in these terms, and are often loosely grouped as 'mixed conditionals', since they incorporate elements of the different types. (Note that all these examples were collected from authentic written sources.)

a) Type 1.
b) Type 2 – although *could*, not *would*, is used in the main clause. The rule, perhaps, should be adjusted to allow for all past modal verbs in this slot.
c) This does not fit any of the three types.
d) Nor does this, since there is no subordinate *if*-clause, although the meaning is conditional, and equivalent to 'If you get me out, I'll give you Terry Waite'.
e) Type 3.
f) This is sometimes called the 'Type 0 conditional': it consists of a main clause in the present, and an *if*-clause also in the present.
g) This is a deviant form of Type 3, minus a main clause. Strictly speaking it should be *If I'd thought...* where *I'd* stands for *I had*, rather than *If I'd have thought...*, where *I'd* stands for *I would*. This variety is quite common in spoken English however, and, as MacAndrew (1991) points out, it is gaining currency in the written form as well.
h) Type 1, in form, at least. The time reference in the *if*-clauses is not future, however, but present: the use of *will* to mean 'it is predictable that...'.

i) A mixture of Type 1 in the *if*-clause and Type 2 in the main clause.
j) Type 2 in form, but not in meaning, since this in fact refers not to an imaginary situation, but a real past (habitual) state of affairs, meaning 'On those occasions when I was in the situation of having no money, I was in the habit of going shop-lifting...'
k) Type 2.
l) Type 2. The use of *would* in the *if*-clause is not hypothetical, but the past of volitional *will*, meaning 'If someone *were willing* to dye greengage jam...'. This is common in business letters, for example, *If you would return the enclosed form...*

6 The exercise focuses on Type 2 conditionals, apart from the first example, which focuses on Type 1. As we have seen in the previous activity, this simple three-type classification doesn't take into account the full variety of conditional constructions, and may give the learner the impression that any form that doesn't fit is automatically 'incorrect'. It may be less misleading to ask, therefore, 'Which two of the following sentences does not fit the Type 1 or Type 2 pattern?' Finally, any judgement about correctness or not has to be based on our interpretation of what the writer or speaker *meant*. In the absence of any context, this is virtually impossible: all the sentences may be correct, or all may be wrong.

7 Because of the difficulties of classifying the wide variety of conditional constructions into groups according to the verb phrase, it is probably easier to adopt a simpler, two-way distinction. For example, look at these two *if*-clauses (from the John Wyndham extract at the beginning of the unit):

(I shall go mad) if I have to sit here

even if we could get there (we'd have to live)

The first of these expresses a 'real' condition (*if I have to sit here* means 'I may well have to sit here'), while the second expresses an 'unreal' condition, i.e. one that is contrary to fact. The implication of *if we could get there* is that 'we can't get there'. Conditional sentences, then, can express either a real condition or an unreal condition. Both real and unreal conditions can refer to past and present/future. For example:

	real	*unreal*
present/future (non-past)	if it snows, what will you do?	if it snowed tomorrow, what would you do?
past	if it snowed (when you were young), what did you do?	if it had snowed (last week), what would you have done?

Accordingly, the extracts in Task 5 divide up thus:
Real: **a, c, d, f, h, j.** (Note that (j) refers to real past time.)
Unreal: **b, e, g, k, l.**

Example (**i**) is the only truly 'mixed' conditional, since it combines both real (*If he never returns...*) and unreal (*...I would not be greatly surprised*) elements.

The tense of the verb in the *if*-clause in unreal conditions is moved back one. Thus, if the reference is to a hypothetical situation in the present or future (non-past), the verb is usually in the past. If the hypothetical situation is in the past, the verb is in the past perfect.

8 Other language functions often realised by conditional constructions include (in the order you might teach them):

Function	Example	Real/Unreal
promises	If you pass the exam, I'll buy dinner.	real
instructions/rules	If you drop the ball, you are out.	real
advice	If you leave now, you'll get a seat.	real
	If I were you, I'd see a doctor.	unreal
imagining/wishing	If I had a room of my own, I'd be really happy.	unreal
regretting	If only I hadn't lost my temper!	unreal
making threats	If you don't go, I'll phone the police!	real

9 Other ways of expressing unreal meaning using the hypothetical past include:

I wish I *hadn't said* that.
I'd rather you *didn't* smoke in here.
It's time you *went* home.
If only she *had phoned*.
You look as if you *had lost* something.
Just imagine if we*'d won*!

22 The noun phrase

1 a) Proper nouns have unique reference, that is, they refer to a person or thing, of which there is no other. Personal and geographical names are typical proper nouns. They do not usually allow the plural nor are they preceded by an article (*the*, *a*). All proper nouns have capital letters, but not all words with capital letters are proper nouns.

Proper nouns in the text are: *Wimbledon*; *the Cup* (because this is short for *The FA Cup*); *Vauxhall* (when it refers to the company, but not to the car, since it is possible to say *a Vauxhall*, just as you can say *a Calibra*). The case of *a Boomtown Rat* is interesting since the name of the group – *The Boomtown Rats* – is a proper name, but by singling out one particular member of the group, *Boomtown Rat* loses its unique status, as evidenced by the use of the indefinite article *a*.

b) Common nouns, then, are all the other nouns in the text, including *Princess* and *Knight*.

c) Count nouns (also called countable nouns) are all the nouns except *the unexpected* (technically an adjective, see (**h**) below), and *thinking*. Note that *industry* in this context is countable (e.g. *There are many different industries, of which the motor industry is one*), but that it has an uncountable use, e.g. *She owes her success to her industry*. For *press* and *public* see (**e**). *Little* is difficult to classify, but is probably best considered as a pronoun in this instance.

d) The only non-count (uncountable) noun, then, is *thinking*.

e) Collective nouns are: *the press* and *the public*. Note that they can take either a singular or a plural verb, and they can be substituted by *it* or *they*, depending on our point of view:

The public was/were there, and it/they approved.

f) The noun modifiers in the text are *Boomtown* and *motor*. Noun modifiers function like adjectives, but do not have the characteristics of adjectives, in that, for example they cannot be used predicatively, that is, in a noun + verb *to be* + adjective construction. So we can say: *It was a motor show*. But we cannot say: **The show was motor*.

Compare, for example, *big*, which can be used predicatively.

g) While it is normally the case that pronouns stand in for a noun – often one that has been previously mentioned – this is not always the case, as some examples in this text demonstrate:

- *it* in *to cap it all* is an example of an 'empty' object, or 'non-referring' *it*, in that it has no real meaning in its own right
- *We* is a personal pronoun, used here to mean both reader and writer – and everyone else, presumably
- *ourselves* is a reflexive pronoun
- *those* is a demonstrative pronoun

– *what* and *which* are relative pronouns
– *it* in *it's not every day* is sometimes called 'anticipatory' *it*, in that it anticipates – and stands for – the whole clause *that a new car appears which bucks so many trends and owes so little to prevailing thinking*
– *little*, as noted above, is best considered a pronoun here

h) An example of an adjective functioning as a noun is *the unexpected*. (Compare: *the rich*, *the unemployed*, etc.)

2 Those items marked with an asterisk are not normally acceptable (although of course it is possible, with a little ingenuity, to think of contexts when they might be possible).

	1	2	3	4
	Kim	*cup	furniture	stone
	*the Kim	the cup	the furniture	the stone
I saw	*a Kim	a cup	*a furniture	a stone
	*some Kim	*some cup	some furniture	some stone
	*Kims	cups	*furnitures	stones

The categories of noun are:

1 Proper nouns, which do not normally take a determiner (*the*, *a*, *some*, etc.) or allow a plural form.
2 Count nouns, that is, those seen as separate, individual entities. Notice that singular count nouns must have a determiner.
3 Non-count nouns, that is, those seen as an undifferentiated mass. They cannot take plural *s*, nor can they be preceded by the indefinite article *a/an*.
4 Those nouns that can be both count and non-count, depending on whether we are talking about individual units (*a stone*, *a coffee*), or simply the material or substance (*stone*, *coffee*, etc.). These can take the full range of determiners.

This exercise demonstrates how critical the two issues of proper noun versus common noun, and of count versus non-count, are in determining article use in English.

3 This exercise focuses learners' attention on the group of nouns represented in category 4 in the previous task, i.e. those that have both 'unit' and 'mass' senses. It also helps remind learners that singular count nouns must have an article.

4 The rule for forming the plural is simply to add *-s* to the singular form (also called the base form), but there are some exceptions. The odd ones out in the exercise are:

a) *watch*: Add *-es*. The rule is: if the base form ends in a sibilant (/s/, /z/, /tʃ/, /dʒ/), add *-es* (unless the base already ends in *-e*).

b) *child*: All have irregular plurals, but *child* is pluralised by adding a suffix (*-ren*), whereas the others change their vowel by a process called 'mutation' – *mice, men, geese*.

c) *chief*: In all the others the final *-f(e)* becomes *-ves*.

d) *skirts*: Skirts has a singular form, whereas the others do not. Other examples of plural-only nouns are *scissors, shorts, binoculars*.

e) *cow*: The plural of *cow* is *cows* whereas the others have the same singular and plural form – *one salmon, hundreds of salmon*.

f) *sheep*: Sheep can be both singular and plural, whereas the others are 'unmarked plural nouns', that is, they are always plural, although they have no *-s* ending. (Of course, *people* can be regular when it means 'nation', as in *the peoples of Asia*.)

Accepting that the *-es* form is hardly an irregularity, since it represents a variation in pronunciation (and learners meet the same variation in verb endings – *I teach, she teaches*, etc.), the first irregular form of pluralisation learners encounter is probably mutation, as in *men, women, feet, teeth*. Also, the very unusual *-ren* suffix, in *children*, and the invariable nouns *trousers, jeans*, etc. will be met at beginner level. Learners at all levels often have trouble remembering that *people* is plural.

5 Among the many and complicated rules for nouns in groups in English, the following simplified rules are the most frequently taught:

1 Where the first noun is a person and the second noun is a thing possessed by that person, the possessive *'s* is preferred.
2 Where the possessor is inanimate, the *of* genitive is preferred.
3 A noun modifier (noun + noun) is preferred where the first noun helps define or classify the second noun.
4 In noun + noun groups the first noun may have a plural meaning, but it does not usually have a plural form.
5 A 'double genitive' is used when the possessor is a person and the thing or person possessed is indefinite (*a/an…*).

The corrected errors, then, are:

a) *my sister's refrigerator* (Rule 1)

b) *Yolanda's hair* (Rule 1)

c) According to the above rules, *policeman's head* is correct. However, the relative clause that follows, modifies the policeman, not his head, and therefore sounds ambiguous as it stands. A more elegant version might be: *This hit the head of the policeman who was standing…* Also: *the corner of the house* (Rule 2)

d) *cinema history* (Rule 3); or *the history of the cinema* (Rule 2)

e) *a car accident* (Rule 3)

f) *a car mechanic* (Rule 3)

g) *a bus network* (Rule 4)

h) *an old friend of Frank's* (Rule 5)

Note that many languages, such as German, have special genitive forms – *das Haus meines Bruders* (my brother's house) – while others, such as French, do not – *la maison de mon frère*. Also, many languages do not use noun modifiers to the extent that English does. Thus, in Spanish, a traffic accident is *un accidente de circulación*, and a cookery book is *un libro de cocina*.

6 Possessive *'s* is typically introduced in the context of family relationships – *Dan is Meryl's sister*. Students' own family photos make good material for practice. Other useful contexts include personal possessions: 'Whose are these keys?' – 'They're Laura's.' This can be demonstrated in class using a selection of students' possessions.

Physical description also includes the use of possessive *'s*: *Birget's hair is dark*; *José's eyes are brown*.

At higher levels, materials and exercises designed to contrast the possessive *'s* with the use of *of* and/or noun modifiers, often involve error recognition, such as the following:

▶ Diagnosis ◀ ◀ ◀

Nouns in groups: the link with 's or s'

Work with a partner to decide which of the following links with *'s* are normal usage. Check your answers in the Key.

a) The President's assassination shocked the
   nation, *normal usage*
b) The lion's cage is open.
c) Have you seen today's paper?
d) The door's knob is broken.
e) They never reached the mountain's top.
f) The government's decision was unexpected.
g) England's decline began long before the war.
h) The idea's origin is unknown to me.
i) The boys' football gear is in the cupboard.

(from *Language Issues* by G. Porter-Ladousse)

7 Examples of pre- and postmodification contained in the text are:

- a case *of finding someone...experience*: postmodification using a prepositional phrase
- someone *with the correct skills and experience*: postmodification using a prepositional phrase
- the *correct* skills: premodification using an adjective
- *Carlyle* Parts: premodification using a (proper) noun modifier
- *damaged coach* windscreens: premodification using an adjective and a noun modifier, respectively
- anyone *suitable for their vacancies*: postmodification using an adjective phrase
- The people *we found*: postmodification using a (defining) relative clause
- a *work* trial: premodification using a noun modifier
- the people *you need*: postmodification using a (defining) relative clause
- your *local* Jobcentre: premodification using an adjective
- all the help *you need*: postmodification using a (defining) relative clause

Note that words like *a*, *the*, *all*, etc. are treated separately in Unit 23.

8 The exercise contrasts defining and non-defining relative clauses. The former identify which person or thing, of several, is being referred to while the latter simply add further information about the noun they postmodify, as in:

- Defining: *The test paper which everyone failed was far too difficult.* (Several test papers were taken. One of the papers was failed by everyone and this is the one that was too difficult.)
- Non-defining: *The test paper, which everyone failed, was far too difficult.*
- Defining: *My brother who is in Canada is an architect.* (As opposed to my other brother who is in Scotland, for example.)
- Non-defining: *My brother, who is in Canada, is an architect.*

Note the use of commas to indicate non-defining relative clauses, implying that the information conveyed is incidental. In speech the same effect is achieved by pausing and changing key, while defining relative clauses tend to be uttered as one continuous tone group.

9 The pronouns in the text are as follows:

personal pronouns:

- subject: *we*; *they*; *you*
- object: *them*; *it*; *you*

possessive pronouns: *their*; *your*
demonstrative pronouns: *this*
relative pronouns: *who*
indefinite pronouns: *someone*; *anyone*

Note that there are two kinds of possessive pronouns: those, like *their* and *your* in the text that are used as determiners, and often called possessive adjectives, and those like *mine*, *yours*, *hers*, etc. that can stand on their own: 'It's not mine, it's hers'.

One popular exercise for focusing on pronoun forms and uses is simply to ask learners to identify the referent in each case, e.g. by circling the pronouns and their referents and connecting them by lines. Note, however, that some pronouns, like *we* and *you* have referents 'outside' the text, while indefinite pronouns have indefinite referents:

Before we sent them fitters we made sure they'd fit.

Filling a gap in an existing team isn't just a

case of finding someone with the correct skills

and experience. So, before we send anyone

for a job, we check they'll fit it.

Carlyle Parts, who amongst other things replace

PIRST SENTENCE

damaged coach windscreens, discovered this recently.

INDEFINITE

They hadn't been able to find anyone suitable for

OUTSIDE TEXT

their vacancies. But we did. The people we found

were offered to Carlyle Parts on a work trial.

Within days they had taken them on permanently.

· · · · · ·

We'll also find the people you need. Whatever

the job. Give your local Jobcentre a call. They'll

give you all the help you need.

10 Rutherford (1987) calculates a noun–verb ratio of roughly three to one in Text 1 (29 nouns, 9 verbs), whereas in Text 2 the ratio is not quite 1.5 to one (13 nouns and 9 verbs). He argues that the relatively low noun–verb ratio is a distinguishing feature of the writing produced by ESL learners.

Exercises and activities aimed at increasing the rate of nominalisation include:

- Word formation exercises, where learners derive nouns from other parts of speech, as in *possess – possession; long – length*.
- Exercises designed to encourage the use of noun modifiers and compound nouns, e.g.

What is one word for these definitions?

e.g. a shop for books is a bookshop

a a shop for shoes
b a place for parking cars
c a place where buses stop
etc.

- Asking students to do noun–verb ratio counts on their own writing, and encouraging them to use nominalising processes to increase the noun ratio.

23 Determiners

1 The determiners in this text are: *a*; *the*; *last*; *a few*; *their*; *first*; *any*; *no*.

Note that *their*, *your*, *my*, etc. are also called possessive adjectives and possessive pronouns as well as possessive determiners; *first* and *last* are sometimes classified separately as ordinals. Note also that some determiners consist of more than one word – *a few*, *a little* – and that, where a noun has two determiners, there is a fixed order as in, for example, *their first roll of film*.

2 The text contains the following zero articles: Ø *London*; Ø *art galleries*; Ø *plantains*; Ø *saltfish*; Ø *sweet potatoes*; Ø *home*. Note that all the other nouns have some form of determiner preceding them: **this** *craving*; **my** *mother's food*; **a** *beacon*; **the** *cold*.

Examples of the rules are as follows:

a) non-count nouns with indefinite reference: Ø *saltfish*
b) plural count nouns with indefinite reference: Ø *art galleries*; Ø *plantains*; Ø *sweet potatoes*
c) proper nouns: Ø *London*
d) common expressions of time, place, transport, etc.: *of* Ø *home*

Here are some more examples of rule (**d**):

time expressions: *at sunset*; *by noon*; *around midnight*
place expressions: *at work*; *at sea*; *to school*; *in prison*; *in hospital*; *to town*
means of transport: *by bus*; *on foot*; *by taxi*

3 The probable article choice in the limericks is the following:

There was *a* young man of Verdun
Who lay several hours in *the* sun.
The people who milled
Round *the* man said: 'He's grilled –
Not just medium-rare, but well done!'

A certain young woman of Thule
Fell in love with *a* man with *a* mule.
Said *the* girl to *the* man:
If we marry, we can
Go to Thule on *the* back of *the* mule.

Information is 'new' if it has not been mentioned before and is not otherwise identifiable, as in *a young man of Verdun*, *a certain young woman*, etc.

Information is 'given' if it is identifiable, either by reference to the shared knowledge of writer and reader, as in *the sun* (there's only one, therefore it is easily identified), or by reference to the text. In this case, the reference can be back in the text (*the mule* refers to the prior mention of *a mule*), or forward, as in 'the people *who milled round the man*', 'the back *of the mule*'. These two kinds of reference are called 'anaphoric' (backward reference) and 'cataphoric' (forward reference) respectively.

Note that the noun can change, although it refers to the same entity: 'a certain young *woman*' -> 'the *girl*'.

4 In the stories, the definite article is used as follows:

a) – *the moon*: The reference outside the text to the shared knowledge of writer and reader makes *moon* a 'given', hence it is definite.
   – *the sky*: Again, the reference is outside the text to shared knowledge – there is only one sky.
   – *the wife*: The reference is back in the text.
   – *the most beautiful*: The reference is to the shared knowledge that superlatives have unique reference.

b) – *the station*: The station is 'given'. The reader can identify it by reference to a mental picture (or 'schema'), shared by writer and reader, which is created by the circumstances of the story – *Carl got off work at three*. People who work often commute by train; they leave from and return to a station, of which there is usually only one in their immediate area. Compare: *He got off at a station in the middle of nowhere…*
   – *the stool…the clerk*: Similarly, the mention of *a shoestore* triggers a mental schema which assumes the presence of stools and clerks in shoestores. Compare, for example: *He put his foot on the stool and let the waiter unlace his workboot*. The question *Which waiter?* is not answered by reference to shared knowledge of the world of the text. The curious reader would need to either backtrack or read ahead in order to answer the question.

5 The first two sentences are general, rather abstract, statements about the typical characteristics of dodos as a whole. *The dodo*, in these sentences, means not one particular dodo, but all dodos. It is a form of 'generic' reference. Sentences three and four describe specific events and specific dodos: *the dodos* that were killed, and *the last dodo*.

6 Generic reference is *not* realised by:

   – Count nouns
      c) *the* + plural: The tigers.

But note that *the* + plural can be used with a count noun for generic reference if it is postmodified: *The tigers of Bengal*.

   – Non-count nouns
      e) *the*: The carbon.

A common mistake made by learners of English is to make generic statements using the above combinations:

*'On average, the women live longer than the men.'
*'The life in big cities is hard.'

7 The articles contained in the text and their uses are as follows:

- *a sunny morning* is a new topic and it is not defined.
- *a man* is a new topic and it is not defined.
- *a breakfast nook* is a new topic and it is not defined.
- *a white unicorn* is a new topic and it is not defined.
- *a gold horn* is a new topic and it is not defined.
- *the roses* are defined by reference forward (*…in the garden*).
- *the garden* is defined by reference outside the text to shared knowledge – the man is in a house; houses have gardens.
- *The man* is defined by reference back in the text.
- *the bedroom* is the same as *the garden* (see above).
- *a unicorn* introduces a new topic (for the listener).
- *the garden* is defined by reference to knowledge shared by the speaker and the listener, i.e. '*our* garden'.
- Ø *roses* is an example of zero article used for plural count nouns with indefinite reference.
- *The unicorn* is generic reference, meaning 'all unicorns'.
- *a mythical beast* is generic reference, meaning 'that's the kind of thing it is'.
- *The man* is defined by reference back in the text.
- *the garden* is defined by reference back in the text as well as by reference to shared knowledge.
- *The unicorn* is a specific unicorn – the one defined by reference back in the text. (Compare: 'The unicorn is a mythical beast'.)
- *the tulips* are defined by reference to shared knowledge – a garden that has roses will have other flowers, possibly tulips.

8 This is how the exercises are answered in *Think First Certificate Self-Study Guide*:

1 1–C 2–B 3–D 4–I 5–G 6–E 7–A 8–F 9–H
2 1–D 2–C 3–B 4–E 5–A

It is arguable that such a preponderance of rules is not that useful – especially when exceptions can be found for each one. Consider, for example, these exceptions to the first four 'rules':

Rule	Example of exception to the rule
A	It was *a* most beautiful day.
B	Is there *a* God?
C	She's a social-worker. She's been *a* social-worker for years now.
D	There's *a* man I know who has a chainsaw.

It may be more effective to sensitise learners to the notion of definiteness through exercises which challenge them to answer the question *Which?* at each instance of *the* in a text (and this suggests that larger contexts than the sentence are necessary for demonstrating article use). Using texts it is not difficult to show that the definite article *the* 'points' in one of three directions:

- backward in the text (anaphoric reference)
- forward in the text (cataphoric reference)
- outside the text, into the knowledge about the world shared by writer and reader – or speaker and listener (exophoric reference)

These three kinds of reference account for many of Naunton's nine 'rules':

anaphoric reference: C
cataphoric reference: D, H
exophoric reference: A, B, G, I

The two instances not covered: E (*She plays the piano well*) and F (*the rich, the poor, the unemployed*) are examples of generic uses of *the* and perhaps do need to be learned separately.

9 The rules for *some* and *any* in *Headway Pre-Intermediate* are syntactic. They generalise uses for each determiner according to the form of both the sentence they are in and of the noun that follows. This is the description that most teachers and learners will be familiar with. The *Out and About* description, however, attempts to get at the underlying semantic meaning of each determiner.

The *Headway* rules account for examples (**a**) and (**c**), but not the others. The *Out and About* rules account not only for (**a**) and (**c**), but for (**d**) and (**e**) as well, and, less obviously perhaps, for (**f**) and (**g**) if we take 'unrestricted' to mean 'it doesn't matter which'. Example (**b**) appears not to fit any of these rules. Chalker (1990) defines this use to mean 'a particular person or thing – though exactly what or which is not stated'. Does Lewis's definition of *some* accommodate Chalker's?

The *some/any* debate is a good example of a case where pedagogical rules may win out over more accurate descriptive rules, simply because they are more learnable, and more easily applicable. The *Headway*-type description is likely to remain in favour, despite its inaccuracy.

10 The activities deal with determiners as follows:

- Activity 1 practises, in a very controlled way, the making of generic statements, using the *zero article + plural count noun* construction.
- Activity 2 focuses on the notion of 'definiteness', and suggests that for each instance of the definite article, the reader should be able to answer the question *Which one?* The reader can do this either by reference back or forward in the text, or by reference to the shared knowledge of reader and writer (e.g. the knowledge that all mountains have tops). Since the exercise does not require the learner to produce examples of the target item (*the*), but simply to understand why *the* is used, it could be classified as a 'consciousness-raising' activity. (It could be made more challenging by omitting the phrases in the box at the end.)
- Activity 3 is designed to practise quantifiers along with *some* and *any*, and the distinction between count and non-count nouns which, in turn, affects the choice of determiner: *how much ice-cream? how many cakes?*

24 Adjectives and adverbs

1 Adjectives: *rude*; *straight*; *angry*; *quiet*; *friendly*; *slow*; *serious*; *lively*; *hard*; *perfect*.

Adverbs: *loudly*; *straight*; *carefully*; *badly*; *quickly*; *slow*; *cleverly*; *hard*; *softly*; *nervously*.

Note that the *-ly* suffix, while a very common way of forming adverbs from adjectives, is also found in some adjectives. Note also that some adverbs and adjectives share the same form (*straight, hard, fast, late*). *Slowly* is one adverbial form of *slow*, but *slow* is also common: *You're driving too slow*.

2 The adjectives in the text are: *terrific*; *soft* (x2); *elusive*; *smooth*; *lined*; *useful*; *grateful*; *everyday*; *indispensable*; *needed* (?); *available*.

Note that words like *our* and *your* are sometimes called possessive adjectives and sometimes possessive determiners (see Unit 11).

House as in *house keys*, and *leather* as in *leather bags* are both nouns, used to modify the nouns they precede (see Unit 22). Noun modifiers do not meet most of the tests of a true adjective (see below).

In this passage *black*, *navy* and *cream* are nouns (and are the complement of *in* in a prepositional phrase). All these words, of course, can, in different contexts, be adjectives, for example, *a black sweater*.

Needed is normally the past participle of the verb *need*, as in 'The video is needed in Room 15 this afternoon'. In the advertising text it has been conscripted to act as an adjective, not unusual for past participles (see also *lined*). However, it fails a number of adjective tests (see below).

Common adjectival suffixes represented here are: *-ic, -ive, -ed, -ful, -able*.

Other common adjectival suffixes are: *-al, -ish, -less, -like, -y*.

3

	Criteria				
	a	b	c	d	e
soft	✔	✔	✔	✔	✔
available	✔	✔	✔	✔	✘
needed	✔	✔?	✘	✘	✘
everyday	✘	✔	✘	✘	✘
house	✘	✔	✘	✘	✘
your	✘	✘	✘	✘	✘

We have already noted that *needed* is normally used as a verb participle.

Note that *everyday* is only normally used before the noun it qualifies, i.e. in the attributive position: *an everyday basis* (but not **the basis is everyday*, which is the predicative position). Other adjectives only used attributively include *lone, former, outright, northern.* Adjectives that are only used predicatively include *alive, well, ready.*

4 Rather than divide *-ing* and *-ed* words into discrete categories, it is probably better to think of them as occupying points on a spectrum, from those that are entirely verb-like in their function, to those that are entirely adjective-like. Nevertheless, for description purposes it is often convenient to make finer distinctions.

   a) verb participles: *illustrated; opening; approached; included*
   b) qualitative participial adjectives: *interesting; inviting*
   c) classifying participial adjectives: *detached; equipped; furnished; curving; sitting*
   d) noun + -ed adjectives: *galleried; three-bedroomed*
   e) compound participial adjectives: *tree-lined; oak-fitted*

5 If noun modifiers are included as classifiers, all the examples follow the pattern, with the exception, perhaps, of *black sticky rice.* Note that qualitative adjectives can have degrees of the quality mentioned – *very soft, less soft* – while classifying adjectives do not normally allow degrees – *?very Victorian, ?less wooden.*

   a) *tight* is a qualitative adjective; *black* is a colour adjective

   b) *comfortable* is qualitative; *Victorian* is a classifying adjective; *country* is a noun modifier

   c) *black* is a colour adjective; *sticky*, in this position, presumably denotes a kind of rice, rather than a quality; *luscious* is qualitative; *nutty* is also qualitative – you can have degrees of nuttiness. To classify something made of nuts you would normally use a noun modifier – *a luscious nut dessert*

   d) *ancient* is qualitative; *Chinese* is classifying; *confectionery* is a noun modifier; *young* is qualitative; *stem* is a noun modifier; *simple* is qualitative; *ice-cream* is a noun modifier; *elaborately decorated* is a classifying adjective (formed from a participle) with a qualitative adverb; *glazed* is a classifying adjective (formed from a participle); *ceramic* is a noun modifier

Note that determiners always come first, and noun modifiers always directly precede the noun they modify – *this comfortable Victorian country house.* Since participles usually have a classifying function, they come after qualitative adjectives.

Many EFL texts and grammars provide elaborate rules for adjectival order, such as:

adjectives of evaluation → size → age → shape → colour → participle → noun-derived (after Broughton 1990).

It is arguable, however, that, not only are such rules difficult to remember, but they encourage the idea that long strings of attributive adjectives are the norm in English. It may be more useful simply to draw learners' attention to these two rules:

- opinion adjectives usually go before fact adjectives, as in *this comfortable Victorian country house*.
- general qualities go before particular qualities, as in *ancient Chinese confectionery*.

6 and 7 'The adverb is an extremely heterogeneous word class. Practically any word that is not easily classed as a noun, an adjective, a verb, a determiner, a preposition or a conjunction, tends to be classified as an adverb.' (Downing and Locke 1992)

These are the adverbs in the text, and their category:

simply:	manner
always:	time
here:	place
together:	place
now:	time
really:	degree
fondly:	manner
again:	time
Then:	linking adverb
warmly:	manner
shrilly:	manner
apart:	place
guiltily:	manner
already:	time
entirely:	degree

8 The adverbials of time and place in the text are:

- on the wide drive: place (prepositional phrase)
- before going back into the house: time (non-finite clause)
- into the house: place (prepositional phrase)
- during the night: time (prepositional phrase)
- after a foully sleepless night: time (prepositional phrase)
- shortly after dawn: time (prepositional phrase)
- through the snow: place (prepositional phrase)

9 Some suggested activities for adverbs and adverbials are as follows:

a) Adverbs of frequency:

Charts showing in diagrammatic form the habits or routines of different people over a week work well. For example, the way each person goes to work:

Helen always takes the bus.
Eric sometimes takes a taxi and sometimes he walks. He never takes the bus...,
etc.

A variation on this is to give the learners sentences along with the chart, and then ask them to arrange the frequency adverbs along a cline, from *always* to *never* according to the information provided by the chart.

b) *Yet*, *still* and *already*:

These time adverbs cause learners a great deal of trouble, not only because of their meaning, but also because of their position in the sentence. One way to present and contrast them is to establish the tour itinerary of a tourist, or of a rock band, for example:

1 May: Bristol
2 May: Cardiff
4 May: Liverpool
6 May: Glasgow
10 May: Newcastle

and then elicit sentences about the present, past and future from the perspective of different dates:

It's May 4th. They're still in Liverpool. They've already been to Cardiff and Bristol. They haven't been to Glasgow or Newcastle yet.

c) *For* and *since*:

Simply write a number of time expressions on the board, such as *five years, 1980, three weeks ago, a week, last Monday, January*, etc. and ask learners to group them according to whether they take *for* or *since*. (Those that are periods of time go with *for*; those that are points of time take *since*.)

10 The corrected sentences and their explanations are as follows:

a) *He looks younger than he really is. More* is redundant with adjectives whose comparative is formed by adding the suffix *-er*.

b) *It all happened when I was much younger.* Comparatives are modified by *much* (or *very much*) but not by *very* on its own.

c) A possible reformulation might be: *He was (quite) different from the boy I had lived with for fifteen years: nicer and more polite. Different* is not usually gradable, hence it doesn't allow the comparative form ?*more different*. *Nice* and *polite*, on the other hand, are gradable, and, since a comparison is being made, should be in their respective comparative forms.

d) *Now, my brother is (much) taller than before.* When only two people are being compared the comparative, not the superlative, is used; *much* can be used to emphasise the difference, if necessary.

e) *Pierre is as intelligent as me. As* is used in this kind of construction. Purists might prefer: *Pierre is as intelligent as I am.*

f) *I was the happiest person in all the world.* Adjectives normally precede the noun; the superlative is used when more than two people or things are being compared.

g) *People don't work as hard as they think.* The correct adverbial form of the adjective *hard* is *hard*; *hardly* has the meaning of 'almost not'.

11 Here is one of many possible reformulations of the composition, focusing specifically on noun phrase problems, but adjusting verbs, etc. for agreement:

They are the same (1) as (2) the other (3) important cities. Living (4) conditions offer good and bad things to Ø citizens (5). The first (6) are for instance, Ø good communication (7) between people by (8) telephone, fax, computer, radio, TV, etc.; Ø public services (9) such as the bus, the train (10), the underground (11), etc.; the leisure (12) to go (13) shopping in the supermarket, to go to the cinema or theatre, etc.

The second (14) are typical, for instance Ø pollution (15), which causes disease (16) and health problems (17); Ø noise (18), which disturbs the old people; living (19) together in the same building (20), which causes noise (21), arguments (22) between neighbours, etc.

Barcelona has advantages and disadvantages, the former (23) are good and the latter (24) are bad. It (25) is very difficult to find any (26) city or village which doesn't have problems. I prefer Ø villages (27) for their calm, (28) natural life, but I prefer Ø cities (29) for their diversions and entertainments. I don't think there's anywhere (30) that (31) doesn't have some (32) disadvantages.

1 the pronoun *same* is invariable, i.e. it has no plural form
2 same + *as*
3 invariable determiner
4 not *life*; use noun modifier since the relation is not possession but classification
5 generic use of plural noun
6 see *same* (1) above; *The former*, in fact, would be better here
7 generic use: non-count noun
8 wrong preposition
9 generic use of plural noun
10 or *buses, trains* – generic use: count noun
11 generic
12 non-count noun: no plural
13 wrong verb
14 see *first* (6) above; *The latter* would be better here
15 indefinite use: non-count
16 non-count form of this noun is probably more appropriate, since specific diseases are not indicated

17 noun modifier – classification rather than possession; alternatively *problems of health*
18 indefinite: non-count
19 *-ing* form is the nominalised form of the verb
20 wrong form
21 non-count
22 spelling
23 see (6) above
24 see (14) above
25 used here to stand in as the subject of the sentence
26 non-restrictive meaning
27 generic
28 *and* is not necessary with two adjectives in attributive position
29 generic
30 unrestrictive
31 preferred to *which* after indefinite pronouns
32 restrictive

25 Prepositions and phrasal verbs

1 and 2 The prepositions in the text, with their associated noun phrase complement, are:

- in 1953: preposition of time (specific time)
- with the Sherpa mountaineer Tenzing Norgay: accompaniment
- to the summit: place (direction)
- of Mount Everest: belonging
- in the same year: (specific) time
- in Auckland: place (position)
- at Auckland University College: place (position)
- on his father's farm: place (position)
- before joining the Royal New Zealand Air Force: (anterior) time
- in 1943: (specific) time
- as a navigator: role
- aboard flying boats: place (position)
- in the Pacific: place (position)
- during the war: (period of) time

Note that *before* is one of a number of prepositions that can also function as a conjunction, i.e. when it introduces a subordinate clause: *...before he joined the air force*; *after we'd had lunch...*

3 The completed chart looks like this:

	POSITIVE		NEGATIVE	
	direction	position	direction	position
DIMENSION-TYPE 0 (point)	*to*	*at*	*(away) from*	*away from*
DIMENSION-TYPE 1/2 (line or surface)	*on(to)*	*on*	*off*	*off*
DIMENSION-TYPE 2/3 (area or volume)	*in(to)*	*in*	*out of*	*out of*

(from *A University Grammar of English* by R. Quirk and S. Greenbaum. Reprinted by permission of Addison Wesley Longman Ltd.)

Note that these are only the most common prepositions that realise these concepts. As well as *to*, for example, *toward(s)* and *up to* can both be used to indicate movement to a point.

4 The activity is designed to practise prepositions of place, specifically those used to indicate direction, both across surfaces, and through areas/volumes, and therefore used with verbs of movement: *The burglar walked along the footpath, in through the front gate, up the path, around the house...*

Apart from the verbs and prepositions, learners would need to know the actual nouns themselves: geographical terms, etc. These could be pre-taught, using the illustrations, or fed in as the learners are doing the exercise itself.

5 The corrections and their explanations are as follows:

a) *in the Caribbean*: for geographical purposes, seas and oceans are seen as being enclosed areas; islands are therefore *in* them, while ships sail *on* them.

b) *on 25th December*: *at* is used for points of time, e.g. clock time, while *on* is used in expressions referring to days – *on Friday, on Christmas Day,* etc.

c) *to school*: movement towards a destination (*to*), as opposed to static position (*at*).

d) *she arrives home*: when *home* is used as an adverb, no preposition is required with verbs of movement; *at one o'clock*; use *at* with clock times (see (**b**) above); *till* (or *until*) *two o'clock*: use *till/until* to mark the end point of a period of time.

e) *for many years*: *during* refers to a point or period of time within the duration of the stated period and answers the question *when?*; *for* refers to the whole period, and answers the question *how long?*, e.g. *We camped on the beach for three weeks during the summer.*

f) *I walked to the job / to work*: *until* is normally only used as a time preposition.

g) *a little different from/to/than my present life*: *from* is British English and is preferred to *to* by purists, while *than* is American English.

h) *they spent the money on buying a house and gave the rest to the poor*: you spend money *on* something, and you give money *to* someone. These are verb-dependent prepositions (see Task 6).

6 The dependent prepositions in the text are: *worried about*; *proud of*; *frightened of*; *pleased with*; *good at*; *disappointed with*.

One way to focus attention on these prepositions might be to give the learners the tapescript with the targeted prepositions deleted. Ask them to predict the prepositions and then play the tape to check, or play the tape and ask the learners to fill in the gaps as they listen (this is in fact the task that is set by the coursebook writers). It may be helpful first to check the learners' overall understanding of the gist of the text by asking some very general questions after an initial hearing: Who's talking to whom? About what?

7 up: adverb
at: preposition
for: preposition
up: adverb
ahead: adverb
with: preposition
back: adverb
on: preposition
for: preposition

of: preposition
up: adverb
together: adverb
on: preposition
through: adverb
to: preposition
at: preposition
by: preposition
up: adverb

Notice that, in this last example, *various loose ends* is not the complement of a preposition *up* but the object of a two-part verb *clearing up*. One proof that *up* is not a preposition is that it can be moved to a position *after* the object: *clearing various loose ends up*. A preposition can never follow its complement.

8 The multi-word verbs in the extracts are as follows:

a) *run away* (verb + adverb): phrasal verb
b) *made for* (verb + preposition): prepositional verb
c) *put...through*: phrasal verb
d) *ran across*: prepositional verb
e) *turn in*: phrasal verb
f) *looking after*: prepositional verb
g) *picked up*: phrasal verb
h) *put up with* (verb + adverb + preposition): phrasal–prepositional verb

Notice that these classifications are syntactic, not semantic. That is, the distinction between phrasal and prepositional verbs, or between phrasal verbs and any other sort of verbs is not made on the basis of, for example, whether the combination of verb and particle is idiomatic. It often *is* idiomatic, but there are many phrasal verbs whose meaning is quite transparent: *sit down*, *stand up*, *eat up*, etc.

9 This four-way classification is a common one and is found in many EFL coursebooks and grammars. It is important to realise, however, that there are essentially only *two* kinds of multi-word verbs: those whose particle is an adverb, and those whose particle is a preposition. The latter are, by definition, always transitive, since prepositions are always followed by a complement which becomes the object of the verb. This is also the case with phrasal–prepositional verbs, which are a combination of both major types. It is only phrasal verbs (verbs + adverb) that can be either transitive or intransitive. And it is only with the transitive phrasal verbs (Type 2) that there is the possibility of separating the verb and its particle as in *Joanna picked a string of pearls up* (see Task 10).

The multi-part verbs in the extracts are:

– *made up* (his mind): verb + adverb, transitive, therefore Type 2
– *pull* (it) *off*: Type 2

- *come into* (it): verb + preposition, therefore Type 3
- *look after* (him): Type 3
- *work out* (a plan): Type 2
- *worked* (everything) *out*: Type 2
- *went off*: verb + adverb, intransitive, therefore Type 1
- *won out*: Type 1
- *goes through with* (it): Type 4

10 Types 3 and 4 multi-word verbs cannot be separated, because a preposition must always precede its object. Type 1 verbs are intransitive and, therefore, have no object to come between the verb and its particle (e.g. *The plane took off*). It is, therefore, only with Type 2 phrasal verbs that the option of separating verb and particle is an issue.

So, in the text, it is clear that *work out* allows both patterns: *trying to work out a plan* – verb + particle + object – and *We worked everything out* – verb + object + particle. *Work out*, then, is 'separable', as is *make up*. Both *he'd made up his mind* and *he'd made his mind up* are possible. Notice that we can say *he'd never pull it off*, but not **he'd never pull off it*. Yet, *he'd never pull off the plan* is possible. Which suggests that the rule for separability is:

'All transitive phrasal verbs allow the particle to come either before or after the object, except when the object is a personal pronoun, in which case the particle must come *after* the object.'

In fact, there is a very small set of transitive phrasal verbs where the particle must *always* follow the object: *I can't tell the twins apart*. Not **I can't tell apart the twins*. However, the rule as stated works in the vast majority of cases.

We can now summarise the main classes of multi-word verb:

- *Verb + adverb*
  1. intransitive: There is no object and the two parts are, therefore, inseparable – 'Tim *got up*'.
  2. transitive: The particle may come before or after the object, unless the object is a personal pronoun – 'I *made up* my mind' or 'I *made* my mind *up*', but not ***'I made up it'.

- *Verb + preposition*
  3. These are always transitive and the particle may never be separated from the verb – 'He *made for* the door'.

- *Verb + adverb + preposition*
  4. These are transitive and inseparable – 'We have got *to go through with* it'.

11 The traditional approach to teaching multi-word verbs is that adopted by the material in the first exercise, whereby they are grouped according to the lexical verb: *get, take, put*, etc. More recently, materials writers have varied this by grouping the verbs according to the particle, and drawing attention to the inherent meanings of the particle. This is, perhaps, based on the assumption that grouping by the particle may facilitate understanding of multi-word verbs, thus aiding memory, and ultimately, production. A third approach is simply to organise multi-word verbs into semantic fields, as is often done with other items of vocabulary, and teach them in their context, e.g. a (disastrous) journey: *fill up*; *set off*; *pick up*; *be held up*; *break down*; *blow out*; *run out of*, etc.

26 Cohesion

1 The correct order is: (e), (a), (f), (b), (d); (c) does not belong in the text.

The original text was:

Cotton is a very useful plant. Inside its round fruits, called bolls, are masses of white fibres. When the fruits ripen, they split and the fibres are blown away. But in the cotton fields, the bolls are picked before this can happen. Cotton grows best in warm, wet lands, including Asia, the southern United States, India, China, Egypt and Brazil.
(from *Pocket Encyclopedia* by A. Jack)

It is possible that the very last sentence could come first, although in this kind of text a very general statement (*Cotton is a very useful plant*) is more likely to precede a less general one (*Cotton grows best…*). It could also take second place in the text, but the repetition of *cotton* so soon after its first mention would seem redundant.

Linguistic clues that might have helped are:

Lexical field: the sentence about copper does not fit into the topic that is suggested by words like *cotton, plant, fruit, fibres, fields*, etc.

Repetition: Inside its round *fruits*…When the *fruits* ripen…

Use of referring devices:
– Pronouns: *Cotton* is a very useful plant. Inside *its* round fruits…
– Articles: …masses of white *fibres…the fibres* are blown away.

Use of linkers: *But* in the cotton fields…

These last three items – pronouns, definite article and linkers – are dependent on the text that precedes them. For this reason, none of the sentences that contain these items could satisfactorily serve as the opening sentence of the text.

This suggests that just as sentences have 'sentence-forming' devices, such as the agreement between a verb and its subject, texts have 'text-forming' devices that function to connect sentences with each other and to bind a text together into a complete whole, i.e. to make it 'cohesive'.

2 There are both lexical and grammatical devices that serve to make texts cohesive.

– Lexical repetition:
  Text 1: *HOSPITAL…Hospital…hospital*; *cleaning…clean*
  Text 2: *mobile phone…mobile phone*

– Indirect repetition:
  e.g. the use of synonyms: *VISITS…inspecting* (Text 1), *using…operate; approval…acclaim* (Text 2); and of more general terms: *hospital…the place* (Text 1)

– Lexical sets:
 Text 1: *hospital...health...casualty...doctor; minister...officials*
 Text 2: *phone...messages...callers...communications; piece of cake...easy as pie...half-baked*

– Tense agreement:
 In Text 1 the first paragraph is narrated in the past simple.
 In Text 2 all the verbs are in the present.

– Pronoun reference:
 Text 1: *The minister...his appointment...he went about*
 Text 2: *...using it...The MT-20...controlling it...the MT-20...it has all the functions; all the functions...They make*

– Article reference:
 Text 1: *Safdarjang Hospital...the hospital...the place*

– Substitution:
 Text 2: *Pick one up...*i.e. pick an MT-20 up

– Ellipsis:
 Text 2: *And several* [functions] *you wouldn't* [expect]*; You'd have to be half-baked not to* [pick one up]

– Conjuncts:
 Text 2: *And...; No wonder*

3 The linkers are categorised as follows:

Addition	Contrast	Cause/effect	Time sequence
Also	However	Therefore	Meanwhile
Moreover	Even so	As a result	Then
Furthermore	On the other hand	So	Later
...too	Yet	Hence	First
...as well	Still	Consequently	Afterwards
And	Nevertheless	Thus	Soon

Note that all of the above can be used to join sentences. There are other linkers that join only clauses: *although; whereas; because; while;* etc.

Note also that there are two kinds of contrast:

– Contrast of surprising facts: *It was a great party. We didn't stay long however.*
– Contrast of opposite facts: *I always wear a tie at work. At home, on the other hand, I never wear one.*

4 In fact, there are no sentence linkers in the text. Possible linkers that *could* be inserted might be, respectively and starting from the second sentence: *That is to say…*; *For example…*; *By contrast…*; *This is because…*; *On the other hand…*

It seems, though, that the sentences *are* logically ordered and that no linkers are necessary. Crewe (1990), among others, argues that too much emphasis is placed on formal linkers at the expense of, for example, lexical repetition, and the use of referential pronouns such as *this* as in *This is because…*

5 The underlined words and their referents are – <u>he</u>: this refers to Hale (this is backward reference using a personal pronoun); <u>they</u>: the reference is presumably to be explained later in the text (thus this is an example of forward reference using a personal pronoun); <u>him</u>: this refers to Hale (this is backward reference using a personal pronoun); <u>That</u>: this refers to all the preceding sentence (this is backward reference using a demonstrative pronoun); <u>his</u>: this refers to Graham Greene (this is forward reference using a possessive determiner); <u>they</u>: this refers to his books (this is backward reference using a personal pronoun); <u>who</u>: this refers to Graham Greene (this is backward reference using a relative pronoun).

There is some debate as to whether this kind of exercise is of value to learners, on the grounds that proficient readers do not, in fact, physically look back or forward to recover the referent of a pronoun. Rather the reader checks the pronoun off against a mental 'picture' (or construct) of the discourse as it develops. Nevertheless, as an exercise in guiding the reader's comprehension of a text it may serve some purpose, as well as raising the learner's awareness of different kinds of pronouns and their uses.

6 A distinction is made between reference to 'co-text' (the surrounding text) and reference to 'context', that is, to the context in which the writer (or speaker) is situated. Contextual reference is known as 'deixis' (which means, in Greek, 'pointing').

There are three main types of 'pointing' outside the text:

– personal deixis: using pronouns to 'point', e.g. *I*; *you*
– spatial deixis: *here/there*; *this/that*, as well as verbs like *come* and *go, bring* and *take*
– temporal deixis: *today*; *yesterday*; *now*; *then*

Here is the extract with the deictic expressions explained in the square brackets:

BENEDICT Now, my [*my*: reference to speaker] guess is, it's somewhere in here [*here*: reference to place]. (*switches on the bedroom light*) Am I [*I*: reference to speaker] right?

POPPY Look, I [*I*:reference to speaker] 'm afraid I [*I*: reference to speaker] must ask you [*you*: reference to addressee] to leave now [*now*: reference to present time], Mr Hough…

BENEDICT (*looks towards cupboard*) What about in here [*here*: reference to place]?...

POPPY My other daughter is here [*here*: reference to place] as well, you [*you*: reference to addressee] know. Just along there [*there*: reference to place]...

BENEDICT (*examining the cupboard*) No, nothing in here [*here*: reference to place].

POPPY I [*I*: reference to speaker] think that [*that*: reference to place] was my [*my*: reference to speaker] husband's car.

The writer's stage directions, as well as the use of names by the speakers, allows us to identify most of the references. Thus *here* in the first sentences refers to the bedroom. Some references are left vague, however – *Just along there* is presumably not in the bedroom; and ...*that was my husband's car* is presumably a reference to the 'sound of' the car.

7 The exercise is designed to practise verbs that have deictic meaning, specifically *bring* and *take* (although *come* and *go* could also be worked in), as well as the deictic adverbials *here* and *there*.

Here refers to the location of the speaker (the 'deictic centre'), *there* can refer to the location of the addressee, or a location away from both speaker and addressee. Some languages maintain a three-way distinction. Thus, in some dialects of Italian *qui* means here (by me), *costí* means there (by you) and *là* means there (away from both of us).

It is not the case, however, that *come* and *bring* refer simply to movement towards the speaker (to *here*), while *go* and *take* refer to movement away from the speaker (to *there*). With these particular verbs the 'deictic centre' is both where *I* am *and* where *you* are, so that it is possible to say both 'Come (to my place) and bring a bottle' and 'I'm coming (to your place), and I'll bring a bottle'. In many languages, such as Spanish, 'I'm coming (to you)' would be translated by the equivalent of the verb *to go*: *voy* (literally 'I go').

8 The answers provided to this exercise are:

A 'I'm going to leave tomorrow,' she said.
B 'This is the record I bought two days ago,' he said.
C 'The parcel will arrive the day after tomorrow,' they said.
D 'Did anyone come yesterday?' he asked.
E 'Your flat will be ready next month,' we told them.
F 'I called this morning but no one answered the door,' he said.
G 'Is today your birthday?' she asked.

  (from *Think First Certificate: Self-Study Guide* by R. Acklam)

It would be possible to report A as *She said she was* (or: *is*) *going to leave tomorrow* if the report is made on the same day as the original utterance. Similarly, B could be reported as *He said this was the record he bought two days ago* for the same reason, and if the record is at hand. This suggests that learners need to have a very clear idea of the context in which the reporting is taking place – one reason why practising transposing sentences in isolation is probably of limited value.

9 The most prominent cohesive feature of this text is the repetition of key words from each immediately preceding sentence (The number in brackets refers to the sentence in which the words occur.):

(1) Television…picture… (2) Television…pictures… (3) …television… camera… (4) …camera…plate… (5) …plate… (6) …signals… (7) …signals… wave… (8) …set…wave… (9) …set…signal…wave… (10) signals… beam…spot… (11) signals…beam…brightness…spot… (12) beam… lines…spots…brightness… (13) …lines…

The only adjacent sentences not connected in this way are (5) and (6). Instead, an explicit link is made using *The result is*…

There are also repetitions of words over longer stretches of the text:

(4) …scene…electrically… (6) …electrical…scene…
(5) …a beam of electrons… (10) … a beam of electrons…

Note also the use of the definite article and *this/these* to 'point' backwards in the text to their referents:

(4) …an electrically charged plate… (5) …this plate…
(6) …electrical signals… (7) These signals…
(7) …a radio wave… (8) …the wave…
(10) …a beam…a spot… (11) …the beam…the spot…

It is also worth noting that there are only two conjuncts (sentence linkers) in the whole text: *then* and *also*. Cohesion from one sentence to the next is signalled almost entirely by lexical means. This suggests that – for this kind of factual writing, at least – exercises and activities to sensitise learners to, and to practise, features of lexical cohesion, such as repetition, may need to be given more prominence than they presently get in EFL materials. Word repetition is often discouraged in writing – used carefully, it can be a very useful device.

10 The word *pig* or *pigs* is repeated ten times and there are another nine pronominal references using *it* or *they*. Of the word-family *died, dead, death*, etc., there are eight instances. *Ate too much* is reformulated as *overfed* and *eaten too much*. There are eight mentions of *the children*, including *they* and *the kids*. *Were engrossed* appears again as *thought this was wonderful, were agog* and *were…very taken*.

These high-frequency words co-occur in two basic patterns: (1) *a pig died because it ate too much* and (2) *the children were engrossed*. (If you had to summarise the text, these two sentences would convey its essence concisely.) These two patterns are interwoven throughout the text with refrain-like regularity. Indeed, this almost rhythmic use of repeated patterns of words has been identified as a feature of a spoken language that, far from being a mark of ill-formedness, actually contributes to the mutual intelligibility of the discourse. Lexical patterning is part of the 'grammar' of texts, both written and spoken, beyond the level of the sentence.

27 Texts

1 Possible cohesive features are:

> Tense consistency: in the first three sentences, at least
> Pronoun reference: *they…they; Hale…he; the place…it*
> Lexical repetition: *morning…morning*
> Indirect repetition: *Brighton…the place*
> Lexical chains: *inspecting…special mention*
> Conjuncts: *And…No wonder*

The text is *cohesive*, but this does not mean that it necessarily makes sense: it is not *coherent*. Coherence is a less tangible quality and less easily defined or accounted for: it is perhaps a 'feeling' the reader (or listener) has, and what may be coherent for one may be incoherent for another. Nevertheless, the task of making sense of a text is made easier if the content of the text is organised in such a way as to make its meaning easily recoverable. The order in which information is presented in a text is an important factor in determining how coherent it is likely to be to the reader.

2 The split texts are:

– 1 and e: The logical relation between the first and the second sentence is a temporal one, e.g. 'Later…'. A causal one is also possible, e.g. 'As a consequence of this…'

– 2 and d: The relation is causal, e.g. 'So…'

– 3 and a: The logical relation is additive, e.g. 'And, what's more…'

– 4 and g: The relation is causal, e.g. 'Because…'

– 5 and f: The relation is an adversative one, e.g. 'However…'

– 6 and c: The relation is additive, e.g. 'And…', or temporal, e.g. 'Then…'

– 7 and b: The relation is causal, e.g. 'Because…'

3 Genre analysis is concerned with identifying the features of specific kinds of texts and accounting for these features with reference to the purposes and readership for which the text was designed. A starting point in genre analysis, therefore, is the identification of the communicative purpose of a text.

	Text type	*Purpose*	*Features*
1/e	news article	to inform	The information is ordered chronologically; the second sentence anticipates the reader's (mental) question: *Whose were they?*; causal linkers are avoided in order not to be seen to prejudge the case, perhaps.

2/d	error message	to explain	The cause comes first, and then the effect. This answers the predicted order of the computer user's questions: *What's wrong?...So what?*
3/a	biography	to inform	The information is presented in chronological order.
4/g	instruction	to request	The request is followed by the reason, to temper the imperative nature of the request, and to answer the reader's question: *Why?*
5/f	advertisement	to persuade	The reader is expected to identify with a problem (which is made to sound very serious), so that he/she is disposed to consider the solution offered.
6/c	dosage directions	to explain	The order follows the sequence of activities and goes from the general to the specific. With articles added, it would read: *take a tablet...chew the tablet...*
7/b	sign	to request	The structure is identical to 4/g, and for the same reasons.

4 These texts are all problem–solution advertising texts, having the same purpose and discourse structure (although more elaborated) as *5/f* above.

The first two sentences of the first text have an adversative relation – problem *but* solution – clearly signalled by *However*. Texts (**b**), (**c**) and (**d**) follow the same pattern, although text (**b**) elaborates the problem by giving an example. Each text uses a different sentence linker to signal the solution: (**b**) *Therefore*; (**c**) *But*; (**d**) *Now*.

The third sentence in text (**a**) has an explanatory and descriptive function, the assumption being that the reader is now interested enough to want to know how the item works. Equivalent explanatory sentences are found in each of the other texts, and occupy the same place in the sequence. Notice that a second advantage is included here in text (**a**), sentence 3. In text (**d**) the second advantage is signalled by the same device: *It can also...* In text (**d**) a separate sentence is devoted to the measurements that, in the other texts, are embedded in the explanatory sentences.

Essentially, though, all four texts follow the same pattern, and it is an archetypical sales talk pattern: 'You probably have this problem. Here's the solution. It works like this. And look! It does this too!'

Notice that the writer cannot assume the reader has the problem or will have considered a solution, hence the use of modality: *life can be difficult*; (this) *could provide instant relief*; *relief may be at hand*, etc.

Notice the use of antonyms to signal a problem–solution dichotomy, e.g. (a) *pain–relief*; (c) *inaccurate–precision*; (d) *suffer–relief*. Note also the high frequency of evaluative language, e.g. *especially useful*, *high quality*, *easy to read*.

Another feature of this text type, which is consistent with its persuading function, is the use of personal pronouns: *we* and *you*. This distinguishes the text type from, for example, the announcement in a specialist magazine of a scientific breakthrough. It creates a degree of personal familiarity, which, perhaps, makes the 'client' more trusting and better disposed to buy: an exaggerated example is the use of the colloquial *us Brits* in text (d).

5 This is the original text:

Dazer – the proven proven dog deterrent

Even the most dedicated canine lover can sometimes encounter unfriendly dogs. Dazer is the safe, humane and non-contact way to repel their advance. At the press of a button it emits harmless ultrasonic sound waves inaudible to the human ear, but very discomforting to the attacking dog. Operates on one PP3 battery, included.

(from *'Self Care'* by *Innovations*)

6 The features of the different text types are as follows:

a) *Recipes*: These typically begin with some introductory comment by the writer, e.g. 'This is a very rich and popular winter dish and is made with veal, beef or hare. It may be cooked in a saucepan but it is better if an earthenware casserole is used.' (Stubbs 1963). Then follows a list of ingredients; then the procedure, each sentence typically introduced with an imperative, and with verb objects omitted if these are understood, even where, normally, they would be obligatory: 'Remove from the fire and stand for at least fifteen minutes before serving' (*ibid*).

b) *Answerphone messages*: These typically begin with a self-identification on the part of the caller, followed by the reason for the call, e.g. 'I'm just calling to ask you if you would be able to…'. This is followed by either a request or an offer, e.g. 'Can you call me on…?'; 'I'll phone back later.'; then some form of closure, e.g. 'Thanks. Bye'. Depending on the relationship between caller and message receiver, the language can range from very informal to relatively formal.

c) *Holiday postcards*: This is probably the least structured of all the text types we have looked at so far, both in terms of what might be considered obligatory features (as opposed to optional ones) and in terms of the order in which these features occur. Usually, however, the reader expects some reference to places visited and some evaluation of the holiday experience as a whole or specific details, such as the weather. In many cultures the postcard serves to convey only minimal information, perhaps just a greeting. Postcards in English tend to be more anecdotal. There is often also some reference to the picture on the reverse side, which may become the 'deictic centre', e.g. 'Arrived here three days ago…'. Notice that redundant subject pronouns and associated auxiliary verbs are often omitted, e.g. '(We are) Having a wonderful time…'.

d) *Newspaper reports*: Typically, these begin with a summary of the story (which is in turn an elaboration of the headline), focusing on its most newsworthy aspect. This often involves using the present perfect, e.g. 'The Prime Minister has resigned' (where the headline is typically in the present simple: 'PM RESIGNS'), thus conveying both recency and relevance to the present. The background is then sketched in, using past tense structures. Because the events are not presented in chronological sequence, you often have to read some way into the text before the full sequence of events becomes clear. Newspaper styles vary widely, however, popular tabloid newspapers opting for shorter, punchier sentences, often one per paragraph. Nevertheless, and especially in opening sentences, there are often very long noun phrases, in which a great deal of background information is condensed, e.g. '*A cheating husband who persuaded a hitman to petrol-bomb his teenage lover's home after she jilted him* was jailed for 10 years yesterday'. (*Daily Mirror*)

7 See above for a summary of the features of a news report. The first sentence of the *Today* report is packed with all the main information, focusing on the result of the crash, rather than on how it occurred. The student, in following a strict chronological sequence of events, has failed to foreground the one fact that makes the story newsworthy, i.e. the fact that the plane crashed. In fact, *crashed* is the very last word mentioned. This is perhaps due to a misunderstanding as to the purpose of the task, which the writer has treated, it seems, as an exercise in displaying accurate past tense forms. This may in turn be due to a general emphasis, in many EFL classrooms and EFL materials, on getting the details right, at the expense of sufficient attention to larger formal features such as text organisation.

8 The paragraph is an excellent example of its own principles. The question, remains, however, as to the usefulness of teaching such very precise rules for text organisation, especially in the absence of any reason *why* such an organisation is the preferred one. Also, novice writers might find these rules rather daunting and such a degree of prescriptiveness might inhibit the expression of their own ideas. On the other hand, some general statement of principles of paragraph and text organisation, especially if they have been discovered by the learners themselves, might serve as a useful instrument for learners to evaluate their own writing.

Activities that might familiarise learners with the formula would include:
– Matching sentences in a paragraph with their categories, e.g. topic
   sentence, transitional sentence, conclusion, etc.
– Ordering jumbled sentences into a paragraph.
– Identifying the sentence that does not fit into a paragraph.
– Fitting a sentence into its appropriate place in an existing paragraph.

28 Conversations

1 Among the differences between spoken and written discourse that are exemplified in this extract are:

- Lack of clear sentence definition: while most written text consists of clearly defined sentences, beginning with a capital letter and ending with a full stop, speech is far less clearly segmented. For this reason, it is often easier to analyse it in terms of tone units, utterances or speakers' turns (see below).
- Lack of clause complexity: utterances are often strung together and joined with co-ordinating conjunctions (*and*, *but*, *so*, etc.), rather than showing the kind of internal complexity typical of much written language, where subordinate clauses are often frequent.
- Vague language: e.g. *that place where you can get water* for 'fountain' or 'hydrant'. Since speaking usually takes place in real time, there is a lot of pressure on speakers to get their message across without too much time spent searching for the most accurate term or expression.
- Repetition: e.g. *she pressed the button*. Repeating yourself is a way of 'buying' extra planning time, (note how she also repeats *she thought he was* as a kind of formulaic sentence frame); or it may be for effect – emphasis, dramatic highlighting, etc.
- Grammatical 'inaccuracy', e.g. *that's all he wanted to know was how the hell do you get water out*. Again, processing constraints mean that utterances are not always fully formulated before they are uttered, and may change tack to adapt to the changing intentions of the speaker.
- Use of such expressive devices as onomatopoeia: e.g. *whack*. This adds immediacy and dramatic effect to anecdotes.

An obvious difference (and not apparent in this transcript) between speaking and writing is, of course, the use of prosodic devices such as stress, rhythm and intonation. For example, in the original narrative, the speaker relates the last stages of the story (from *filled the bucket…*) with an intonation pattern of mock resignation, to emphasise the repetitive nature of the events and their inevitable consequence.

2 Like many features of conversation, it is not easy to define exactly what constitutes a turn. For convenience I have simply numbered utterances in the transcript, but this ignores occasions when a speaker is momentarily interrupted but manages to retain control of the floor (e.g. C in turns 6 and 8). It is clear, however, that, in this extract, C bids successfully to get the floor in order to tell her story. Speakers do not simply interrupt at random to get a turn, however, but wait for key intonational and paralinguistic clues (e.g. a marked drop in pitch, pausing, eye contact), as well as linguistic clues (e.g. 'but erm'), which signal that a speaker is relinquishing a turn. This may mean, however, that two speakers may attempt to fill the vacant slot simultaneously.

The speakers in this extract use none of the more explicit devices for turn-taking, such as 'that reminds me', 'funny you should mention that'. Perhaps these are more characteristic of less informal talk. C, in introducing the topic of her story simply says *like kedgeree...Kedgeree* and uses a 'high key' to signal a new topic.

3 Using the criteria for gauging text cohesion outlined in Unit 26, there is evidence in the extract of the following:

Lexical cohesion:

- Repetition: *junket* (four mentions); *kedgeree* (eleven mentions); *making kedgeree...make kedgeree...make it...*; *comprehensive school...comprehensive school*.
- Lexical sets: old-fashioned English and/or colonial dishes such as *junket*; *stewed rhubarb*; *kedgeree*; *spotted dick*; *toad-in-the-hole*; *egg and bacon*; *galub jalum*.

Grammatical cohesion:

- Pronoun reference: I'm going to have to try *it*; I couldn't make *it*.
- Substitution: I had to sit there while everybody else *did* (i.e. made it).
- Ellipsis: Might be great (i.e. It might be great).
- Conjuncts: *And* I had to take a note...; *So* I couldn't make it...; *But* kedgeree...

Notice also the use of deixis, i.e. reference to the immediate context: *This is really nice this Rioja*.

The conversation, then, features at least some of the same cohesive devices as written text. These devices occur, perhaps, in different proportions, e.g. there is more use of lexical repetition than of pronouns. They are also realised in different or less linguistically sophisticated ways, as in the case of conjuncts.

4 Apart from *Well, here's my bus*, this conversation consists entirely of adjacency pairs, most of which are opening and closing sequences – *Well, here's my bus* is, technically, a pre-closing turn.

Telephone conversations often begin with opening sequences in the form of adjacency pairs:

(1) A: Hello?
(2) B: Hello?

(3) B: A?
(4) A: Yes, speaking.

(5) B: It's B.
(6) A: Oh, hi, B.

A typical pre-closing and closing sequence might be:

(7) A: Well, better go.

(8) B: Uh-huh.

(9) A: So. Speak to you soon.

(10) B: Yeah.

(11) A: Bye then.

(12) B: Bye.

Other two-part exchanges that can usefully be taught to elementary students include:

Service encounters:

A: Can I help you?

B: Yes, have you got a map of...?

Offers and invitations:

A: Would you like to go to the movies?

B: I'd love to.

Requests:

A: Can you open the door?

B: Sure.

5 A typical service encounter, according to this model, might go:

(1) A: Good morning.

(2) B: Good morning. Can I help you?

(3) A: Yes, can I have a carton of milk?

(4) B: Here you are. Anything else?

(5) A: No thanks.

(6) B: That's seventy-five cents.

(7) A: Seventy-five. Thanks a lot.

(8) B: Thank you. Have a nice day.

(9) A: You too.

Note that, in reality, some of the 'moves' in this dialogue might not be realised in speech, e.g. the payment in (7). The obligatory moves are probably the following:

Shopkeeper: Offer service.

Customer: Ask for something.

Shopkeeper: Respond affirmatively or negatively; make another offer.

Customer: Decline.

Shopkeeper: Give total price.

Customer: Make payment and thank shopkeeper.

These models are probably most useful in the case of 'ritualised' exchanges such as shopping encounters. They provide the learner with a 'schema' for the interaction. They are also a useful tool for setting up classroom role plays: students are given the model and have to map on to it a dialogue. The danger of any kind of model, though, is that it may make learners less equipped to respond to the unpredictable in such encounters.

Models (or schemata) for the other situations might be:

a) Asking street directions:

    A: Attract attention; ask directions.

    B: Give directions.

    A: Repeat directions.

    B: Confirm or correct.

    A: Thank.

b) Phoning a restaurant to make a booking:

    (*phone rings*)

    A: Answer, giving name of restaurant.

    B: Greet. Make request, stating time/date and number of people.

    A: Acknowledge and confirm.

    B: Thank.

    A: Respond. Take leave.

    B: Take leave.

c) Phoning a friend to invite him/her round for a meal:

This is obviously a much more loosely structured conversation, but will probably include these elements:

– Caller identifies him/herself.

– Exchange of greetings.

– Preliminary chat, e.g. about recent activities.

– Caller asks friend if he/she is free at a certain time.

– If 'yes', caller makes invitation.

– Friend accepts or declines (the latter is unlikely if he/she is already committed to being free; but he/she may hedge).

– Further instructions, e.g. what to bring, how to get there, who else to bring, etc.

– Pre-closing.

– Closing.

6 The exercise is designed to practise ways of making requests in two different registers: informal and formal. It is doubly misleading, however. The exponents it suggests for each register are all but interchangeable, and it is possible to imagine the exercise working just as well with the exponents reversed, especially when factors such as intonation are taken into account.

More importantly, requests – especially those made to strangers – are seldom, if ever, made without some preamble. Asking someone to do something for you is 'face-threatening', and every care is taken to reduce the likelihood of the request being refused, to the point that, ideally, the request is never actually voiced. Asking someone to move their car, for example, might be preceded with a query 'Are you going to be here for a while?', to which they might (ideally) reply, 'Why? Am I in your way? Here, let me move it and let you out…'. As it stands, the material gives learners no guidance in this kind of interaction. Instead, it suggests that sounding polite requires nothing more than a single unadorned (albeit syntactically complex) sentence.

7 Topic can loosely be defined as 'what is being talked about over a series of turns'. 'Traditional dishes' is the general topic, but within this, C uses one of these dishes to introduce the topic of domestic science classes in comprehensive schools.

As noted above, there are no very explicit devices of topic initiation in the extract, although C's *I remember* (verb + *-ing*)… is a common sentence starter for introducing an anecdote. Often all that is needed in order to signal a new topic is a change to a higher key. Some more explicit devices include:

By the way…; *That reminds me…*; *Did you read/hear about…*; *Speaking of which…*; *Before I forget…*

Notice also the use of 'left-displacement' – when the speaker announces the topic of the sentence by placing it at the beginning (or on the left) of the sentence:

(1) Junket, I mean you have junket and stewed rhubarb
(8) Kedgeree, I remember saying to my mum

Classroom activities designed to help learners recognise topic shift require, ideally, recordings of authentic conversations, of which, unfortunately, there is little commercially available material. However, even scripted material such as news broadcasts, or monologue material such as interviews, have some value for ear training. Activities such as counting the topics, or ordering the topics in a list, require learners to attend to such cues as high key and pausing, as well as lexical clues. The same tasks can be used with authentic conversations, if available, as well as more language-focused tasks, such as making transcriptions of key points in the recording, e.g. at points of interruption or topic shift.

One activity that provides practice of conversational agenda management is 'Obsessions': students are given (or choose) cards on which is written their personal 'obsession', e.g. *My baby*, *Running*, *Football*, etc. In small groups they have conversations in which each person tries to steer the conversation back to his or her obsession, using devices such as 'That reminds me...', 'Speaking of which...', etc.

8 The ability to tell stories, jokes or anecdotes is an important conversational skill (as long as it is not overdone). Anecdotes, like any other genre, have a structure. For example, both stories, very briefly announce what they are going to be about (the 'abstract'):

Task 2 (8)   Kedgeree
Task 8 (1)   They take them to the park

Then follows the background to the story (or 'orientation'):

Task 2 (8) and (10)   I remember saying to my mum I've got to take a pound of fish next week we're making kedgeree

Task 8 (3)   this mother took her child to the park and he had a, she gave him a bucket of water

Then follows the 'complicating event':

Task 2 (10)   'n she said 'you don't want to be making kedgeree' 'n she said 'we don't like it' And I had to take a note to my domestic science taitch teacher saying 'Kathleen can't made kedgeree because we don't like it'

Task 8 (3)   so he had like sand and making a mush

Then some kind of 'resolution':

Task 2 (10)   So I couldn't make it. I had to sit there while everybody else did

Task 8 (3) and (4)   she said 'No t'embrutis! Prou!' He got a smack

Both stories draw a kind of moral (or 'coda') which gives the story some point:

Task 2 (20) and (21)   it was so inappropriate for the first year comprehensive school kids to be making

Task 8 (5)   if you give if you give a two-year-old a bucket of water what do you want, no?

The 'kedgeree' story also includes an element of 'evaluation':

Task 2 (10)   Awful.

Note also that both speakers use direct speech and 'put on' funny accents in order to heighten the dramatic and comic effect.

These are elements common to most anecdotes – they may well be common to story-telling worldwide. What learners will need help with is ways of realising these different story elements in English. This means exposing them to authentic examples, if possible, of anecdotes and drawing their attention not only to the structure, but to the linguistic realisations of these structures. For example, there are a number of formulaic ways of opening and closing stories, and, in the light of what has been said about the importance of acquiring effective turn-taking skills, it may be worth highlighting these. For example:

- That reminds me of the story about...
- I still remember once when...
- Someone was telling me about...

and

- It just goes to show, doesn't it?
- It takes all types.
- It makes you think, doesn't it?

For more ideas about how to use stories in class, see *Once Upon a Time* by Morgan and Rinvolucri.

9 a) There is very little coursebook material which encourages learners to attend to the discourse features of authentic conversation in English – this is a rare example. Whether or not they can go on to apply these features in fluent conversation, once they have had them pointed out, is debatable, but the progression from recognition to production is a logical one.

b) This advice might apply to a conversation in any language. What is missing is advice as to how to achieve these objectives in English. How do you sound interested, for example? How do you keep the conversation going? How do you talk about the weather? Some examples of common conversational gambits in English might be more helpful.

c) Practising free-flowing conversation in classroom conditions may be a contradiction in terms; certainly the best discussions that take place in class are often unplanned and spontaneous. This is why teachers often resort to role plays and simulations – useful up to a point but no substitute for the real thing. Further ideas for practising conversational skills can be found in *Conversation* by Nolasco and Arthur.

d) This exercise focuses on what are called 'backchannel signals', i.e. the things listeners say to show they are listening, and to demonstrate conversational involvement, even when not holding the floor. The intonation typical of each response would need to be demonstrated before learners went on to produce these. The prompts for practising these might form the basis for extension into longer conversations.

Bibliography

Books and articles referred to in the text

Brazil, D., Coulthard, M. and Johns, C. (1980) *Discourse Intonation and Language Teaching*. Addison Wesley Longman.

Broughton, G. (1990) *The Penguin English Grammar A–Z for Advanced Students*. Penguin.

Brown, G. (1974) Practical phonetics and phonology. In *The Edinburgh Course in Applied Linguistics. Volume 3: Techniques in Applied Linguistics*. Oxford University Press.

Carter, R. and McCarthy, M. (1988) *Vocabulary and Language Teaching*. Addison Wesley Longman.

Chalker, S. (1990) *English Grammar Word by Word*. Addison Wesley Longman.

Close, R. (1975) *A Reference Grammar for Students of English*. Addison Wesley Longman.

Collins COBUILD English Grammar. (1990) Collins.

Collins COBUILD English Language Dictionary. (1987) HarperCollins.

Collins COBUILD Student's Grammar. (1991) HarperCollins.

Comrie, B. (1976) *Aspect*. Cambridge University Press.

Comrie, B. (1985) *Tense*. Cambridge University Press.

Crewe, W. (1990) The illogic of logical connectives. *English Language Teaching Journal*, **44**, 4.

Crystal, D. (1980) *A First Dictionary of Linguistics and Phonetics*. André Deutsch.

Crystal, D. (1987) *The Cambridge Encyclopedia of Language*. Cambridge University Press.

Crystal, D. and Davy, D. (1975) *Advanced Conversational English*. Addison Wesley Longman

Downing, A. and Locke, P. (1992) *A University Course in English Grammar*. Pheonix ELT.

Gimson, A. C. (second edition 1970) *An Introduction to the Pronunciation of English*. Edward Arnold.

Halliday, M. and Hasan, R. (1976) *Cohesion in English*. Addison Wesley Longman.

Hatch, E. (1992) *Discourse and Language Education*. Cambridge University Press.

Huddleston, R. (1988) *English Grammar: An Outline*. Cambridge University Press.

Krashen, S. and Terrell, T. (1983) *The Natural Approach*. Pergamon.

Leech, G. (1989) *An A–Z of English Grammar and Usage*. Edward Arnold.

Leech, G. and Svartvik, J. (1975) *A Communicative Grammar of English*. Addison Wesley Longman

Lewis, M. (1986) *The English Verb*. Language Teaching Publications.

Longman Active Study Dictionary of English. (1983) Addison Wesley Longman.

Longman Language Activator. (1993) Addison Wesley Longman.

MacAndrew, R. (1991) *English Observed*. Language Teaching Publications.

McCarthy, M. (1990) *Vocabulary*. Oxford University Press.

Morgan, J. and Rinvolucri, M. (1988) *The Q Book*. Addison Wesley Longman.

Nolasco, R. and Arthur, L. (1987) *Conversation*. Oxford University Press.

O'Connor, J. D. (second edition 1980) *Better English Pronunciation*. Cambridge University Press.

Palmer, F. (1988) *Modality and the English Modals*. Addison Wesley Longman.

Penguin Spelling Dictionary. (1990) Penguin.

Quirk, R. and Greenbaum S. (1973) *A University Grammar of English*. Addison Wesley Longman.

Quirk, R., Greenbaum, S., Leech, G. and Svartvik, J. (1985) *A Comprehensive Grammar of the English Language*. Addison Wesley Longman.

Richards, J. (1985) *The Context of Language Teaching*. Cambridge University Press.

Rutherford, W. E. (1987) *Second Language Grammar: Learning and Teaching*. Addison Wesley Longman.

Stannard Allen, W. (1959, 1974) *Living English Structure*. Addison Wesley Longman.

Swan, M. (1980) *Practical English Usage*. Oxford University Press.

Swan, M., and Smith, B. (eds) (1987) *Learner English*. Cambridge University Press.

Thomson, A. and Martinet, A. (1986) *A Practical English Grammar*. Oxford University Press.

Ur, P. (1988) *Grammar Practice Activities*. Cambridge University Press.

Ur, P. and Wright, A. (1992) *Five-Minute Activities*. Cambridge University Press.

Wells, J. and Colson, G. (1987) *Practical Phonetics*. Pitman.

Willis, D. (1990) *The Lexical Syllabus*. HarperCollins.

EFL texts used in tasks

Abbs, B., Cook, V. and Underwood, M. (new edition 1978) *Realistic English Drills*. Oxford University Press.

Abbs, B. and Freebairn, I. (1981) *Developing Strategies*. Addison Wesley Longman.

Abbs, B. and Freebairn, I. (1982) *Opening Strategies*. Addison Wesley Longman.

Abbs, B. and Freebairn, I. (1991) *Blueprint 2: Teacher's Book*. Addison Wesley Longman.

Acklam, R. (1990) *Think First Certificate Self-Study Guide*. Addison Wesley Longman

Alexander, L. G. (1990) *Longman English Grammar Exercises*. Addison Wesley Longman.

Baker, A. (1981) *Ship or Sheep?* Cambridge University Press.

Bell, J. and Gower, R. (1991) *Intermediate Matters*. Addison Wesley Longman.

Black, V., McNorton, M., Malderez, A. and Parker, S. (1986) *Fast Forward 1*. Oxford University Press.

Bowler, B. and Cunningham, S. (1990) *Headway Intermediate Pronunciation*. Oxford University Press.

Bowler, B. and Cunningham, S. (1991) *Headway Upper-Intermediate Pronunciation*. Oxford University Press.

Bradford, B. (1988) *Intonation in Context*. Cambridge University Press.

Coe, N., Rycroft, R. and Ernest, P. (1983) *Writing Skills*. Cambridge University Press.

Dalzell, S. and Edgar, I. (1988) *English in Perspective*. Oxford University Press.

Doff, A. and Jones, C. (1991) *Language in Use: Pre-Intermediate*. Cambridge University Press.

Doff, A., Jones, C. and Mitchell, K. (1983) *Meanings into Words: Intermediate*. Cambridge University Press.

Fowler, W. S. and Pidcock, J. (1985) *New Proficiency English Book 1*. Addison Wesley Longman.

Garton-Sprenger, J. and Greenall, S. (1991) *Flying Colours 2*. Heinemann.

Gilbert, J. B. (second edition 1993) *Clear Speech*. Cambridge University Press.

Hartley, B. and Viney, P. (1980) *Streamline English*. Oxford University Press.

Hughes, G. (1981) *A Handbook of Classroom English*. Oxford University Press.

Jones, L. (1977) *Functions of English*. Cambridge University Press.

Kenny, N. and Johnson, R. (1983) *Target First Certificate*. Heinemann.

Lewis, M. (1982) *Out and About*. Language Teaching Publications.

May, P. (1991) *First Choice for Proficiency*. Heinemann.

Mortimer, G. (1977) *Clusters: A Pronunciation Practice Book*. Cambridge University Press.

Naunton, J. (1989) *Think First Certificate*. Addison Wesley Longman.

O'Connor, J. and Fletcher, C. (1989) *Sounds English: A Pronunciation Practice Book*. Addison Wesley Longman.

O'Neill, R. (1971) *Kernel Lessons Intermediate*. Addison Wesley Longman.

Ponsonby, M. (1987) *How Now Brown Cow?* Pheonix ELT.

Porter-Ladousse, G. (1993) *Language Issues*. Addison Wesley Longman.

Radley, O. and Burke, K. (1994) *Workout Advanced*. Addison Wesley Longman.

Redman, S. and Ellis, R. (1989) *A Way with Words: 1*. Cambridge University Press.

Redman, S. and Ellis, R. (1990) *A Way with Words: 2*. Cambridge University Press.

Roach, P. (second edition 1991) *English Phonetics and Phonology*. Cambridge University Press.

Rogerson, P. and Gilbert, J. (1990) *Speaking Clearly*. Cambridge University Press.

Shepherd, J. and Cox, F. (1991) *The Sourcebook*. Addison Wesley Longman.

Soars, J. and Soars, L. (1986) *Headway Intermediate*. Oxford University Press.

Soars, J. and Soars, L. (1987) *Headway Upper-Intermediate*. Oxford University Press.

Soars, J. and Soars, L. (1991) *Headway Pre-Intermediate*. Oxford University Press.

Swan, M. and Walter, C. (1984) *The Cambridge English Course 1*. Cambridge University Press.

Swan, M. and Walter, C. (1985) *The Cambridge English Course 2*. Cambridge University Press.

Swan, M. and Walter, C. (1990) *The New Cambridge English Course 1*. Cambridge University Press.

Swan, M. and Walter, C. (1990) *The New Cambridge English Course 2*. Cambridge University Press.

Thornbury, S. (1992) *Beginners' Choice Workbook*. Addison Wesley Longman.

Underhill, A. (1994) *Sound Foundations*. Heinemann.

Vince, M. (1989) *Excel at First Certificate*. Heinemann.

Viney, P. and Viney, K. (1989) *Grapevine 1*. Oxford University Press.

Willis, J. and Willis, D. (1988) *Collins COBUILD English Course: Practice Book 1*. Collins.

Ayckbourn, A. (1987) *A Small Family Business*. Faber and Faber.

Carter, A. (ed.) (1991) *The Virago Book of Fairy Tales*. Virago Press.

Christie, A. (1953) *Death on the Nile*. Penguin.

Fitzgerald, P. (1990) *The Gate of Angels*. HarperCollins.

George, E. (1989) *Payment in Blood*. Bantam Books.

Jack, A. (1983, 1987) *Pocket Encyclopedia*. Kingfisher Books.

Orton, J. (1976) *The Complete Plays*. Methuen.

Pinter, H. (1967) *Tea Party and Other Plays*. Faber and Faber.

Pym, B. (1983) *An Unsuitable Attachment*. Macmillan.

Stubbs, J. (1963) *The Home Book of Greek Cookery*. Faber and Faber.

Thurber, J. (1945) *The Thurber Carnival*. Hamish Hamilton.

Townsend, S. (1983) *The Secret Diary of Adrian Mole aged 13¾*. Methuen.

Welch, D. (1984) *I Left My Grandfather's House*. Allison & Busby.

Wyndham, J. (1963) *The Kraken Wakes*. Michael Joseph.

Index